THE LIFE & MUSIC OF
LOUREED
WAITING FOR THE MAN

THE LIFE & MUSIC OF
LOU REED
WAITING FOR THE MAN
JEREMY REED

OMNIBUS PRESS

London / New York / Paris / Sydney / Copenhagen / Berlin / Madrid / Tokyo

Exclusive Distributors
Music Sales Limited,
14/15 Berners Street,
London, W1T 3LJ.

Music Sales Corporation
180 Madison Avenue, 24th Floor,
New York,
NY 10016,
USA.

Macmillan Distribution Services
56 Parkwest Drive
Derrimut, Vic 3030,
Australia.

Every effort has been made to trace the copyright holders of the photographs in
this book but one or two were unreachable. We would be grateful if the
photographers concerned would contact us.

Printed in the EU

A catalogue record for this book is available from the British Library.

Visit Omnibus Press on the web at www.omnibuspress.com

This book is dedicated to John Robinson and Mark Jackson with love.

Contents

1

Waiting For The Man

THE enigma gated by raybans or black reflective aviators, his typically implacable sunglassed cool facing down audiences and music journalists with apparent contempt is the typical rude-boy Lou Reed image associated over the years with the artist's notoriously defensive hostility towards his public. Among my favourite Lou photos is the one taken by Gary Gross used on the jacket of this book. It epitomises Reed's continued focus on sexual ambiguity in the late-seventies, both in his private life and as a recurrent theme in his gossipy anecdotal songs about New York friends and generic lowlife.

It is of course the man in black, soon after the acrimonious breakup with his transvestite partner Rachel in 1978, a de facto gay partnership that had survived five years of chronic speed and alcohol on Reed's distempered, resolutely self-destructive part. Something of Reed's unchecked dissipation is squeezed out of this highly charged black and white shot in which his characteristic conflicting bisexual energies are the focus for the cover shot of his indifferently received 1979 album *The Bells*.

No matter the controversial, almost draggy look, there's no obvious sense of feminine queer in Reed, despite the fastidiously waved hairdo, and the fact that out shot he's holding a girl's hand mirror in his right hand, presumably to check his makeup. There's a distinctly nocturnal aura to the shot, as though the subject is a night person, rearranged for the day. And of course there's a recognisable angularity to Reed's features and personality that resists straight identity, like his sexuality remains unresolved, and his attitude implies you don't come too close without risking aggression or possible verbal abuse.

From the release in 1957 of his first record 'So Blue' with a high school group called the Shades, to the naively formatted pop of 'Sneaky Pete' and 'The Ostrich', released by Lou's band the Primitives – the subversive garage-oriented noise of the Velvet Underground, and through to the regularly shape-shifting timeline of his solo career, Lou Reed has been a presence synonymous with the cutting edge music of our times over the duration of 50 years of combatively innovative creativity.

My interest in Lou Reed in this book focuses partly on his singular concern to turn rock into an intelligently literate medium of expression. He's arguably, like Bob Dylan, the novelist in rock music, his songs often condensed into micro-novellas, cut-up narratives twisted out of the raw experience of street poetry and squeezed into the compressed space of a record lyric. In method he's closer to William Burroughs' deconstruction of linear time into randomised visual frames as disarranged storytelling, and in generational sensibility to the Beats, Ginsberg, Kerouac and Corso, than he is to the more sophisticated New York school of poets characterised by John Ashbery, Frank O'Hara, James Schuyler and Kenneth Koch. The best of Reed's songs, like Dylan's, hold up as poems on the page, lyrics which while they make no concessions to formal poetic technique possess sufficient economy of phrasing and image to hang together independent of the music for which they were written. In Reed, identification of work and place are so acute, that during his lifetime he was popularly conceived as the unofficial Poet Laureate of New York, the man who in the lyrics of his songs turned urban dirt into gold.

The resilient defiance in lyrics like 'Sweet Jane' and 'Heroin', archetypal Reed songwriting, carry Lou's stated intention of integrating aspects of the novel into rock. 'Sweet Jane', with the familiar gender switch, 'Jack's in his corset/Jane is in her vest', and with the song's protagonist cool in his take it or leave it identity, 'I'm in a rock'n'roll band', makes clear that Lou's place, like all other outlaws, is not in a study, but on the street corner, in the urban theatre of experience. I instance 'Sweet Jane' as classical Lou, with its reference to poets studying rules of verse, something he partially adapted to a corresponding acumen in rock.

Others have shown a similar awareness: Bob Dylan, Leonard Cohen, Joni Mitchell, the best of the Jagger/Richards songs from the sixties and seventies, Lennon/McCartney, Ray Davies' domestic mini-dramas, Pete Townshend's construction of rock operas, Peter Perrett of the Only Ones druggy morbidity, Marc Almond's glitzy lyricisation of sleaze, Morrissey's social realism, Pete Doherty's evocation of dodgy outlaws; but the man in black remains an altogether more dangerous edge-walker when the lyric's an impacted social target.

For all his privileged millionaire tax accountant parents' upbringing and education, a typical Lou Reed song nearly always originates on the street, the platform for big city experience, drawing on blues as inner resources of protest, and voyaging in search of rock's still undiscovered potential, as in 'Heroin' which is in a way his answer to Baudelaire's journeying into drug-induced imaginative geography: 'anywhere out of the world', rather than suffer the boredom of the socially accepted view of reality. Baudelaire, a disillusioned, disinherited, syphilitic opium addict, known as the Paris Prowler for his stalking of prostitutes he was impotent to fuck, lived like a spook throwing shapes over a red light in a Paris alley, and made the city the essentially urban grid of his poetry, in the way Lou Reed capitalises on New York, as resources for lyrical incentive. Reed's drug narratives are arguably the rock equivalent of Baudelaire's inner voyaging to imaginary islands in poems like 'The Voyage', and 'Voyage To Cythera', where sensory reward is provided by a lawless offworld ethos. In Reed's 'Heroin', intravenously mainlined diamorphine fuels a drug-induced voyage towards states Baudelaire would have recognised as biomarkers to visionary experience. Part of the song's greatness, apart from the terminal-junky references, with which Reed could so easily identify in the sixties and seventies, is its exploration of the frontiers of altered state conscious-ness pushing death.

Baudelaire in 'The Voyage' praised those who 'Plonger au fond du gouffre, Enfer ou Ciel, qu'importe?/Au fond de l'inconnu pour trouver du nouveau!', those who risked plunging into the gulf, down or up, deep into the unknown to discover the new; and Lou Reed's drug journey in 'Heroin' is no less extreme. The user liberated into smack's dopamine rush is bonded by opioid receptor sites into affirming 'it's my wife and it's my life', an individuated choice in contrast to war-bent hawkish politicians, having 'dead bodies pile up in mounds' as part of unstoppable US global military imperialism. Reed's link to Baudelaire in thematic pointers, as a state of total indifference settles after the initial feel-good high, is in the narrated wish to 'put on a sailor's suit and cap' and sail 'the darkest seas', questing through an injected drug for a visionary high. Reed's seminal delivery, in which a monotone drawl registers little or no emotional response was, right from the start, the punkishly indifferent signature to a whole generation of garage, punk and indie, in which resigned nonchalant vocals front two and three-chord guitar aggro. Only Lou's insouciant tone is prototypical ennui, massaged by a literacy he often assumed separated him from his audience; and in reality at New York's Felt Forum in 1975, while performing 'Dirt' live, stopping after the word 'psychological' to demean the audience by suggesting the 'big word' was beyond their language grasp. It was an imperious attitude Reed adopted throughout the seventies, an arrogating superiority facing down the assumed vacancy of his fans.

The legitimacy of Reed's claim to be rock's premier lyricist, a self-created title that stuck, was enforced by his implication that the medium in which he excelled was somehow too superficial for his intellectual type. Certainly, the power and originality of a song like 'Heroin' was formidably controversial when Reed first recorded it in 1965 and played it for the first time onstage as part of Warhol's Exploding Plastic Inevitable, in an event staged on January 13, 1966 at a dinner for the New York Society for Clinical Psychiatry. This was the multi-media function called *Up-Tight*, to which the Velvet Underground and Nico contributed with a series of shows staged in The Gymnasium in New York, ads in the *Village Voice* reading 'The Silver Dream Factory presents the Exploding Plastic Inevitable with Andy Warhol /The Velvet Underground/and Nico'.

Aficionados of early Velvet Undergound noise, studio and live, can find excerpted tracks of the Exploding Plastic Inevitable on bootleg recordings like *Screen Test: Falling In Love With The Falling Spikes, The Warlocks/The Falling Spikes, Untitled Caka Black Banana, A Symphony Of Sound, Yesterday's Parties Exploding Plastic Inevitable*, and on the Nico bootleg *Death Of The Maiden*, which includes a 3:00 excerpt of 'Melody Laughter', one of two long improvisations performed by the Velvet Underground during the EPI show at Valleydale Ballroom in Columbus Ohio on November 4, 1966, as well as on the Velvet Underground box set *Peel Slowly And See.* Randomised experimentation on the part of Reed and Cale, as a sort of series of I Ching sonic accidents, together with the ingestion of available Factory drugs, mostly speed, is central to an understanding of the Velvet Underground's early music in initialising a sound so deconstructively focussed that while it has been ubiquitously emulated, it has never been copied; the prototype always keeping ahead of the copyist at illusory Formula One distancing.

And with my point here being Lou's deliberate attempt to craft literary rock, inspired by his reading of the likes of Raymond Chandler, Nelson Algren, William Burroughs, Allen Ginsberg and Hubert Selby Jnr, his argument for the validity of introducing subcultures into rock as mandatory to the Velvet Underground's expression, rang presciently true. 'That's the kind of stuff you might read, why wouldn't you listen to it? You have the fun of reading that, and you get the fun of rock on top of it.'

Reed was of course equally cogent arguing for the band's full on use of distortion, aggressive feedback and drone as integral to their cult sound:

> 'What the music really has to do with is electricity. Electricity and different types of machines. One of the ideas we had was like, for instance, John would be playing one of his viola solos and we'd have two jack-cords coming out of the viola; in other words, he'd have two, three, four contact-mikes on the viola, put into two, three, four different amplifiers, and then Nico and me and Mo would control each amplifier. One amplifier would be concerned with bass and another amplifier would be concerned with volume, and another one . . . or we could have a mixer, or we could have lots of mixers and what we would all be playing is John, which is what it would amount to.'

Intimations of Reed's tech-head deviations, later characterised by 1975's unlistenable drone-assault, *Metal Machine Music*, were apparent right from the start of his involvement with the Velvet Underground, as a sort of

13

unanalysable metaphysical weaponry employed to confuse critics and fans alike by its apparent irrational rightness of method.

If Reed's themes of drugs, social alienation, deviancy and S&M, all in evidence on *The Velvet Underground And Nico* (1966) initially met with commercial and critical failure, then 'Heroin' became a song programmed into its writer's identity, as a live construct to which audiences attached and an assumed slice of confessional autobiography. As a key song in Reed's seventies solo sets, 'Heroin' was to undergo radical mutations in arrangements to fit with the particular image Lou adopted for a tour and his band at the time. From its demo origins, as acoustic folk-rock, through to its stratospheric orgasmic peak, *Live With The Velvet Underground*, 'Heroin' graduated in 1973 to a heavy metal wall-to-wall speeded up epic, enhanced by Steve Hunter and Dick Wagner's crunching licks on the 1973 *Rock'n'Roll Animal* tour. Incessant travel, poor diet, injected crystal meth and marital stress (Reed was at the time married to Bettye Kronsdat, the blonde cocktail waitress whom his gay friends derided as 'Betty Boop' and 'Betty' – like Archie and Veronica), had reduced him to a physical shape described by Wayne Robins in *Zoo* as 'a cross between a mad executioner and an overgrown rodent'. Intent of ridding himself of the association with Bowie and glam rock brought about by the collaboration on *Transformer* (1972), Reed's persona as a butch leather boy fronting cyclonic power-chords was a radical reinvention of 'Heroin' live.

Parting company in 1974 with his guitar core, Hunter and Wagner, the incorporation of a wind section provided a slightly modulated and jazzier feel to 'Heroin', Reed with his bleached hair and size zero figure looking 'far better off dead' as the personification of the lyrics, the performance having Timothy Ferris in *Rolling Stone* compare the ritual surrounding the song to 'the atmosphere of a cathedral at black mass'.

In 1975, with a less emaciated Lou morphed from post-human to a more recognisably natural identity, 'Heroin' as the gig's anticipated lawless focus was toned down to a part-acoustic song, an edgy, liverish Reed still appearing to court self-immolation despite the consolidation of his relationship with the Mexican transvestite Rachel, before being reconstructed in 1976 by brilliant improvisation in Lou's energised *Rock'n'Roll Heart* jazz tour of the States. The song reached a chilling zero in nonchalant disasso-ciation in the 1977 live sets, Reed appropriately introducing the line 'falling off the edge of the world' to describe his own mental state, the conflict that was starting to come up in his relationship with Rachel, his displacement in the music scene at the time of punk, and the flagrantly anarchic youth culture the latter entailed, at a time when Reed, its pro-genitor, was in his mid-thirties. By 1978 'Heroin' was delivered almost as a spoken word song, Reed in tears onstage while performing it in Amster-dam, before the lyrics lost their sensitive reading in the big-band sound that Reed adopted for a year of continuous touring in 1979.

The feel of Reed's songs delivered live throughout the seventies was invariably interpreted by his visual image, the two combining to form an approximate composite of his mental state at the time. The butch-looking black-lipsticked black nail-lacquered Lou Reed who toured in 1973 as the 'Rock'n'Roll Animal', revamping Velvet's classics like 'Sweet Jane', 'Waiting For The Man' and 'Heroin', was the unleashed personification of his songs. The peroxided, anorexic Reed who toured in 1974 with a new band, gated by hostile raybans, and incorporating a stripped down 'Sister Ray' into the set, was a hybrid speed-freak so dependent on speed that he would be forced offstage at intervals with chronic tachycardia.

By 1975, a still blond but physically cleaned up Lou, was back playing guitar for the first time since 1972, in a band that featured Doug Yule on lead guitar as a throwback to the Velvet Underground, with songs like 'Leave Me Alone', 'Dirt', 'Kicks' and 'I Wanna Be Black' given airings for the first time prior to their eventual incorporation into the *Coney Island* and *Street Hassle* albums (1976 & 1978). It was a year of unpredictable numbers, the most powerful of which proved to be the psychopathic character study in 'Kicks', a song that advocates murder as an alternative to sex. The partying voices used as a backdrop to the new version of the song when it was recorded with Godfrey Diamond, for *Coney Island Baby*, retain the homicidal fury to which the number builds, but there is nothing quite like the pathological orgasmic shriek of 'Kicks' as it was performed live in the mid-seventies.

The man was mutant. After a year without touring, and having released the commercially disastrous *Metal Machine Music*, four sides of disruptive electronic drone, in July 1975, Reed embarked on a jazz tour across the States, hiking up still another controversial morph in his live presentation of old and new material. There's little in Lou's live oeuvre to match the cool, improvised spontaneity of these gigs, the semi-spoken, often rushed monotone working the lyrics across a frenetic jazz given cold indigo colour by the likes of Don Cherry.

However, when Reed toured Europe in 1977, when punk rock was using him as its seminal influence on its raw garage subversion of pop formatting and ironically labelling him its 'godfather', Reed had never sounded more dissociated and disengaged from punk's hyper-energised core. Partly parodying the inarticulate vocals that characterised punk, he sounded angry, morose and drunkenly alienated from his audience. The sets were short and antagonistic: the man wasn't going to deliver when everywhere his music was being abused, ripped off – its inimitably nonchalant vocals copied. Reed was also booze-drenched, irascible and uncompromisingly hostile to interviewers, declaring onstage, as a warning to clones, 'I do Lou Reed better than anyone.'

Reed's 1978 live sound, his look remaining little different from 1977's implacable anti-hero dressed all in black, featured Marty Fogel on a dominant horn section and Angela Howell and Chrissy Faith on backing vocals, and introduced self-comment, self-critique, repartee and confessional candour, a talkative Lou Reed, in savage contrast to the previous year's chilling silence where the songs went unannounced and the man seemed bored by his own presence onstage.

Reed's adoption of conversational anecdote and black humour into his 1978 and 1979 live repertoire seem in part to have originated from frustration, and with it the need to situate himself within the historic present. Throughout most of the seventies, his cutting edge spearheading work with the Velvet Underground remained undervalued, and while his formative music inspired the likes of David Bowie, Iggy Pop, Patti Smith and the New York CBGBs explosive punk rock scene, Reed as archetypal one-chord deconstructionist was in danger of being left in the shadow of a new generation of garage anarchists. An increasing strain of cynicism infiltrated his late seventies performance, with self-deprecation a weaponised means of launching offensive. Maintaining invincible mystique as progenitor to most forms of literate pop and rock, Reed's self-adopted role as unacknowledged avatar to youth, John Rockwell writing in the *New York Times*, 13 March 1978, found Lou in a singularly perverse state of conflict with himself:

> 'Mixed with his purely artistic experimentation, however, is a streak of sometimes self-defeating perversity which leads him deliberately into styles that look almost as if they were chosen because his admirers would be offended by them . . . Mr Reed's singing voice remains what it always has been, an instrument that seems almost defiantly shy about carrying a tune precisely, yet makes a remarkable impact when turned to declamatory uses. As a public performer he is at least as much an image and an icon as he is a musician.'

It is important to remember that acceptance by the media and television was still a thing of the improbable future, to a Lou Reed saturated in notoriety touring relentlessly throughout the seventies. His survival with integrity through resources of constant reinvention, without any least compromise, while it won him a consolidated fanbase, did little to appease the artist's sense of lack of recognition from a systemised mainstream to which he didn't in any aspect belong.

By the end of the seventies Reed was in his late thirties, and questioned by Lisa Caine Fando for *Album Tracking* about his punk and insurgently youthful imitators, said: 'I don't know what you mean by the term. I don't believe in it. If there is a punk scene there are some awfully intelligent punks.' Reed, while he appeared disinterested in punk, and dismissively so – he'd done it ten years earlier from a more sophisticated musical platform – refused to namecheck any likes in contemporary music, preferring to look to literary influences, like Rimbaud, as compatible with his own experimental objectives. The presumptuously disdainful runaway teen, Arthur Rimbaud, arguably the most antagonistic counterculture poet of early modernism, who gave up writing poetry in 1870 at the age of 20, and was frequently cited as a seminal influence on punk music and intransigent attitude, was as incurably disrespectful as the seventies Reed in his contemptuous diffidence towards poetry itself and his contemporaries. Rimbaud's contradictory method of deconstructing his own work in the process of writing it, and of imaginatively recreating the accepted view of reality through what he called 'the systematic derangement of the senses', was in part the product of explosive visionary imagination, and in part the hallucinated documentation of absinthe binges with his alcoholic lover and partner on the road, Paul Verlaine.

It was Rimbaud who wrote, with typically punk defiance, 'Work is further from me than my fingernail from my eye. Shit for me. When you see me eat shit, only then will you find how little it costs to feed me.' You would be forgiven for thinking this is a quotation from a mid-seventies Lou Reed interview, but it is in fact an extract from one of Rimbaud's letters to Verlaine about his predicament as a poet. Rimbaud with his stick-up hair, scatological mind and contempt for society, was a proto-typical punk who launched an offensive on bourgeois values and main-stream poetry with the hot plume of a re-entry fire, only to walk out on his art, disillusioned by its limitations and to end up as an Abyssinian arms-dealer, dead at 39 from an incurably gangrenous leg.

If Reed's polarisation in the seventies was inextricably linked to a cult anticipating his death onstage from drugs/drink related excesses, then both the man and his stage image underwent radical transformation in the eighties, a decade which found him improbably married to Sylvia Morales. They'd met at a gay S&M club in New York, and lived part of the time on a substantially landed farm in New Jersey. Partially media-friendly in a way that couldn't have happened in the seventies, and undergoing detoxification from alcohol, Reed after recording *Growing Up In Public* (1980), an indifferent, laconic album that lacked characteristic bite and seemed to be his final comment on the seventies, and making a brief tour of France and Italy in 1980, disbanded the musicians who had toured with him as an integral unit since the mid-seventies, went into semi-reclusion, reporting that he would never tour again, and that if he played future dates they would be restricted to the Bottom Line in New York. The speed-freak, overwired, self-destructive Reed myth was losing credibility by the end of the seventies, and a hostilely voiced frustration and anger at the lack of promotional support given him by his record company Arista, combined with poor record sales and a tongue willing to vilify everyone, including his Arista boss Clive Davis, seemed to have brought his disparaged, drunkenly skewed momentum to a temporary halt.

There was also the psychological adjustment to be made in terms of sexual orientation. Reed had become more willing to speak about his homosexuality in interviews given in the late seventies, and for a long time had lived in an apartment on Christopher Street, the acknowledged epicentre of New York's gay life. But on Valentine's Day 1980 Reed married Sylvia Morales, his self-confessed decadence and being into 'drug masturbation' having to be substantially revised in the process of rethinking his public front. Of his decision to marry on the rebound of his acrimonious split with Rachel, Reed told Steve Dupier in *International Musician*:

> 'There's this real myth, as if by getting married you suddenly become old and senile and move to the suburbs and never do a meaningful piece of work again. I envision marriage as the great romantic thing it is. How can you write about love when you don't believe in it?'

The silence was broken with the release of *The Blue Mask* in 1982, and a return for Reed to his old label RCA. The album's artwork, a blue–black revamp of the original *Transformer* sleeve, suggested an uneasy transitioning between the decades, with Reed using his newly won emotional stability to maintain a tension between past and present with his signature firepower and derisively controversial lyricism only really kicking in on the propulsively angry title track.

I see *The Blue Mask* as a mid-life album, with its reflective rather than confrontational tone proving pivotal to the artist's development, as well as a psychic reintegration; and in finding an affirmative aspect to growing older, as a process of deepening. The grainy, binaural, often directionless modalities of the critically acclaimed *Street Hassle* (1978), and the questioningly eclectic *The Bells* (1979), were replaced by a mellower vocal line, and a confirmation, particularly in 'My House', of the poet's craft. This song was dedicated to Reed's tutor at Syracuse University, Delmore Schwartz, a Jewish, seriously alcoholic writer, who remained a lifelong avatar to Reed's aspirations to make pop lyricism into a serious literary expression. Reed credited Schwartz with showing him how 'with the simplest language possible, and very short, you can accomplish the most astonishing heights.'

Schwartz, who suffered periodically from mental illness and was incurably dependent on alcohol, had published his first book of short stories, *In Dreams Begin Responsibilities*, in 1938 when he was only 26, but booze, breakdowns and personal alienation had seriously disrupted his trajectory as a writer, and his isolation was so acute that when he died of a heart attack on July 11, 1966, two days passed before his body was officially identified at the mortuary. It seemed fitting that Lou's inspirational tutor should be both Jewish and alcoholic and highly focussed into compressed poetic form and, like Reed, the subject of electro-shock, in Schwartz's case for alcoholic depression and in Reed's for homosexual tendencies.

As a psychological litany to perversion, 'The Blue Mask', with its detailed catalogue of sexual pathologies including incest, patricide, and fratricide was up there with other epic Lou deviant narratives like 'Heroin', 'Sister Ray' and 'Kicks', the dissociated narrator climaxing on a psychopathic focus on atrocities worthy of Caligula, Nero or Heliogabalus in their serial killing for perverse, maniacal kicks.

But the man, the rehab Lou Reed, appeared to have cleaned up his act in the attempt to reconstruct his identity and to have got off drugs and drink as metabolic biomarkers without serious loss to his creativity, other than that angular appeared less edgy, and subject matter more regulated to fit in with the times; 'The Gun' as a pointer to John Lennon's assassination by Mark David Chapman on December 8, 1980 outside the Dakota Building on the West Side of Manhattan; 'Women', as an unconvincing disclaimer to his gay identity; and the autobiographical 'Underneath The Bottle', as attempted re-evaluation of his chronically alcoholic past aggravated by recurrent hepatitis.

By early 1983 Lou Reed was back in action with a series of dates at the Bottom Line backed by a new band, Fred Maher (drums), Fernando Saunders (bass) and Robert Quine, ex-Voidoids (lead guitar), from which the live video *A Night With Lou Reed* was shot. Outwardly, Reed was still dressed in black leather, black shades, interchangeable with the retro wire-rimmed professional eyewear he came to adopt as he grew older, but his professionally clean live sound, mechanical, and without any of his antagonistic verbal interaction with audiences sounded frigid, like a detoxed Reed doing little more than go through the motions to reaffirm his live presence after three years away from touring.

Without drinks as the mediator between himself and the audience, Reed sounded locked into formulaic cold and determined to return to basics. In 1983 he told the writer Chris Bohn:

> 'I've always liked those very basic, very simple rock'n'roll changes. I've never heard anything I like more than that. Not in opera, not in classical music, not in jazz, nor in show tunes. Not movie music. Nothing. Nothing has impressed me as much as the most basic rock'n'roll chord change, and by that I mean, say E to A. And to this day, when I hear that change done right – and it can be done wrong – I get an abnormal degree of pleasure from it. Wouldn't it be wonderful to put a melody over that, something that would stick like grease? And then wouldn't it be great if the lyrics also had some substance to them, were as simple and as elegant in that change from one chord to the other?'

I saw Lou Reed play at the Brixton Academy in 1984 as part of his glacial clean-up act, having last seen him at the Hammersmith Odeon in 1979, and the transformation was acutely uncomfortable in that the man was someone else, a dissociated automaton playing basic rock with little emotional expression and with songs like 'Street Hassle' cleaned of offensive language and simply performed rather than lived.

The man was clearly somewhere else and to combat his dependencies had integrated Wu-style Tai Chi Chuan, or Chinese boxing, into his life as a spiritual discipline, remarking, 'It's an aesthetic and physical discipline that I find exquisite . . . the discipline is in the ability to relax. It's very beautiful to watch.' And as a contrasting means of relaxation, Reed had become a biker, burning up the country roads near his Jersey farm, doubtless in the psychological attempt to outstrip his past and confront the present through helmeted speed.

That Reed's creative impetus had fallen away in this period of largely flat transitioning is evident by the uninspired succession of albums it generated: *Legendary Hearts* (1983), *New Sensations* (1984), and *Mistrial* (1986), none of which suggested his marriage or rehabilitated lifestyle had in any way enhanced his creative energies, but instead alienated him from the deviant resources he romanticised as the subject of his writing. Only occasionally did Reed come alive with songs like 'The Last Shot' from *Legendary Hearts*, an examination of the terrors of withdrawal from alcohol, but overall the albums beginning with *The Blue Mask* (1982) were for the next four years, state of the art synthesiser product, so anodyne as to suggest Reed was now living on past reputation, a used-up directionless escape from the sixties and seventies, and institutionalised in that he produced his records for Sister Ray Enterprises Inc, as part of the factored Lou Reed emporium.

On the back of *Mistrial* (1986), with the title track arguing the defendant's rights to bring his ambiguously unresolved case before the people of New York City, and with the termination of his contractual obligations to RCA, Reed appeared at the time a self-parodying survivor of a legend sustained by the continuous re-evaluation of the Velvet Underground as seminal to rock's cultural development as artistic expression. His regeneration instanced by the grittily energised *New York* (1989), and his reunion with John Cale for the beautifully elegiac *Songs For Drella* (1990), as a tribute to Andy Warhol, had a lot to do with Reed signing to Sire, originally Seymour Stein's custom indie label, now affiliated to the giant WEA group, and providing him with the incentive of a conducive restart, if approaching 50, he could reboot his creative faculties with integral Reed menace, rather than deliver another album of multi-focussed songs compromised by attempting to win mainstream acceptance after decades of acute edge-walking credibility.

New York, arguably Reed's last great album, realistically evoked the city's extreme social inequalities, depredation and the Reagan Republican policy of suppressing welfare programmes and benefits, the Federal government's labelling of AIDS as the gay pandemic, the proliferation of homeless children, junkies and psycho Vietnam veterans begging from behind cardboard signs. It was a record that bannered through the smog of the Reagan/Thatcher coalition of ruthless materialism and corrupt profiteering, as the ideological directive to wipe out the last traces of creative idealism and community, the founding principles of sixties and seventies youth culture.

The man, no matter how financially privileged or secure in his elevated status as notorious anti-hero to three generations of leftfield garage subversives, was back with a mission to document a city in crisis, his lived-in voice and rumbled guitar spook as weaponry with which to impact the times, no matter Reed was growing richer by writing about the deprived and New York's financially penalised underbelly.

Reed's *New York* in part personified the questionable issue of the rock star capitalising on concerns of social deprivation to benefit on sales, and using empathy as a monetised faculty to still further the gap in inequality. But that's to deny the supremacy of the artistic achievement, and the individual's finely tuned sensitivity in using a heightened personal gift to alert the collective to its predicament through the awareness created by common suffering expressed as art.

Lou's *New York* came at the right moment to redeem a career that seemed irremediably sold out to compromise without commercial success, mediocrity as a substitute for risk, and the cultivation of celebrity at the expense of outlaw banditry. The no-colour, no-person Lou Reed was back as reconstructed rock mugger to the record buying public through revitalising awareness of his own high-end skyscrapered city in which floor levels represented wealth on an ascending financial scale.

New York, coming unexpectedly at a time when Reed appeared to have grown complacent, and to be living off a bad boy image consigned to the past, restored his artistic credibility after a decade of directionless compromise, and a string of unmemorable albums rarely accessed even by hard core Lou Reed fans. The eighties were a low point in the man's career, a clean-up act in which the tired licks of car paint quickly oxidised, and in which the attempt for mainstream acceptance was depressingly misguided, attracting no new audience and simply alienating those looking to recover the legend.

Contemporaneous with *New York*, and clearly stimulated by conceiving the epic he'd so long configured but never quite delivered, Reed temporarily re-united with John Cale to consolidate his reconstructed songwriting facilities on *Songs For Drella*, a 14-song cycle tribute to Andy Warhol, the Factory mastermind Reed had fired as the Velvet Underground's manager in 1966, and who had died unexpectedly in 1987 after a routine gall bladder operation. A brief musical series of snapshots of Andy Warhol's highly idiosyncratic, phobic, star-struck life as pop artist and factory celebrity, *Songs For Drella*, one of Reed's best crafted and finest albums, was again oxygenated by the return to form and eloquent expression he'd lacked since the mid-seventies, as the basis of his attempt to compress the idea of the Great American Novel into rock.

The album, an inventive mixture of fact and fiction, presented partly through Lou's Andy persona, and partly through the distillation of Reed's guilt at having ostracised Warhol from his circle, and being pejoratively remarked on in Warhol's *Diaries*, found Lou principally enthused 'by the amount of power just two people could do without needing drums'. But part of Reed's enduring conflict with Cale, the hostilities dating back to Cale being ignominiously fired from the Velvet Underground in 1968, is alluded to by Cale summarily in his ambivalent note to the *Drella* album: 'Although I think he did most of the work, he has allowed me to keep a position of dignity in the process.'

Issued in May 1990, to singularly affirming reviews as to the deepening modality of Reed's songwriting resources, *Songs For Drella* was renewed evidence of Lou's inspired creative renaissance, a facility consolidated by its successor, *Magic And Loss* (1993), Lou's last major album, a sustained lyric cycle that has him attempting to find transcendent qualities in the harrowing cancer-related deaths of two friends, the songwriter Doc Pomus and Rita – real name Kenneth Rapp – a gender-bending fixture of Warhol's Factory entourage. *Magic And Loss* is a totally intensified and unflinching suite of songs, documenting terminal illness coshed by chemotherapy: 'I saw isotopes introduced into his lungs/To stop the cancerous spread/It made me think of *Leda and the Swan*/And gold being made from lead.' A genuinely magnanimous work delivered with inflexionless gravity and his usual angle of detachment, the rock elegy's forensic scoping finds Reed inimitably on top of his art, in his early fifties, delivering an album comparable in structure to *New York*, but more intense in its conceptual seriousness to confront issues that demanded superlative lyricism. Reed, however, remained indomitably cool about the contents, placing the emphasis on tech, and telling Q's Mark Cooper: 'I wanted you to be able to walk round the sound, to be able to pick out the people playing and locate them, even pick out different instruments if you want.'

In May 1993 the four original Velvet Underground musicians reconvened for rehearsals in New York for one of rock's more unlikely reunion tours, almost 30 years after their spontaneously untutored noise distortion and controversial lyricism had become the pioneering template for most garage and indie graduates with a cool pair of reflective shades and aspirations to lay down a similarly epochal abrasive beat, albeit one you can never get.

Opening the tour at the Playhouse, Edinburgh on June 1, 1993, Reed, Claale Sterling Morrison and Mo Tucker played the Wembley Arena and a series of European festivals including the Glastonbury Festival on June 25 and the Roskilde Festival, before the inevitable disruptive hostilities between Reed and Cale exploded into irreconcilable tensions and splitting the band into terminal fallout. Both Reed and Cale looked and sounded resistantly menacing, their raw energised firepower still sufficiently noise-driven, aggressive and melodic to give audiences a rumble as to why the band were considered rock's educated hoodlums, who'd accidentally jumped into tomorrow, an unacknowledged mid-sixties phenomenon. Continually pushing tech frontiers, Reed's new weapon, his 'toy', was an LED constellated matt black and chrome stack, possibly fashioned on the desk at Mission Control, cased in violet plastic, together with a huge semi-circular foot-pedal console as state-of-the-art VU primed tech. The contentious reunion had the camps split into two, Reed and Tucker, Cale and Morrison, Lou having always singled out his female drummer as the only member of the band with whom he retained a sustained friendship surviving the decades, with Mo regularly sending Lou a Valentines card by way of admiration. According to the disillusioned and financially disappointed John Cale, 'We could have done anything we wanted. We could have stood on our heads, but it all suddenly became an exercise in revitalising a catalogue. And instead of doing something that everyone would look up to, and maintain the standard we had, we compromised. I hated that!' To monetise the aborted reunion and document its historic significance a CD and a DVD of the band's reformation was released as *The Velvet Underground: Live MCMXCIII*, as obligatory listening to diehard fans, still hoping to extract sufficient of the legend in the band's reinvention to carry the music forward.

By the mid-nineties, having divorced Sylvia Morales in 1993 for predictable emotional incompatibility, Reed's deepening relationship with the performance artist Laurie Anderson gave rise to two confessional albums, fictitiously mapping the complexities of this new relationship, *Set The Twilight Reeling* (1996) and *Ecstasy* (2000), both commercial failures, but valuable as the continued extension of Reed's selective autobiography translated into songs signposting the emotional turbulence and periodic equanimity churning through his nerves, and made public by his music. As Reed told Nick Johnstone, of his songwriting methods:

> 'When you're dealing with real people in life – it's complicated. The songs try to capture that odd push-and-pull going on, that can sometimes push you into a more extreme position than you would have realised. And you've gone and opened your mouth and you're stuck over there. And trying to have a balance with these things when you're dealing with emotion, its difficult.'

No more difficult than any other artistic expression that makes private subject matter public, only that rock music has a wider audience than most cultural modalities, and what may be concealed in a book by the silent and private nature of reading, is exposed and mediated through the nature of listening. Part of Lou's irreconcilable problem is that he constantly wants it both ways, the remove of the writer who is only read and the celebrity of the rock star whose private life is exhaustively scrutinised for sensation.

Why else make records if you don't want your issues made public?

Set The Twilight Reeling and *Ecstasy* are albums for Lou completists, but neither of these, nor *The Raven* (2003), Reed's epically scaled homage to Poe, a fundamental mismatch of sensibilities and expressions, build on the optimally crafted and conceptual integrity of *New York*, *Songs For Drella* and *Magic And Loss*. They were conceived as a trilogy, where a rock format seems to partner Reed's often overstated ambition to make his music the equivalent of contemporary literary expression. Reed's vision and its application never fully cohere on *The Raven*, although Reed stokes squalls of abrasive feedback into 'Fire Music' and is suitably focussed for his time of life on 'A Thousand Departed Friends' and surprisingly generous in allowing Antony Hegarty to remake 'Perfect Day' from *Transformer*, as part of Lou's theatrical schematics for the project that somehow fails to connect with Poe's opiated, metaphysical trickiness, as an early practitioner of crime horror and spook fiction.

A two-hour long conceptual work, *The Raven* is ultimately muddied, unfocused and lacking in original alacrity, despite Lou's claim that it represented 'the culmination of everything I've ever done'. While the work represented his creative tech present, there's little evidence either lyrically or musically of Reed finding any genuine empathy with Poe, outside of his intended association with Poe as outlaw, ruined by drink and drugs, and the hallucinated casualty dying in the streets of Baltimore. Reed could have been in the late seventies with his dependency on alcohol and substances.

Anticipating *The Raven* as likely to be as critically misconstrued as his electronic deviation *Metal Machine Music* (1975), he aligned the two albums as self-indulgent slabs, radically ahead of their time. He told Gavin Martin:

'Let me tell you something. I put out a thing called *Metal Machine Music*, and 20 years after the fact they put out an anniversary edition of it and it's performed live by an orchestra in Berlin. It's the sort of thing I've had happen with a bunch of records. I would hate to see that happen with this. If people don't get into it because of its length

27

and complexity then you'll just continue to have what you have. And you'll deserve it.'

Lou's conviction that he was always light years apart from his rock contemporaries, combined with invincible intellectual attitude when discussing his work, allowed him always to maintain a position of arrogating over potential critics of his work. His method is usually to place his form outside the accepted limitations of his art and to demand it is reviewed as rock literature rather than rock music. It's a category Reed nominated as his own, with no other inclusions in his singular genre, and with angular affront to anyone who dared challenge his status as rock's sneering smart boy with all the academic answers.

Expanding his Poe theme that Lou conceived of his ultimate fusion of rock and literature, he spoke of the aging process as a deepening of experience and creative resources rather than loss of dynamic.

> 'But I do know that, before, my understanding was only superficial. That's one of the nice things about getting older – you can read something like that and have a better chance of taking it how it was meant. In his essay, *The Imp Of The Perverse*, he's saying: '"Why are we drawn to that which we know is bad for us?" Now if there's a human being on Earth with a pulse who doesn't understand that, hasn't experienced that or doesn't know what that is about, I haven't met them.'

Reed's 2007 anomaly, a no guitar, no colour piece of hypnotic electronics *Hudson River Wind Meditations*, largely formulated to be used as meditative aids to accompany his Tai Chi practice, a series of low-key drone sketches that simmer noise, rather than release it, went largely unnoticed except to attentive fans hoping to find in the instrumentation the coding to an ambient *Metal Machine Music* remake.

Reed's pioneering experimentation persisted to the end, so too his often misconceived attempts to superimpose literature on the more elementary basics of rock, with *Lulu*, an 87-minute song cycle based on two plays by the German writer Frank Wedekind (1864–1918), *Earth Spirit*

(1895) and *Pandora's Box* (1904), forming the basis of a story in which Lulu, a lowlife escort and street hooker, ends up with her throat slashed by Jack the Ripper. A character study in depredation and moral ruin, Lou chose heavy metal pulverising warlords Metallica as his unlikely collaborators, the whole album being recorded in ten days at Metallica's San Rafael studio and projected at the listener like a sonic dirty bomb, an assault of atrocious riff pyrotechnics by the most notorious terrorists of guitar trash, pointing up noise as though recording at optimal time on a runway. Inviting immediate critical ridicule, and almost unanimous hostility for its apparent incongruous components, the album charted at 36 in the US and the UK respectively, reconfirming Reed's status as inveterate mainstream antagonist, his unpredictability seriously throwing his critics into a position of deriding the same sort of uncompromising sound liberated by the Velvet Underground in the mid-sixties, as a serious aberration on the uncategorisable *Lulu*.

What's so impressive on *Lulu* is Reed's lyric writing, probably his most intensely sustained since *Magic And Loss*, and suggesting at 70 his talents of reinvention and spearheading controversy were still unapologetically charged to keep on pushing frontiers. That his last album proved as controversial as anything he'd done, and was as much an irritant to both his admirers and detractors as the infamous *Metal Machine Music*, seemed an appropriate end to an iconoclastic career interrupted by death from liver failure on October 21, 2013.

2

Kill Your Sons

A GENERIC New Yorker, Lewis Allan Reed, aka Lou, was born a Piscean on March 2, 1942 at Beth El hospital in Brooklyn, New York, the son of Jewish tax accountant parents, Toby Futterman and Sidney Joseph Reed, and grew up in the family home at Freeport, Long Island. Like all angular gay outlaws, including Jean Genet, Lou never endorsed his date of birth, preferring to live independent of facts, distanced from his family background by reinventing himself through music. Filtered through layers of self-mythologised fictions, Lou, talking about his parents, explained in 1976:

> 'My parents were self-made millionaires. On paper they were very rich. I know what it's like to have money. They would love me to take over their companies. It's tax law – it all has to do with numbers. If United Steel is your client you can save them millions.'

There's also the suggestion that Lou's real name was Louis Firbank and that he changed his name to reconstruct a butch identity – 'Lou' feminine, 'Reed' masculine – as an integrated sexual identity in the face of hetero-normative parents. A fundamental problem for biographers is that Lou resists biography, his dominant expression being his art as the fictitious narration of his life, at the expense of chronological facts. To certain sensibilities, dissociation from family and formative conditioning is a necessary part of liberation into a self-created identity of the type Lou Reed projected, and one that seeks to reject the past by disowning it.

Growing up with a draconian father and an ex-beauty queen mother, with the father as an unquestionably authoritative voice, Lou was given obligatory piano lessons: 'I was a tot – eight, ten, something like that. I just had a natural affinity for music. Playing the classical piano, I forgot it all.' But it wasn't the piano that led the way to opening Lou's musical pathways, it was the ubiquitous radio that for Americans in the forties and fifties provided music, news and entertainment much like television today. Popular radio shows like Red Skeleton, Abbott & Costello, Jack Benny, Bob Hope and Truth or Consequences, transmitted not only doo-wop, but also rhythm and blues influenced early rock'n'roll artists like Chuck Berry, Elvis Presley, Bo Diddley, Fats Domino, Little Richard, Jerry Lee Lewis, Big Joe Turner and Gene Vincent, as prototypes of sexualised youth culture. Radio was as seminal an introduction to new music for Lou as it is to the five-year-old Candy in his song 'Rock'n'Roll' from *Loaded* (1970) whose life like Lou's was literally 'saved by rock'n'roll'.

Learning to play three-chord guitar from the radio, Reed was to say later, 'My god is rock'n'roll. It's an obscure power that can change your life. The most important part of my religion is to play guitar.' Lou's other enduring love picked up at the time from the radio was doo-wop, a genre onamatopoeically named from the harmonies provided by the backup singers for the tenor lead vocalist. Doo-wop had mixed origins derived from New York, Philadelphia, Chicago, Baltimore, Newark, Pittsburgh, Cincinnati, Detroit and Washington, flooded American radio in the fifties, and Lou's pop education was formed listening to the likes of The Elegants, Dion & The Belmonts, The Four Seasons, The Platters, The Coasters, The Drifters, The Silhouettes. And there was innovative jazz on the airwaves: John Coltrane, Miles Davis and Thelonius Monk linked to the musical underbelly, and the more experimental atonal improvisations of Don Cherry, who was to play on Reed's 1976 tour, Ornette Coleman and Artie Schwepp.

But undermining Lou Reed's youth, and as a potential social disgrace to his Jewish parents, was his homosexuality, the same-sex attraction listed by the American Psychiatric Association (APA) as a mental disorder, until it was declassified in 1973, largely due to the consolidated work of activists. According to B. Richard Peterson, writing for *Christianity Today* in 1960, homosexuals were to his moralistic thinking notably identified by certain key features. They are:

a third sex
born with the bodies of the wrong sex
hereditarily incapable of normal love
easily recognised by one another
impotent men and frigid women
feminine men and masculine women
highly talented and creative

This endemic misconception of homosexuals as a sick threat to the community was a belief shared by Lou's parents, who looked to conversion therapy or reparative therapy, through the brutal application of electro-shocks, as a way of correcting their son's same-sex attraction. Aversion therapy, the subject of Lou's 'Kill Your Sons', written for but never recorded by the Velvet Underground, and finally surfacing as the stand-out track on *Sally Can't Dance* (1974), was accompanied by the projection of 35mm colour stimulus slides. According to Farall Slides the manufacturer of shock devices: 'In reinforcing heterosexual preference in latent male homosexuals, male slides give a shock while the stimulus relief slides of females do not give shock.'

According to Lou, recollecting his experience of aversion at Creedmore State Psychiatric Hospital,

> 'They put the thing down your throat so that you don't swallow your tongue and they put electrodes on your head. That was what was recommended in Rockland County to discourage homosexual feelings. The effect is that you lose your memory and become a vegetable. You can't read a book because you get to page 17 and have to go right back to page one again.'

He later described the inefficacious treatment as 'like a very prolonged bad acid trip with none of the benefits'. Reed, like other diagnosed psychotic outpatients, attended Building 25, Creedmore State Hospital in Queens Village, Queens, New York, opened in 1912, which was initially the farm colony of Brooklyn State Hospital with 32 patients who worked the farmland as part of their treatment. In the seventies, crime infected the campus with three rapes, 22 assaults, 52 fires, 130 burglaries, six suicides, a shooting and a riot occurring within 20 months of each other. A crowded, understaffed institution, Creedmore is the subject of Susan Sheehan's *Is There No Place On Earth For Me?* (1982), a biography of a patient pseudonymously called Sylvia Frumkin.

To reinforce shock aversion, nausea-inducing drugs were used on the patient and in Lou's case Thorazine, a dopamine antagonist of the typical class of antipsychotic drugs possessing active ingredients to treat schizophrenia, the side effects of the drug named in 'Kill Your Sons', being intolerable restlessness, giving name to the Thorazine shuffle in which the user finds it impossible to ever rest or sit still.

As additional weaponry to convert his son to straight orientation, Lou's father insisted on him having a Farall Instruments Visually Keyed Shocker home device, the idea being that once the patient has received supportive therapy and a successful conditioning technique has been established, most patients can reinforce themselves with little or no supervision. The device targeted automated behaviour conditioning for 'Addiction, Masochism, Alcoholism, Aggression, Transvestism, Exhibitionism, Sexual Preference', using a self-buttoned device displaying 35mm slides of the patient's fantasy as stimulus, useful, according to the makers, 'for reinforcing sexual preference, reduction of anxiety associated with sexual frigidity and in treating homosexuality and some types of sex offenders.'

The barbarity of reparative therapy gunned into an intelligent, sensitive, confused youth, may account in part for the irreparably cold, invincibly hostile attitude Lou showed his public for most of his career, making no apology for his disdain of critics, journalists, admirers and three-chord imitative clones, and remaining understandably unapologetic about his acute dislike of his father.

In more brutal therapy sessions, shock was delivered to the male patient's genitals every time the person experienced gay positive response to the presentation of homoerotic stimuli. And despite the pioneering sexual studies of Charles Kinsey and Evelyn Hooker's seminal study published in 1957, *The Adjustment Of The Overt Male Homosexual*, in which she reported that 'homosexuals were not inherently abnormal and that there was no difference between homosexual and heterosexual men in terms of pathology', America's consolidated anti-gay bias made a forensic sweep on Lou's type as pathological gay.

The US's anti-homosexual legal system was spat back by Lou, ridiculing its authoritative methods in 'Kill Your Sons': 'All your two-bit psychiatrists/Are giving you electroshock/They said they'd let you live at home with mom and dad/Instead of mental hospitals/But every time you tried to read a book/You couldn't get to page seventeen/Cause you forgot where you were/So you couldn't even read.' According to John Cale the song was set up for demoing by the Velvet Underground in 1965, but vetoed as lacking commercial appeal.

Lou's only liberation from psychiatric drug coshes used on his homosexuality was to escape his disciplinarian family by attending Syracuse University in 1960 to study journalism, film directing and creative writing, the latter under the supervision of Delmore Schwartz, an already burnt-out self-destructive Jewish poet and writer. Reed, an ROTC platoon leader, was expelled from the programme, at the intervention of the State police, for holding a revolver to his superior's head, suggesting the combination of electroshock and Thorazine had left him seriously behaviourally disturbed. In the same year as Reed began his studies at Syracuse, a campaign to rid New York City of gay bars was put into full operation by order of Mayor Robert F Wagner Jr, who was concerned about the image of the city in preparation for the 1964 World's Fair. Undercover officers, as they did in London's West End, worked on entrapment, unlawfully coercing and then arresting unsuspecting gays for solicitation.

During the typical raid Lou would have experienced in a gay bar, the lights were turned on, and customers were lined up and their identification cards checked. Those without ID or in full drag were arrested; others were allowed to leave.

The persistent persecution of gay men in the workspace or in recreational bars or clubs continued throughout the sixties, the turning point arriving on Saturday, June 28, 1969, when at 1.20 a.m., four plainclothes policemen in dark suits, two patrol officers in uniform, and Detective

Charles Smythe and Deputy Inspector Pine, met with concerted resistance while attempting to raid the Stonewall Inn, located at 51 and 53 Christopher Street, a recognised gay residential zone where Lou was to buy an apartment in the mid-seventies.

Announcing their arrival with 'We're taking the place', the police officers were met with solid resistance, quickly losing control to the faggots they despised, and having attracted in the process a crowd that was incited to riot, they were persistently beaten back. The Stonewall Inn, whose patrons included the gay community, drag queens, newly self-aware transgender folk, male prostitutes and homeless youth, suddenly became the epicentre of activism, with tension between New York City Police and gay residents erupting into further serious riots the next evening, and again several nights later. For the first time the ruthlessly discriminated against Greenwich Village gay community gained sympathy, and Village residents were motivated to form activist groups to concentrate efforts on establishing places for gays and lesbians to be open about same-sex orientation without fear of being arrested.

From Lou's own account, his first serious gay affair, opening a pathway for his same-sex orientation, happened at 19:

> 'It was just the most amazing experience. It was never consummated. I felt very bad about it because I had a girlfriend and I was always going out on the side – and subterfuge is not my hard-on. I couldn't figure out what was wrong. I wanted to fix it up and make it OK. I figured if I sat around and thought about it I could straighten it out.'

In the same 1979 interview, and Reed was most vocal about his gay life in the late seventies, he expressed the excruciating emotional pain of 'trying to make yourself feel something towards women when you can't'. Sadly, Reed's repeated attempts to marry at intervals in his life, as a spurious, invariably failed compromise, seemed like periodic shock reminders of his teenage reparative therapy warning him away from natural gay into unnatural straight, in the way Farrall's corrective stimulus slides shocked him for responding to homoerotic stimuli, and rewarded him for acknowledging women as correct orientation. The same pattern tracked

Lou as a musician, whatever he was into he wasn't, whatever he achieved he deconstructed with no stabilised resting point. Arguably, it all pointed back to the pretend choices needed to avert shock and admit to being gay.

In 1961, while still at Syracuse University, Lou began hosting with pioneering intrepidity a late-night radio programme on WAER called *Excursions On A Wobbly Rail*. With its name lifted from a song by avant-garde pianist Cecil Taylor, the programme typically featured Lou's obsessions at the time, doo-wop, rhythm & blues and jazz variants, particularly the off-the-wall free jazz developed in the late fifties as part of atonal modernism. In retrospect we could argue that many of Lou's guitar figures such as the guitar–drum roll, were initially inspired by free-form jazz saxophonists like Ornette Coleman and Don Cherry, with something of their wonky disarrangements being incorporated into Lou's jazz impro-vised *Rock'n'Roll Heart* tour of the States in 1976, his most audacious attempt to mix jazz into his recognisably unpredictable rock format.

Given Reed's troubled, rebellious angle on life, it seemed natural he would gravitate to the degenerate campus sexual predator and drunk Delmore Schwartz as avatar. Recalling his mentor in 1978, Reed observed:

> 'Delmore Schwartz was the unhappiest man who I ever met in my life, and the smartest – till I met Andy Warhol. He didn't use curse words until he was 30. His mother wouldn't allow him. His worst fears were realised when he died and they put him in a plot next to her. Once, drunk in a Syracuse bar, he said, "If you sell out, Lou, I'm gonna get ya." I hadn't thought about doing anything, let alone selling out. Two years later, he was gone. I'm just delighted I got to know him. It would have been tragic not to have met him. But things have occurred where Delmore's words float right across. Very few people do it to you. He was one.'

There's no evidence, given Lou's defensiveness, that he ever came out at Syracuse, and certainly not to Schwartz, a skirt-chasing member of the faculty already in disrepute for his notably heavy drinking. Schwartz's fuckedness quotient as a speed-freak who combined amphetamine with alcohol, who had been institutionalised for drug abuse, and as a poet who'd recklessly accelerated a continuous self-destructive binge, could arguably have been the prototype for Lou's similar attempted assassination of his songwriting facilities throughout much of the seventies, when the same cocktail of speed and booze seriously damaged his health, and he was forced regularly to reconstruct songs he'd originally written in the sixties for the Velvet Underground as new album material. Reed was already experimenting with weaponised noise at Syracuse, his Gretsch guitar bled into distortion as he worked out figures to shock using improvised feed-back. A natural punk, who early on recognised noise as optimal attractor, Reed in tune with the increasingly war-driven tech-overloaded 20th-century picked up early on the idea of guitar being his chosen instrument to shatter noise-limitations.

It was while creating noise patterns on his guitar on campus that Reed's sonic directive attracted another literature student, Sterling Morrison, who having been sent down from Illinois University for consistently bypassing ROTC training, was temporarily staying at Syracuse before beginning a course at City College, New York. The accident of his passing through was by a prescient time-slip, and the introduction it affected, his randomly selective reason for being in the original Velvet Underground. If Lou spent a lot of time drinking in the local bar, the Orange, with Schwartz, then he was also writing poetry, short stories and rock lyrics themed around anti-authority, dysfunctional families and gay subculture. Originally, Reed wrote future Velvet Underground signature songs like 'The Gift', 'Heroin' and 'Waiting For The Man' as stories that he later downsized into rock lyrics, as part of his belief that rock was the new transporter of oxygen through the blood. Reed's debt at the time to William Burroughs, outlaw junky novelist, whose heroin novel *Naked Lunch*, published in 1959, quickly gained underground notoriety, is particularly apparent in songs like 'Heroin' and 'Waiting For The Man'. In *Naked Lunch*, Dr Benway who presides over the allegorical Freeland Republic, talks of 'those junkies standing around waiting for the Man', or the dealer.

William Seward Burroughs (1914–1997), the major literary influence on Reed's lyric writing, was, like Lou, born to a wealthy family in St Louis, Missouri, grandson of the creator and founder of the Burroughs

Corporation. He attended Harvard University in 1932, studying English and anthropology and later spent time at a medical school in Vienna. Discharged from the US army in 1942 on account of civilian disability, Burroughs – a homosexual pretending to be straight – became seriously addicted to morphine and heroin by the mid-forties, selling heroin in Greenwich Village to support his habit. While living in Mexico in 1951, Burroughs shot and killed his common-law-wife, Joan Vollmer, in a drunken game of William Tell at a party above the American-owned Bounty Bar in Mexico City. While awaiting trial he fled to the United States, and was convicted in absentia of homicide and given a two-year suspended sentence.

Burroughs published his first novel *Junkie* (1953) under the alias William Lee, but it was the publication of a postmodern drugs manual in the form of *Naked Lunch* (1959), a novel that redefined subject matter for fiction, that brought him to Reed's attention, as dystopian chronicler of drugs creating alternative realities in contemporary culture. On its publication *Naked Lunch* was subjected to a court case under US sodomy laws, and the extensive, randomised, unedited manuscript from which the book was extracted provided the material for the subsequent Nova trilogy, *Soft Machine* (1961), *The Ticket That Exploded* (1962) and *Nova Express* (1963).

Reed, who regardless of his early talent lacked the sustained imaginative discipline necessary to write prose, scrambled his talents into writing lyrics with the same sort of disconnected cut-up technique adopted by Burroughs in books like *Naked Lunch*, *The Wild Boys* and *Nova Express*. But partly due to lack of concentration as a side effect of the shock treatment, and the fact that he was being prescribed the tranquilliser Placidyl, Reed was put on academic probation at the end of his first year at Syracuse as a clearly troubled and disturbed student. Apart from drinking a lot of alcohol to keep pace with Schwartz, Reed had already devised his own pharmaceutical menu, and reportedly experimented with hallucinogenics like peyote, LSD and magic mushrooms and, like most students of his generation, regularly smoked marihuana. He also picked up on a Burroughs recommendation, the codeine-based cough syrup Turpenhydrate, an opiate he alternated with heroin.

Lou's roommate at Syracuse, Lincoln Swados, was also a significant influence on his deviated mind-set, an agoraphobic, astutely intelligent schizophrenic, like Lou into altered states, and who lost an arm and a leg in a failed suicide attempt in 1964, throwing himself under an incoming subway train. Both students were control freaks, into head-games and radically opposed to authority and campus regulations, and used downers like Seconal and Thorazine to further alienate themselves from student activities, while remaining unnervingly intellectually smart.

But almost in compliance with the sexual punishment given him at Creedmore State Psychiatric Hospital for same-sex orientation, Reed pursued an on/off relationship with a girl called Shelley Albin, which was never consummated, but established Reed's lifelong alternation between the sexes in a conditioned pattern of guilt and reward. Reed's unpredictable mood swings and antagonism drove Albin away, although it's rumoured 'I'll Be Your Mirror' was written with her in mind, as a creative point of re-focussing a predominantly failed relationship.

By 1963–64 Reed was fronting short-lived college bands, integrating doo-wop and generic rock'n'roll into basic three-chord structures, and also playing for a time in a folk quartet. It was while a member of the performing rock band LA & the Eldorados that Reed wrote early versions of 'Coney Island Baby', 'Heroin' and 'Waiting For The Man', but chose to perform standard covers onstage, like The Kingsmen's 'Louie Louie' and The Premiers' 'Farmer John'. Whatever innovative template Reed had formulated for experimental sound was kept concealed in his college years, and would in part need John Cale's provocative avant-garde classical training to be fully unleashed in the Velvet Underground's signature experimentation with rock as art form.

In 1964 Reed graduated from Syracuse with a degree in English, and faced with an indeterminate future – his parents were pushing him for a career in legal accountancy – decided as a better option to remain as a student and do postgraduate studies in journalism and drama production. After producing Fernando Arrabal's *The Car Cemetery*, he was asked to leave Syracuse, probably because of drugs, and according to him 'by the Tactical Police Force of the city which housed my large eastern university, to leave town well before graduation because of various clandestine operations I was alleged to have been involved in.'

Abruptly terminating his postgraduate studies, after a spell back home on Long Island, a period of anxious inactivity, Reed took up an in-house post at Pickwick International Records, based on Staten Island, as one of the label's songwriting team charged with imitating current hits, be it surf music, rock, girl groups, biker songs, pop, cynically copying the sound without artistic merit. The job benefitted Lou in that it allowed him to analyse the components of commercial hits, and by stripping the originals apart like a motorcycle to learn the basics of formulaic rock and pop, as well as gain valuable studio experience. Among the songs written by Lou during his Pickwick residency were 'You're Driving Me Insane' by The Roughnecks, 'This Rose' by Terry Phillips, 'Flowers For The Lady' by Terry Phillips, 'Wild One' by Ronnie Dove, 'Johnny Won't Surf No More' by Jeannie Larimore, 'I've Got A Tiger In My Tank' by The Beechnuts, 'Cycle Annie' by The Beechnuts, 'The Ostrich' by The Primitives, 'Tell Mama Not To Cry' by Robertha Williams and 'Why Don't You Smile?' by The All Night Workers. 'The Ostrich', a dance number inspired by a fashion revival of ostrich feathers, released in late 1964 by The Primitives, was singled out by Pickwick executive Terry Phillips as potential chart material if recorded by the right innovative band.

In 1972, Reed recollected his time at Pickwick Records:

> 'I was working as a songwriter for Pickwick. We just churned out songs; that's all. Never a hit song – what we were doing was churning out these rip-off albums. In other words, the album would say it featured four groups and it wouldn't really be four groups, it would just be permutations of us, and they would sell them in supermarkets for 99 cents or a dollar. While I was doing that I was doing my own stuff and trying to get by, but the material I was doing, people wouldn't go near me with it at the time. I mean, we wrote "Johnny Can't Surf No More" and "The Wedding Bells Ring" and "Hot Rod Song".'

At the time of their first meeting in 1964, John Cale, a classical music student, was sharing an apartment on dodgy Ludlow Street, on New

York's Lower East Side, with Tony Conrad, Lamonte Young's wacky violinist, and when he moved out Lou moved in. Working now only part time for Pickwick, due to some of his progressively extreme ideas going off radar, Lou reportedly earned money from selling his blood and from modelling for photographs of wanted criminals to illustrate sensationally fictitious stories marketed by the tabloids for supermarket consumption. With lack of money an acute issue, and Reed's parents unwilling to assist unless he conformed to regular employment, the two musicians, both lived on an improvised diet of oatmeal and junk food when they could afford it. The two also busked for money outside the Club Baby Grand on 125th Street in Harlem. If there were tensions between the two, they were sexual: Lou clearly wanted a relationship with Cale, who relates in his autobiography *What's Welsh for Zen?* how he quickly realised Lou's sexual orientation when Reed placed his hand on his cock. Lou's bisexuality seems to have lacked singular focus, as an oscillating pivot, and it's arguable that his failure to make it with Cale was the emotional basis of the conflicts between the two that drove the volatile Cale out of the Velvet Underground in 1968.

Briefly calling themselves the Falling Spikes, Reed ran into his old friend Sterling Morrison on the subway in April 1965, enlisting him in the band, now renamed the Warlocks, before adding Angus MacLise on drums and recording a demo tape featuring 'Heroin', 'Venus In Furs', 'The Black Angel's Death Song', 'Wrap Your Troubles In Dreams' and a song with a typically punkish Reed title, 'Never Get Emotionally Involved With Man, Woman, Beast Or Child'. The only surviving recordings from the Warlocks incarnation, called Ludlow Street demos, minus Angus MacLise, surfaced on the *Peel Slowly And See* boxed set, as acoustic, folksy, unvitaminised versions of early Velvet songs, largely stripped of all weirdness. Instrumentally subdued, and with 'Heroin' delivered in a flat Dylan-cloned nasal delivery, the formative Ludlow Street demos offer no hint of the authentic, monumentally lived-in menace of the version recorded on *The Velvet Underground And Nico*; so coldly self-realised, Lou sounds as if in the course of phrasing the song, he has literally injected the drug into his neural pathways. The Ludlow Street demos are interesting for their partial restraint, their excruciating failure to deliver the optimised potential of the Velvet Underground. 'When the smack begins to flow/I really don't care any more' was Reed's as we know it on record, and in his personal life, total conviction of an alienated young man buying drugs in Lexington and mainlining H for exhilarated dopamine acceleration as the molecules bound to his opioid receptors, kicks orgasmically depressed by a hypodermic plunger with hepatitis as the organic knock on.

The protein building blocks of any song are of course the lyrics, and Reed's romanticisation of the urban underbelly through street poetry and a dystopian terminology picked up from William Burroughs and the Beats, as cool countercultural expression dosed with drug references was, no matter Cale's drone emphasis, the basis of the Velvet Underground's shocking originality. 'Up to Lexington 125/feel sick and dirty more dead than alive' was Lou's confessional dictum in 'Waiting For The Man', a lyric that found no direct counterpart in British rock, with its heavily censored surveillance: 'Hey white boy what you doing uptown/ you chase all my coloured women around,' or is it men in Lou's case, the smart college kid with an unresolved sexual identity? The man waiting for the man, what's a blowjob but another sort of chemical combination?

It was Tony Conrad who picked up a second hand paperback of *The Velvet Underground*, a 1963 book by Mike Leigh, a book about wife-swapping with a blurb that read: 'It will shock and amaze you. But as documentary on the sexual corruption of our age, it is a must for every thinking adult' and passed it on to Lou as an interesting curiosity. The Warlocks' immersion in underground film, art and literature seemed appropriate to the book's title, and the name stuck as the oblique expression of their unclassifiable cultural genre. *The Velvet Underground*, a mass market paperback published by MacFadden Books in September 1963, investigates paraphilia or aberrant sexual behaviour among consenting adults, with the title alone suggesting something of the decadence implied by the Velvets music. Published in the UK in 1967 as *Bizarre Sex Underground*, the author brought out a sequel in 1968 *The Velvet Underground Revisited* to capitalise on the success of his investigative social phenomenon.

Of the initial demos recorded at raw brownstone 56 Ludlow Street (with Lou only decamping there at weekends, and living on tins of Dinty Moore meatball stew), and Cale burning scavenged crates and wood to keep warm, Cale recalls, 'We rehearsed, we experimented, and the six songs we taped in the apartment in July '65 on our Wollensak recorder wound up being the basis of our first album in 1967'. Cale additionally throws valuable light on the inception of drone, as a Velvets characteristic, particularly in relation to its incorporation into 'Heroin':

> 'It's the first song where we decided drone would work. The song was pretty much the same in 1965; Lou just changed the key when I played the violin, because that's the dominant instrument – the landscape. Everything was dominated and distorted with the Velvets in those days. We used cheapish guitars. Lou had a Gretsch Country Gentlemen; I used a classic viola with mandolin and guitar strings that were eaten into with clips and pick-ups – really scarred, but it got better as time went on.'

Meanwhile, interfacing Lou's penalised homosexuality, activist events occurring on the gay radar, were small, but highly significant in mediatised impact. In 1965, homophile activists picketed the White House on April 17, and the United Nations on April 18, after hearing that Cuba was illegally placing homosexuals into forced labour camps. As a further ripple of increasing opposition to discrimination, on April 25, 1965, an estimated 150 people participated in a sit-in when the manager of Dewey's restaurant in Philadelphia refused service to several people it thought were gay.

On May 29, 1965, the White House was again the target for activists in a protest organised by ECHO, as one of a series of pickets focussed on discrimination, which also took up the cause outside the Civil Service Commission, the State Department and The Pentagon. The increased wave of resentment at anti-gay legislation was indirectly buried in the Velvets' dissonant sound, with Lou's choppy disarranged guitar starting to be stoked into aggressive weaponry. To an uptown graduate, coshed by the State for his sexual orientation, and saturated in rock as an art form, Lou's writing and playing was plugged into the dangerous countercultural subversion of the accelerated times.

Of the improvised guitar surgery at Ludlow Street where the band, looking like street Arabs posed for photo shoots outside and on the roof, Sterling Morrison admitted:

> 'The thing is, Lou and I never saw blues as a religion, something where you had to learn every riff and play it just that. There was no danger either Lou or I would become the next Mike Bloomfield. We didn't care enough about the blues as a form. I like Chuck Berry as a guitar player. But I liked him better as a lyricist. There was a lot more depth there, and the rhythm of his lyrics was fabulous.'

Morrison could have said the same of Lou, that it was the metric drive of his street poetry that superseded his playing, and that verbal thrust was the nose cone of the Velvet Underground's offensive. With the integration of Maureen Tucker into the band, after MacLise summarily quit, and with Tucker's kit costing 50 dollars, comprising one snare, a bass drum, a floor tom and a beaten up cymbal, the Velvet's debuted their new line up on November 11, 1965 at the Summit High School and moved on to a residency arranged by Al Aronowitz at a Greenwich Village dive, the Café Bizarre, attracting immediate controversy through their sleaze-themed music, and actually getting fired for playing 'The Black Angel's Death Song', a number that provoked hostility on the part of the café management.

By luck, Gerard Malanga, one of Andy Warhol's Factory assistants, was in the audience to experience the band's unusually punkish menace and edgy avant-garde propulsion, and was to impart his enthusiasm to Warhol, New York's pop art guru, with a particular interest in collecting weird people, including a transgender retinue, and giving them space to express themselves at The Factory.

John Cale, recollecting the Velvets policy of detuning instruments and playing with state-of-the-art gadgets, also recognised 'what Lou was singing was not what rock'n'roll was generally about. Yet there was no reason why this other hybrid could not exist. We were all of a single mind about that.' But what Lou was singing about – sexual tensions, drug para-phernalia, the underworld, and the basic problems of human identity – fitted perfectly with the gay, platinum-haired Czech immigrant and generally uncategorisable celebrity, Andy Warhol, who was constantly experimenting with new media, including the movie *Blow Job* (1963), a continuous shot of someone receiving oral sex, typical of Warhol's voyeuristic fixation in which physical content was substituted by vicarious reward through observing others.

According to Lou Reed, whose relationship with Warhol was always emotionally ambivalent, 'Andy told me that what we were doing with music was the same thing he was doing with painting and movies, i.e. kidding around.' Whether Warhol regarded the Velvet Underground as a long term proposition, or a short-lived sensational phenomenon isn't clear, only that Warhol – nicknamed 'Drella', a combination of Dracula and Cinderella – was addicted to reinventing the concept of fame as a transiently superficial marketing brand that, unable to sustain its shock value, was instantly superseded by something more shocking. His HQ, the Factory, was a metaphorical assembly line, not only for his own art but for the contributions of others, big in the moment, but without any antici-pated durability. This certainly wasn't Lou's event horizon and Warhol's bitterly acerbic wit, annihilative in its content, threw Lou out of his customary control freakery into still another of Drella's put downs. That the two were on a collision course from the start was obvious in that both were inexorably controlling – Lou in an overt way, Andy from a subtler angle – neither willing to concede or delegate power. But Reed learned smartness from his and the Velvet Underground's patron, and how to parallel process who you are with who your public wants you to be while remaining intrinsically impartial to both.

Rehearsing at the Factory, where Warhol's regulars included Gerard Malanga, Billy Name, Edie Sedgwick, Paul Morrissey, Ondine, Brigid Polk and Mary Woronov, most of whom were gay or bisexual, with the addition of the German model, actress and singer Christa Päffgen, aka Nico, a depressive blonde looker with the affected vocal gravitas of Marlene Dietrich, the Velvet Underground began musically experimenting in what was known euphemistically as the Silver Factory. The original fifth-floor Factory, located at 231 East 47th Street in midtown Manhattan, with a rent of $100 dollars, was done out in a space age silver by Billy Name, with fractured mirrors and walls covered in silver foil, giving an arthouse feel to an industrial structure, and also incorporated as a centre-piece a red couch that Billy Name found on the sidewalk of 47th Street and salvaged for the Factory.

But despite the Factory attracting speed users and a gender-bending entourage, Warhol maintained a highly disciplined work ethic, and his assistants would make silkscreens and lithographs under his direction. John Cale recollected, 'It wasn't called the Factory for nothing. It was where the assembly line for the silkscreens happened. While one person was making a silkscreen, somebody else would be filming a screen test. Every day something new.' Warhol promoted hard work as the effort needed for significant creative achievement, and as part of the process using silkscreen to mass-produce images in the same way corporations mass-produced consumer goods. Attracting a druggy ménage, known as the Warhol Superstars, Andy was unsparing in making work the price of being incorporated into the Factory, with him as industrial foreman. It was there that Lou Reed not only became dependent on speed, but met the cast of characters documented in his first commercial hit 'Walk On The Wild Side', Holly Woodlawn, Candy Darling, Joe Dellesandro, Jackie Curtis and Joe Campbell with his factory name, Sugar Plum Fairy.

Things too were happening to politicise the gay scene by seriously opposing the brutal discrimination, to the extent that the New York state Liquor Authority banned homosexuals from being served in licensed bars in the state under penalty of revocation of the bar's license to trade. By 1965, influenced by Frank Kameny's proto-activist addresses in the early sixties, Dick Leitsch, the President of the New York Mattachine Society, advocated direct confrontation of the authorities, and the group staged the first openly gay demonstration and picket lines, arguing to legalise homosexuality.

At the time of Lou's immersion in the Factory ethos, under Warhol's tutelage, Greenwich Village, with its diverse mix of subcultures, was the hub of gay street youth. Largely young effeminate runaways rejected by their families, society and the gay community, they were often openly gay, wore makeup, sold their bodies, took drugs, mostly mephedrone, shoplifted and hustled older gay men in order to survive. Reflecting the prevalent counterculture, they were Lou's generation of young gay men finding their own identity and voice, without being punished by reparative therapy of the sort Reed had undergone in his traumatised teens.

Although Warhol had never produced a record, he offered to attach his name as producer to the first Velvet Underground LP, the 'Banana' album, and pay for the sessions, the material being largely the live set performed regularly by the Velvets as part of Warhol's multimedia Exploding Plastic Inevitable. Lou, meanwhile, used the Factory's decadent resources as direct inspiration for writing.

> 'I kept notes of what people said, what went on, and those notes would go directly into songs. There would be a line, and I could go from there. It would suggest a title or a situation. I was writing everything in these notebooks.'

Realising that trying to get the Velvet Underground a commercial recording deal might present insurmountable difficulties, Warhol personally financed sessions to produce a finished album to offer to the industry. Andy put up $700 of his own money on top of $800 from Norman Dolph, a former sales executive at Columbia Records. The small sum which was raised allowed for two days of recording in Sceptre Records' studio, located in a derelict Manhattan facility that was under order for demolition; a suitably appropriate site for the band's pre-industrial punkish noise. With Dolph and the inept Warhol on the desk, in a studio that was wrecked, the Velvets, hot from playing live, didn't need more than two takes of any song, with 'Heroin' the compelling centrepiece, although later, when a young black producer, Tom Wilson, signed the band to MGM's subsidiary label Verve, they re-recorded three numbers with Wilson at T.T.G. Studios in Los Angeles and, back in New York, 'Sunday Morning' under his direct supervision.

The distinctive jangly chop of Lou Reed's guitar, achieved by tuning all his strings down to the same note, possibly as a spin-off from speed abuse, gave emphasis to Cale's highly idiosyncratic viola playing. According to Sterling Morrison's cataloguing of the band's technical facilities, 'If we played in a normal E tuning, for John to get the pitch he wanted in an open modal style, he would have to uptune, which would put too much strain on the neck and the bridge of the viola. To prevent that from happening, we down tuned a half tone, sometimes a whole tone.' And from Cale's viewpoint, 'Downtuning was better for Lou's voice and better for all the instruments. It gave everything a squelched, slightly squashed sound, creating more sustain.'

The album, recorded in 1966, and held back by Verve as a vote of no confidence until March 1967, despite the Warhol designed banana sleeve giving it instant appeal as eye candy, failed to make any commercial impact. Verve, largely insensitive to the band's uncompromising experimentation, attempted to focus the album's selling point on Warhol's pop art credentials. One ad read: 'What happens when the Daddy of Pop Art goes Pop Music? The most underground album of all. It's Andy Warhol's new hip trip to the subterranean scene.' Reaching number 71 on the *Billboard* album chart in mid-May and signally under-promoted by Verve, the album quickly disappeared from stores to become an oddity to be rediscovered decades later, and in a genre of its own; in much the same way as was given the sort of continuous cult acclaim as surrounded the originally obscure publication of Arthur Rimbaud's *A Season In Hell*, privately published by the author in 1870, at the time known to ten or 20 people and later acclaimed as one of the seminal texts of underground modernism and transgressive counterculture spearheading.

The Velvet Underground And Nico, now universally known as the 'Banana' album, was released shortly after the cyclonic furore surrounding the Beatles *Sgt Pepper's Lonely Hearts Club Band*, as period psychedelia. Undeterred by its lack of commercial success, the Velvets moved on, minus Nico, an easily disposable supernumerary, but more surprisingly without Warhol, summarily fired by Reed for trying to impose systems on the band in their commercial interests. According to Reed:

'When he told me I should start making decisions about the future, and what could be a career, I decided to leave him. He did not try to stop me, legally or otherwise. He did, however, tell me I was a rat. I think it was the worst word he could think of.'

Essentially, Warhol lacked serious commitment to the Velvet Underground as a manager, knew little of record company politics, and was anyhow totally centred in his own creative programme to make art into lucrative commodity and himself a celebrity. The Velvet Underground as an art gallery project wasn't central on his self-preoccupied atlas and Lou's similar absorption into his own songwriting stimulus demanded the full attention he expected of the work's marketable potential.

Sexually and recreationally, according to Edie Sedgwick, Lou Reed and Billy Name used the backroom in a bar called Ernie's, which may have been the Bon Soir, 40 West 8th Street in Greenwich Village – gay bars were often known to their habitués by their patron's name – and for Lou there was also 'Julius' at 159 West 10th Street, also known as the Express, on account of the rapidity of the transient sex, largely blow jobs, that took place on the premises of this established gay meeting place. Also on the fugitive gay map was the Sanctuary, Le Jardin (that Lou references on 'Sally Can't Dance') and the precursor of Studio 54, the Tenth Floor, David's Loft, the Stud on Greenwich Street, the Ninth Circle, and Kellers on West Street, all accommodating a world of clandestine coding targeted by frequent police raids, vicious arrests and panicked getaways, like Lou's line, 'You gotta run, run, run' or end up in a police van.

When the Velvet Underground came to record their second album, the punk noir *White Light/White Heat*, the ultimate in feedback distortion and volume overload, the band were recognised sound-bandits, with nothing to lose as outlaws wallowing in their still uncategorisable generic punk with an intellectually sophisticated twist. It's a bit like William Burroughs fucking a virtual Raymond Chandler into lyrical realisation that there's noise on the other side of words. By the time they came to record *White Light/White Heat*, Reed's black leather jacket and wraparound shades was now his signature image, with the band having originally been requested by Andy Warhol to wear dark clothes onstage, so he could project films and bright lights on them as a reflective contrast.

Begun in September 1967, the often directionless *White Light/White Heat*, a sonic car-chase, reflected not only warring tensions in the band, but drugs, most notably speed and heroin. According to John Cale, 'It was a very rapid record. The first one had some gentility, some beauty. The second one was consciously anti-beauty.' Produced by Tom Wilson, who according to Reed walked out of the sessions and left them to it, the album's high noise quotient or 'power-cubed' to use Reed's term, is as flagrantly anti-user friendly as an album could be in 1967 in terms of trying to sell hostility as attitude. Exploring Reed's typically dystopian urban landscape, the record's urgent antagonism placed it at the time in a menacing rock wasteland, an uncommercial interzone between intelligent experimentation and an explosive assault on noise limitations. Radical experiments like 'The Gift', a short story Lou wrote at Syracuse as part of a creative writing module, and read by John Cale with an incongruous Welsh cadence, and 'Lady Godiva's Operation', a sort of cut-up narrative in which Reed and Cale scrambled alternate lines, fed by drone, sounded like the first genuine attempt to apply Burroughs' literary collage method to rock music as raw, disjointed verbal energies. Grainily mixed, whining with guitar feedback like an airport runway, *White Light/White Heat* also contains numbers like 'Here She Comes Now' and 'I Heard Her Call My Name' that hint in their melodic undertow at Reed's forthcoming about-turn to write pretty songs for the Velvet's eponymous third album, in which tuneful hooks replace insurgent guitar phrasing as the record's melodic focus. To Lou the album's power-pointed distortion fell considerably short of the abrasive sound the band achieved live.

> 'You can hear it on some bootleg. That never came across on record. They couldn't get the bottom end of it in those days. No engineer was going to come out and put a really good mike on a guitar like that, assuming they knew where to put it anyway. I wanted to control that noise – to get only the stuff I wanted to get out of it, even it was arbitrary.'

The album's unrepeatable, epic metal centrepiece, 'Sister Ray', stands out as a competitive band assault, as much on each other, as conventional modalities of accepted subject matter for rock music. A lyric written by Reed, on the road between gigs, describing a number of drag queens having an orgy broken up by the police, 'Sister Ray' best exemplifies the cool indifferent tone Reed had picked by from Burroughs' cold dissociation from experience on junk. Lou's flatly narrated account of deviated sex, murder and drugs is delivered glacially, nonchalantly over a soundtrack of angry guitars and organ drone in collisional conflict. Of 'Sister Ray', with its cocksucking drag queens too busily engaged in fellatio to note proceedings, Lou said:

> 'It has such an attitude and feel to it, even if you don't understand a word of it . . . it's just a parade of New York night denizens. But of course, it's hard to understand a word of it, which is a shame, because it's really a compressed movie.'

We have Duck and Sally, Miss Rayon, Rosie, Sister Ray, the dealer from Alabama, what is in essence a novella submerged in catastrophically gunned noise that sounds like a subway roar. With Reed and Morrison's guitars maxed to overload against a sonic wall of Cale's organ, Morrison recalls the unpredictable thunder of the track:

> 'When Cale came surging through the wall of sound on his first solo I remember thinking "where's John getting all that noise from?" I see him fumbling over there with all the stops on his organ. I expected it more to stay at the same volume. And all of a sudden the organ is way louder than me or Lou. I couldn't turn up; I was already maxed out. At one point, I was down at the bridge pickup on my Stratocaster, so I decided to get a little more oomph on the neck pickup. So I switched to that, which was good. I can hear it in there.'

The indomitable sleaze factor theming 'Sister Ray' was unknown in rock lyricism in 1967, in what was in fact 'the summer of love', the peak of psychedelic flower power and idealistic hippy community both in the US and the UK. Reed's mining of his city's underbelly, and particularly its gay and altered gender coterie, would have bypassed British youth, whose pop/rock parameters at the time were still dominated by largely unrequited love and the social revolution implied by countercultural dominants like fashion, soft drugs including LSD, and the iconoclastic subversion of class. Although homosexuality was conditionally decriminalised in the UK on July 21, 1967 following the findings of the Wolfenden report, the Sexual Offences Act applied official sanction only to two consenting adults in private who had attained the age of 21, with the introduction of a third party considered a criminal offence. Blackmail and entrapment, particularly in the capital's recognised sites for male prostitution, like Piccadilly Circus and Leicester Square, and in bars and public toilets, was still a police focus and the punishment and humiliation of queers remained high on the public agenda of moral offences to be scandalously sensationalised and redressed.

Reed's Greenwich Village gay scene, subjected to equal police brutality, was draggier and more outrageous than anything in the UK, while the topic of his liberated lyric writing at a time had no British counterpart in rock, nothing that openly narrated stories of gay life and its fugitive subculture. Released in the US in December 1967, *White Light/White Heat* reached number 199 on the *Billboard* chart for one week in March before sliding into the commercial abyss. Its legacy, largely the result of the accelerated, pre-punk warhead 'Sister Ray' is now and forever recognised as possibly the most deviantly shattering inimitable noise drone ever released outside of the US military.

3

Put Jelly On Your Shoulder

IN September 1968, Lou Reed convened a meeting in a Greenwich Village café attended by Morrison and Tucker, specifically to fire John Cale from the band, due to their continuing conflict of interests. Cale wanted the band to go louder, more menacingly disruptive and cultishly alienated, and Reed realised that if they adopted this course his song-writing facilities would be harnessed to just one aspect of his creative resources, and denied the poppier, soft-focussed sound that now interested him. Lou didn't want to go on repeating a polarised formula:

> 'I thought it would be a terrible mistake and I really believe that. I thought we had to demonstrate the other side of us. Otherwise we would become this one-dimensional thing, and that had to be avoided at all costs.'

Throughout the period 1967–1970 Reed's extraordinary prolific output as a songwriter reached its apogee, with much of the unreleased material written for the Velvet Underground fuelling the basis of his solo career from *Lou Reed* (1972) to *Street Hassle* (1978) as well as two Velvet Underground albums of previously unavailable recordings, *VU* recorded 1967–1969, and *Another View* recorded 1967–1969, released in 1985 and 1986 respectively, documenting a continuing mixed legacy of Reed's peak, speed-fuelled creativity in the late sixties.

To replace John Cale, the band brought in Doug Yule, a 21-year-old bass player from Boston, who like Reed with his astrological bias, obsessively strong at the time, was a Piscean, balancing the fact that Morisson and Tucker were both Virgos. Yule had been discovered by Morrison via the Velvets' road manager, Hans Onsager, and proved to be a sensitive multi-instrumentalist, less aggressively flamboyant than Cale, but capable of creating big surf rolls of surging organ as a Velvets' live characteristic.

According to Sterling Morrison, the sound of the band's third album, known as the 'Grey' album, was a consequence of having most of their sound effects stolen at JFK Airport in New York, which left them with no option but to compromise with a more rounded pop curve.

> 'Nobody has ever accepted that as a reason for anything, but it is true. We used to keep all our special effects boxes in these ammunition cases. You could kick them around and nothing would happen to them. And they were stolen at JFK Airport in New York which was too bad.'

True or not, and there's no reason to doubt Morrison's account, Reed had clearly decided he was locked into a systemised garage noise that he had to break to reinvent the band's identity. With Reed and Morrison both using twin Fender 12-string guitars, the band under the management of Steve Sesnick sojourned at the Chateau Marmont in Los Angeles to feel their way into the dreamily introspective material they were pulling up as a third album. From a management point of view, Reed's intellectual diffidence and innate anti-social attitude was never going to be a commercial selling point to youth – Lou was born middle-aged – and so the switch in musical direction towards listener-friendly rock looked like an opportunity to move on, even though MGM, after countenancing two commercially failed albums, had almost given up on the band and the hard drugs reputation that sat on their backs like a black halo.

White Light/White Heat had unintentionally formed the template for albums without singles; there wasn't a promotable song on its metal-dense aggro, and so the 'Grey' album was prepared with a certain resignation on Reed's part: the band were never going to chart or get air play. It may have come out of the drugs, but there's a genuinely mystical feel to Lou's writing on the third album in songs like 'Jesus', 'Beginning To See The Light', 'Some Kinda Love' and 'Pale Blue Eyes', as though transcendent altered states had opened a pathway into intangible but perceptible light in his brain's neural pathways. It wasn't just the psychedelic times: Reed hated

West Cost psychedelia with its self-indulgent etherealised expression of acid dimension; the change was happening in Reed's own awareness of himself and his inner creative potentialities. The tone is intimate, confiding, Reed's semi-spoken delivery is at its best when he appears to be narrating from a bar stool with just the right quotient of whiskey, while 'Murder Mystery' continues in the tradition of the Velvet Underground's spoken narrations in which the short story gets minimally crunched into adaptive rock-noir format. And Reed's sexual orientation surfaces in the beautiful 'Candy Says', a song about Candy Darling, one of Warhol's retinue of Factory transvestites who didn't make it into 'Walk On The Wild Side'.

Even if Reed appeared to have dampened down the Velvets sound from sonic assault to coercive pop ballad, his themes remained singularly perverse. In one of the album's stand out tracks, 'Some Kinda Love', he sings, 'Put jelly on your shoulder/lie down upon the carpet/between thought and expression/let us now kill the culprit.' You don't get more lyrically ambiguous than that in phrasing the sort of love that most people don't entertain – the jelly presumably being KY.

The whole album pivots on sexual ambiguity and the dissolving of gender into a gay/bi context, a mode of writing that was to come to perfection on *Transformer* (1972) where gay and transgender themed songs feed directly into an ethos of seventies liberation. The enduringly beautiful balled 'Pale Blue Eyes' is another classic example of Lou's ability to write about non-specific gender as a substitute for gay relations. Avoiding the issue of sexing a casual partner, Lou sings 'It was good what we did yesterday/and I'd do it once again/the fact that you are married/only proves you're my best friend/but it's truly truly a sin.' In gay coding the word 'friend' is recognised as implicitly same-sex and can be used generically, or to imply a short or long term partner. The overall tone of the album is 'down for you is up', as opposed to its predecessor that annihilated all mainstream pretensions totally with its druggy, lawless, nihilistic directives overwritten by noise.

Recorded November-December 1968, at TTG Studios in Hollywood, the album's official mix by MGM/Verve staff recording engineer Val Valentin was subverted by Reed's clandestine Closet Mix, mixing down the sound into box compression, something done without the band's knowledge, and typical of Lou's head games, partly methamphetamine fuelled, the result being significant sonic differences in the versions, with 'Some Kinda Love' an entirely different take. While the Closet Mix made up the majority of the album's pressings, copies of the Velvets Mix also got onto the market and was the mix used when the album was reissued in 1985, while Lou's Closet Mix, available on disc four of the 1995 CD box set, *Peel Slowly And See*, is how Reed originally intended the album to be heard, with the voices up front and the instruments mixed down.

Little promoted and badly distributed, the album made no impact on the charts, consolidating Reed's often distraught conviction that the band was ultimately a one-off kamikaze unit consigned to play small clubs and crash. Reed had also grown paranoid about Steve Sesnick's management of the band, and given his propensity for control freakery, read machinations into Sesnick's policies, at worst to exclude him as the band's frontman and to replace him with the younger and more easily manipulated Yule.

Between May and October 1969, the band went back into the studio at the Record Plant in New York to record material, often referred to as their lost MGM/Verve album, most of which Lou re-recorded for his first solo album *Lou Reed* (1972), the original studio material appearing regularly on bootlegs, before finding official release decades later on the albums *Velvet Underground* and *Another View*. Entirely disillusioned by the lack of promotional chutzpah attached to their first three albums, and MGM's evident lack of interest in their career, the band was understandably reluctant to have yet another album die on them due to record company indifference. The Velvet Underground's ghost album, as we know it from splinter rather than composite releases, comprised 'Foggy Notion', 'Coney Island Steeplechase', 'Andy's Chest' (which Reed was to re-record for *Transformer*), 'I'm Sticking With You', 'She's My Best Friend' (re-recorded for *Coney Island Baby*), 'I Can't Stand It', 'Ocean', 'Ride Into The Sun', 'One Of These Days' and 'Lisa Says' (all re-recorded for Reed's debut solo album), 'Ferryboat Bill', 'I'm Gonna Move Right In' and 'Real Good Time Together' (re-recorded for *Street Hassle*). He was reading the mystic writings of Alice Bailey, a condensed extension of Madame Blavatsky's seminal work of theosophy, *The Secret Doctrine*, and the value he attached to these Record Plant sessions at a time when he was right at the peak of his songwriting facilities and prolificacy, is apparent in the way he treated almost all of the material as prototypes for re-recorded solo excursions.

According to Sterling Morrison, MGM were just hanging fire on demanding closure of the band's contractual obligations.

> 'We were in and out of the Record Plant doing this stuff. And then Mike Curb wanted us off the label. He took over as head of MGM and wanted all the druggies and weirdos off the label – the Mothers, the Velvets etc . . . So we said OK, without much regard for what was in the can. And that was that. We said to hell with it.'

Three months after being fired by MGM, the band signed a two-album contract with Atlantic's Ahmet Ertegun on condition that there would be no drug or sleaze-themed songs on future recordings – live they were free to be persuasively subversive – and they worked at Atlantic Studios in the evenings between April and July 1970, recording the poppy, altogether more euphoric *Loaded* that liberated the band, minus Mo Tucker, who was pregnant. She was replaced by Doug Yule's brother, Billy, on drums for Lou's continued melodic curve of memorably hooky pop songs, his last consistently sustained surge of creative writing for nearly a decade.

Meanwhile, the Velvets were performing five nights a week during a ten-week residency at Max's Kansas City, a counterculture hangout in Times Square, and Lou's voice was shot from the strain of these performances. Also, he felt his central role in the band as focal point and sole songwriter was being challenged by the Yule brothers' attempt to hijack *Loaded*, abetted by Steve Sesnick who looked upon them as prodigies for a new-look, new-sound band with Reed and Morrison as suppressed passengers as opposed to an alliance that was criminally dangerous.

While Lou discredited the production of *Loaded*, he put his life-affirming heartbeat into the autobiographical 'Rock'n'Roll' as a redemptive slice of how music first heard on the radio had offered him a window to escape from home restraint and parental discipline against which the new music generationally rebelled.

> 'If I hadn't heard rock'n'roll on the radio, I would have had no idea there was life on this planet. You know what I'm saying? Which would have been devastating – to think that everything everywhere was like it was where I came from. That would have been profoundly discouraging. Movies didn't do it for me. TV didn't do it for me. It was the radio that did it.'

In August 1970, contemporaneous with the recording and release of *Loaded*, thousands of gay men and women staged a protest march from Times Square to Greenwich Village demanding complete civil rights and equal treatment, with activists belonging to the Gay and Lesbian Alliance, and Gay United, harassing the anti-gay papers and hassling conservative media moguls. It was during this period that Lou discovered the predominantly gay Le Jardin, situated on two separate floors, the basement – once known as the Oubliette – and the penthouse of the Diplomat Hotel located on 110 West 43rd Street where cute waiters dressed in tank tops and gym shorts sashayed on skates and the stoned lay on waterbeds on the outdoor roof terrace, searching through soupy smog for stars. New York's explosive, condomless, reckless gay scene was firing up for the liberated seventies with clubs like The Mineshaft, The Toilet (located on the third floor of 400 West 14th Street), Central Park's The Ramble, and the steamy gay mecca New St Marks Baths as compulsive magnets.

For two summer months in 1970, until the night Lou walked out on the band, the Velvet Underground played their residency upstairs at Mickey Ruskin's Max's Kansas City, now a focus for New York's newly launched creative celebrities. Ruskin, a lawyer with a gold-chipped tooth, was a genuine patron of the arts with a legacy of establishing bohemian hangouts like the Tenth Street Coffeehouse, which featured nightly poetry readings, Les Deux Magots on East 9th Street, the Ninth Circle Steakhouse and a venture run parallel with Max's, the Longview Country Club on 19th Street and Park Avenue South diagonally across the street from Max's.

Max's opened on December 6, 1965, and originally attracted the likes of

Allen Ginsberg, William Burroughs, Willem de Kooning, Jackson Pollock, Dennis Hopper and Diana Vreeland, all largely in the front room, with Warhol and his androgynous entourage almost nightly occupying the red wall-papered backroom. Max's was split like the two hemispheres of the brain, with Lou inevitably destined for the backroom and the Velvet Underground playing to an in-house, cultishly partisan audience. According to music biz exec and writer Danny Fields, drugs were a no-no. 'You went around the corner to smoke a joint out of respect for the club.' One could argue that the claustrophobic vampirism of Max's, the nightly routine of always playing to an appreciative audience of friends in a boxy room, no matter how outwardly cool, precipitated Lou's impulsive decision to jettison the band he'd created as art house punks and recapitulate on his losses before going forward solo with his reputation intact.

Lou quit after the show on August 23, 1970, the same night that Brigid Polk allegedly made her seminal cassette recording, released for lack of any other recording facility and put out as the 1972 budget priced album *The Velvet Underground Live at Max's Kansas City*. Sterling Morrison wasn't ever sure if the Polk tape really was the last night or near to it. 'As far as I can tell it sounds awful, although the conversations around Brigid are interesting – people trying to buy drugs, talking about things. But I don't know if it's the last night or not.' With Doug Yule and Steve Selsnick embarrassingly attempting to legitimise a deputised continuity of the Velvet Underground, a burnt-out and disillusioned Lou Reed went back home to Freeport on Long Island to recuperate and work for his father's accountancy firm as a typist for $40 a week. But whatever his generally depressed state at the Velvet Underground's lack of recognition for their pioneering attempts to enhance rock with literate sensibilities, to push out the frontiers of accepted subject matter, Lou continued to write songs and re-shape unreleased material in a format that would suit a solo career.

Unofficially released recordings of demos made for Lisa and Richard Robinson and recorded at their New York apartment on May 16, 1971, show that Reed had written much of the material that would later be released on his first three solo albums. The acoustic set ('Berlin', 'I Love

You', 'Wild Child', 'Ride Into The Sun', 'Lisa Says', 'She's My Best Friend', 'Hangin' Round', 'Walk On The Wild Side', 'The Kids' and 'What Goes On/Follow The Leader') is executed with authoritative panache, while an electric set recorded in the same month for the Robinsons, a mixture of old and new songs, hints at Lou's wanting to get back to live performance and his possible choice of set if he had: 'Rock'n'Roll', 'Sweet Jane', 'The Bed', 'Berlin', 'New York Telephone Conversation', 'Honky Tonk Women', 'Wild Child', 'Some Kinda Love', 'Jesus', 'Who Loves The Sun', 'Wagon Wheel' and 'Waiting For The Man'.

Photos of Lou at the time show him looking butch and skinny, his naturally wavy hair cropped short, his black T-shirt and choice of hip-length denim jacket and jeans compatible with the new liberated urban gay look as he struggled to reintegrate an affirmative identity. Glenn O'Brien, a Velvet's aficionado who was working for *Interview* magazine at the time, invited him over to Warhol's Factory in order to discuss his new projects and has left a valuable account of Lou's clearly mentally deranged state at the time:

> 'He was very nice and open, but he seemed strangely damaged. He had been living in Long Island and working for his father's accounting office. I wondered how this could have happened to him. But the good news was he was making music again. He was recording his first solo album with Richard Robinson producing for RCA records. I suggested that Lou write something about the record for *Interview*. He sent me a piece and I thought it was embarrassingly earnest, but also kind of lobotomized. I told Lou it wasn't really what I had in mind and he apologized to me. I felt awful.'

O'Brien also noted Reed's heavy drinking, how whenever they met for brunch Lou drank double bloody Marys before noon and seemed dependent on self-medicating uppers and downers, creating unpredictably contrary moods. Clearly still suffering the residual damage of his upbringing, the drug coshes given to him as reparative therapy, and the rejection of the Velvet Underground as a commercial venture, Reed was set on a highly self-destructive stabilising pattern of keeping above depression by abusing alcohol as a depressant in an escalating quotient as the seventies progressed.

As a tentative restart, Reed gave a poetry reading at St Mark's Church in the Bowery, attended by Allen Ginsberg, published the lyrics to 'The Murder Mystery' in the *Paris Review* and was reputedly working on songs for a Broadway adaptation of Nelson Algren's *A Walk On The Wild Side*. By accident he began dating a young Long Island Jewish woman, Bettye Kronsdat, whom he'd met while shopping in a department store, a prescription for potentially abusive disaster. Given Lou's emotional and sexual conflicts at the time, marriage, which he quickly proposed, seemed the worst possible option. Living in a Greenwich Village apartment with ugly shag carpeting and tasteless furniture, Lou waged an emotional war on Bettye who stayed with him only until after the recording of *Berlin* in 1973. According to Bettye:

> 'He gave me a black eye the second time he hit me. Then I gave him a black eye, too, and that stopped him using his fists. Everybody knew he was abusive, abusive with his drinking, his drugs, his emotions, with me. He was also incredibly self-destructive then.'

Bettye's characterisation of Lou's brutal misogyny, coupled with self-loathing, suggests how deeply he'd been distressed by a violent father and a mother who was herself subjected to marital beatings. All his repressed anger was focussed on Bettye because she wasn't a man and the only sex Lou would consent to was blowjobs. There's an insoluble problem for gay men who recognise in a woman the feminine aspects they would wish to have themselves. The issue of sexual conflict ceased to exist when Lou met Rachel (or Tommy) in late 1973, as Rachel, a transvestite with a drag queen's overcharged feminine glamour, was physically a man. With Rachel Lou was able to conduct gay relations with a pretend, rather than real woman, so hostilities were dissolved. The marriage to Bettye quickly broke up because of Lou's pathologically irrational behaviour dosed by Johnnie Walker and speed.

According to Bettye:

'Being around him was tearing me up, but I stuck by him because I had given my word to and that meant something to me then and it does now. I was in my early twenties, though. Had married, divorced and gone back to Lou because he and I had decided to try and work it out again. Then I promised his managers I would see him through the recording of *Berlin*. They said he wouldn't be able to finish it if I left. I stayed as long as I could take it.'

Bettye, who didn't break her silence until 2007, was adamant that she wasn't the suicidal protagonist of *Berlin* as passive, self-harming Sylvia Plath sacrificial wannabe, but that the remorselessly moribund album was themed partly on what she'd related to Lou about her mother's life and most definitely not her own:

'I have read in newspaper and magazine reports that I tried to kill myself during the recording of *Berlin*. That's a lie. Everyone around at the time knows I would never do that or didn't. I was too involved in keeping Lewis straight to get through the recording sessions. Sometimes when the recording sessions went on for a long time and he didn't come home yet, I either stayed in the hotel room or took the hired car to St James' Park at dawn and walked through the beautiful gardens to keep myself sane.'

Although the overtly gay-themed 'Walk On The Wild Side' never made it on to Lou's first solo endeavour, a radically different lyric with the same choral hook was taped by Richard Robinson in his apartment on May 16, 1971, as the hooky blueprint Lou would work on and craft into the polished version that epitomised draggy androgyny on *Transformer*. The more ragged, thematically disconnected demo lacks the Factory characterisation, but it is interesting for being weird. 'Dolly Horning walking down the street/looking so far he's got no place to put his feet/off to Broadway by the top/you never know it until you get a red mop/take a walk on the wild side . . .' While the song owes its title to Nelson Algren's novel *A Walk On The Wild Side* (1956), the original carries nothing of the ambivalently sexed allure of the highly-crafted finished version that incorporates real Factory drag queens into its serenely controversial, chart-climbing remit.

Meanwhile, events on the politically gay frontline in New York were reaching a crisis point that would directly affect Lou's songwriting. The song 'Make Up', written at the time and recorded for *Transformer*, took up the gay declaration 'Out of the closets and into the streets' that was a demonstrative part of the gay protest. The drive for gay liberation was taken up by *Life* magazine, in its December 1971 issue, with an 11-page photo essay called *Homosexuals In Revolt* that focussed on increasing angry and prolific 'zaps' on the part of the gay community in their desire to be heard. According to *Life* magazine:

> 'They resent what they consider to be savage discrimination against them on the basis of a preference which they did not choose and which they cannot – and do not want to – change. And while most will admit that straight society's attitudes have caused them unhappiness, they respond to the charge that all homosexuals are guilt-ridden and miserable with the defiant rallying cry 'Gay is Good.' Never before have homosexuals been so visible.'

The article went on to point out that most of the young gay militants were affiliated to New York's dynamic Gay Activists Alliance, (GAA), who had developed a significant form of protest called 'zap', part picket-line and part sit-in which was in itself a sort of active group therapy for the humiliations inflicted on them by heterosexual society. 'One good zap,' they say, 'is worth six months on the psychiatrist's couch.'

To produce his first solo album for RCA, Richard Robinson elected to take Lou to London and utilise Morgan Studios in Willesden. Lou felt understandably time-warped in that his musical contemporaries hardly knew of his work with the Velvet Underground or, like David Bowie, were just starting to catch up with it. Lou told *Melody Maker*'s Richard Williams:

> 'What I was writing about was just what was going on around me. I didn't realise it was a whole new world for everybody else.

Everybody else is now in the point I was in 1967. Makes me wonder where they'll be in five years' time. Come to that, makes me wonder where I'm at now.'

With a personnel of reputable session musicians, Steve Howe and Rick Wakeman of Yes, guitarist Caleb Quaye, a mainstay of Elton John's studio band, the veteran Clem Cattini on drums, Les Hurdle or Brian Odgers on bass, and John McLaughlin and Paul Keogh on guitars, Lou entered into the studio forensics of attempted folk rock hit making, a displaced czar of pioneering avant-garde looking to validate a still unrecognised past by a compromised present. It was a catch up that proved hard, because Lou had already done it, with six of the songs, 'I Can't Stand It', 'Lisa Says', 'Ocean', 'Ride Into The Sun', 'Walk And Talk It' and 'I Love You' which had been recorded in the last months of the Velvets' existence. Lou was already ahead of the moment when he was obliged to recreate his past for hardcore fans who still principally identified him with the Velvet Underground.

Despite the indifferent reception given the album by the music press and unpredictably disappointing sales, the eponymously titled *Lou Reed* is a superb showcase of hooky pop songs, less commercially on the moment than its successor *Transformer*, but containing outstanding, lyrically engaging numbers like 'I Can't Stand It' and 'Wild Child', a neglected Lou narrative up there with his finest compressed storytelling as rock novella, reflecting his ability to create singular snapshots of a character that leaves the listener to complete the story via his imagination. The album was picked up for its merits by Stephen Holden, whose review for *Rolling Stone* highlighted Reed's quintessential laconic vocal style, in which his phrasing is neither spoken nor sung, but at a gradient in between, thickened by cigarette smoke. Noting its familiar signature, Holden remarked:

'Reed's voice hasn't changed much since the early days. Outrageously unmusical, it combines the sass of Jagger and the mockery of early Bob Dylan, but it is lower-pitched than either. It is a voice so incapable of bullshit that it makes even an artsy arrangement work by turning the whole thing into a joyous travesty. Just as arresting as Reed's voice are his lyrics, which combine a New York street punk sensibility and rock song clichés with a poetic gift.'

If fans were looking for a rehabilitation of Velvet Underground avionic noise, they were instead met by a hybrid folk-rock/pop album sounding distinctly modern and crunchily cool, with the hangover of Reed's post-Velvets' depression surfacing only on 'Ocean', with its expressed terminal death-wish accelerated by prescription drugs and indefatigable touring.

Contemporaneous with the release of his first solo album, Reed contributed a confessional essay, 'Fallen Knights And Fallen Ladies', to a book called *No One Waved Goodbye*, a casualty report on rock'n'roll edited by Robert Stone, in which he discussed the influence of the Beatles and the Stones on his life and the tragically ruined lives and premature deaths of Brian Epstein, Jimi Hendrix and Janis Joplin. Writing with fine-tuned psychological acumen about the erroneous audience expectation that the artist knows the answers that they don't, Reed touched on his own perniciously harmful introduction to needle-injected drugs in his Long Island neighbourhood 'where sophisticated elderly townies came to prey on callow youth' – a reference of course to predatory older gays.

'I had recently been introduced to drugs at this time by a mashed-in faced Negro whose features were in two sections (like a split-level house) named Jaw. Jaw gave me hepatitis immediately, which is pathetic and laughable at once, considering I wrote a famous amplified version of the experience for a song. Anyway, his bad blood put an end to my abortive excursions and consequently tempered whatever enthusiasm I had for pop music at the time.'

You could read this as the origins of Reed's classic junkie song 'Heroin', not on any dumb, unresponsive, passive level, but on an acutely self-analytic one, in which Reed the performer is optimally, almost uncomfortably, aware of the dichotomy between personal and stage identity. 'It simply requires,' he writes, 'a very secure ego to allow yourself to be loved

65

for what you do rather than what you are, and an even larger one to realise you are what you do.'

The unresolved debate in Lou – whether he should have pursued a career in literature, and if he was a frustrated poet rather than rock lyricist – doesn't really arise, as his integral contribution was to music, in itself a legitimate art expression he tried always to transcend, as though the form didn't do him intellectual justice, but was his acclaimed identity. Reed is best described as rock's novelist, not in the tradition of the Great American Novel pursued by Scott Fitzgerald, William Faulkner, John Steinbeck, Ernest Hemingway, Jack Kerouac or William Burroughs, but in the postmodern immediacy of presenting characters with no history or developed continuity in the minimal space of a pop song. An intended Reed novella is maybe 30 lines spatialised into 300 by musical accompaniment. Songs arguably never end and we keep on adding to them by repeat listening.

Reed was in good fractured storytelling form on his first solo effort, kicking into 'Wild Child' with 'I was talking to Chuck in his Genghis Khan suit/and his wizard's hat/he spoke of his movie and how he was makin'/a new sound track/and then we spoke of kids on the coast/and different types of organic soap/and the way suicides don't leave notes/ then we spoke of Lorraine/always back to Lorraine.' This random introduction to both Chuck and Lorraine, and what comes up as topical conversation typifies Reed's ability to engage us in character studies too brief to be developed and the more intriguing for their enigmatic qualities. Who is Chuck and who is Lorraine? We don't know and don't need to, but they dominate the song. 'I Can't Stand It' drives a surreal narrative with an incisive bent that could arguably have been a hit single, as Lou declares, 'It's hard being a man/living in a garbage pail/my landlady called me up/ she hit me with a mop', and goes on with the curious admission, 'I live with thirteen dead cats/a purple dog that wears spats/they're all out living in the hall/and I can't stand it anymore.'

The album did nothing commercially, scraping the *Billboard* Top 200 at 189, selling as little as 7,000 copies and failing to chart at all in the UK: a signal disappointment to Lou and Dennis Katz at RCA, both of whom were left to contemplate the familiar quandary of how to separate the singer from the band with which he was identified by fans, and endorse a credible profile as a solo artist. The record deserved better, and like most Lou time-slips, *Lou Reed* has proved a slow burner classic, and is to my mind without a bad song, and even given the homogenous session musician fill-ins, Lou's undervalued debut kicks up a storm of finely crafted appeal, including the optimised 'Love Makes You Feel', a euphorically inflected scorcher that sits with his best.

While Lou stayed in London, living in an apartment on the fashionable Kings Road in Chelsea, RCA was seriously thinking of dropping him on account of the resounding commercial failure of the solo album. In January 1972 Lou flew to Paris to reunite with John Cale and Nico for a gig at Le Bataclan in Paris, a *salle de spectacle* at 50 Boulevard Voltaire in the 11th Arrondissement, named after Ba-Ta-Clan, an operetta by Jacques Offenbach. They rehearsed for several days and performed songs from *The Velvet Underground And Nico*, including a stripped-down, no-colour, minatory 'Heroin', while Lou authorised newer, unknown songs at the time, like 'Berlin' and 'Wild Child', and Nico concluded the set with a tunnel-vision vocalised 'Janitor Of Lunacy' not as a band reunion, but as tentative solo artists on trial. Cale performed material like 'Ghost Story' from his debut album *Vintage Violence*, and Reed retained the reflective mood by singing 'Femme Fatale' and 'I'll Be Your Mirror'.

As some indication of his mental state at the time, and as something of a resume of his fractured career to date, Reed had prepared a selective account of his dominant aspects for RCA as a mini character synopsis:

Played in Long Island hoodlum bands where there were fights
Attended many schools – always had bands i.e. Pasha and the
    Prophets, L.A. and the Eldorados
Expelled from ROTC for threatening to shoot officer
Rejected from army – deemed mentally unfit – X5. Worked as
    songwriter and met rejection.
Worked with Warhol and Velvet Underground through various
    permutations and helped create earlier mixed media
    environment also known in the happy sixties as "psychedelic".'

Left Warhol, realigned band and ultimately realigned self
Exile and great pondering
Lawsuits and depression
RCA, solo album, satisfaction

Reed's selective, salient points are of course the aspects of his personality he chose to present, and he understandably chose to ignore his homosexuality, university education and, more pertinently, his wealthy background in the interests of his punk hoodlum image, as the myth subscribed to and perpetuated by fans.

Initiating a US tour with a backing band called the Tots, comprising Eddie Reynolds and Winnie Latorta on guitars, bassist Bobby Reseigno and drummer Scott Clark, with Lou abandoning guitar, the ensemble activated their rock weaponry at Hillard Fillmore Room at the University of Buffalo in April 1972, mixing material from Lou's upcoming solo album with Velvet Underground favourites like 'Heroin', 'I'm Waiting For The Man' and the epic cocksucking narrative 'Sister Ray'. If Lou's recently embarked upon solo venture appeared to have commercially dipped, redemption on his return to England came through his confirmed admirer and fellow RCA artist, David Bowie, currently riding the apogee of his cross-dressing glam personification of Ziggy Stardust, androgynous leather messiah and faggot who ritually suicides onstage.

Bowie had in 1971 regularly incorporated Reed's 'Waiting For The Man' and 'White Light/White Heat' into his live sets and BBC sessions, iconising Reed for his intelligent lyricism and economic phrasing, and the Velvet Underground as Warholian avant garde artboys bending the dimension of rock. Bowie, who claimed to have recorded an unissued cover of 'Waiting For The Man' in 1967, featured the song on BBC Show *Sounds Of The 70s* on January 18, 1972, broadcast three weeks later, and released on the 2000 compilation, *Bowie At The Beeb*. Not only did Bowie and his guitarist Mick Ronson redeem Lou at RCA by offering to produce his next album, but radically upped his British profile by having Reed guest at a Save The Whale benefit gig at the Royal Festival Hall in London on July 8, when Reed performed three Velvets' numbers, 'White

Light/White Heat', 'I'm Waiting For The Man' and 'Sweet Jane' as a scorching reminder in part of Bowie's indebtedness to his adapted origins.

Reed, meanwhile, had been approached by Andy Warhol to write songs for a proposed Broadway musical he was planning with fashion designer Yves St Laurent, and it was the material for this aborted project, largely gay-themed songs about cross-dressing and camp bitching, that formed the basis of his next album, *Transformer*. For this, Reed specifically wrote the songs 'Vicious', 'New York Telephone Conversation', 'Wake Up,' and a radically revised 'Walk On The Wild Side'. According to Lou, 'Andy said, "Why don't you write a song called 'Vicious'? I said "What kind of vicious?" "Oh, you know, like I hit you with a flower." And I wrote it down, literally.'

Lou temporarily adapted a draggy glam rock look in place of leather butch for a British tour that took in London's Kings Cross Scala Cinema on July 14, with a second date there arranged due to popular demand two weeks later. His set for the tour mostly comprised 'White Light/White Heat', 'Waiting For The Man', 'Ride Into The Sun', 'New Age', 'Walk And Talk It', 'Sweet Jane', 'Going Down', 'I Can't Stand It', 'Berlin', 'Cool It Down', 'Wild Child', 'Rock'n'Roll' and 'Heroin'. The recording of *Transformer*, arguably the campest package of 1972, took place under Bowie and Ronson's direction at Trident Studios in St Ann's Court in London's Soho, where Bowie had recorded *The Rise And Fall Of Ziggy Stardust And The Spiders From Mars*, referencing his own transitioning kamikaze persona in the title.

On the gay radar, the record couldn't have been better timed to intersect with the increasing politicisation of gay rights, not only in the US but also on the emerging gay scene in Britain, where Lou was temporarily resident. June 1972 saw the inception of the pioneering London-based newspaper, *Gay News*, a collaboration between members of the Gay Liberation Front and the Campaign for Homosexual Equality, as the first openly published gay newspaper that, despite being banned by the UK biggest newsagent WH Smith's, was successfully sold by independent outlets. The fortnightly paper excavated a gay cultural past, presenting new developments in the arts, and campaigning for further law reform, including parity with the heterosexual age of consent of 16, and against the medical profession's pronouncing homosexuality as a disease. Under the memorably courageous editorship of Dennis Lemon, the paper played a pivotal role in the struggle for gay rights in the seventies, and both it and the first UK Gay Pride Rally on July 1, 1972 which attracted 2,000 participants, coincided with Lou recording *Transformer* as an upbeat colour moment in the lives of the capital's gay community. Recollecting the turbulent but liberating times, Peter Tatchell wrote of 1972:

> 'Being involved in the GLF was incredibly empowering because it turned the tables on every smug straight assumption. Whereas society problematized homosexuality, we said society's homophobia was the problem. Contradicting heterosexual presumptions of superiority, the GLF dared to question straight supremacy, likening it to racism and misogyny.'

Lou's message was more coded. Confessing to *Disc & Music Echo* that 'Walk On The Wild Side' was an outright gay song, he referred to the songs on *Transformer* diplomatically as 'worded so the straights can miss out on the implications and enjoy them without being offended'. Although much of the album's camp New York terminology was lost on the British record buying public, the record's pervasive mood of sexual ambiguity linked to the bisexual thermal of the early seventies with both Bowie and Roxy Music affecting drenched camp to their commercial profile of scoping variant sexual orientations. Sass was cool and Lou rather than Bowie was its consummately stylish prototype. With Herbie Flowers playing the inimitable interlocking slide bass lines for a session fee of £17, and female backing vocals provided by the Thunderthighs' Karen Friedman, Dari Lalou and Casey Singer, as the coloured girls, Lou's casual, mellow, dissociated phrasing made him sound unshockably dissipated, as though he'd done it all, known it all, experienced every degeneracy with Holly Woodlawn, Candy Darling, Little Joe Dellesandro and Joseph Campbell, the Sugar Plum Fairy. As salacious as it was hummable, 'Walk On The Wild Side' secured him his first Top Ten UK single at number 10, and reached number 16 on *Billboard*'s Hot 100.

If *Transformer* gave Reed his first commercial credibility, then the artist viewed it ambivalently as a compromise: a partial sell-out with the album largely a transgressive recapitulation of time spent with Warhol's queenish Factory superstars, all of it lip-glossed by Bowie's indomitably glam signature. Part of *Transformer*'s success was also dependent on the album's obtrusively camp Mick Rock designed sleeve, with a panda-eyed Reed on the cover personifying the gay lib-themed 'Make Up' and other same-sex songs like 'Vicious' and 'Andy's Chest', and on the rear as a split image, Ernie Thormalen dragged up on the left as a pouty transvestite, and on the right as a butch gay clone in a black leather cap, white-on-white T-shirt and phallically enhanced jeans emphasising cock. Reed, though, was quick to pronounce that men wearing makeup wasn't necessarily a sign of being gay, but perhaps just an accessory, and Lou as butch conquistador was by now familiar with the scene. 'Just because you're gay doesn't mean you have to camp around in makeup. The makeup thing is just a style thing now. If people have homosexuality in them, it won't necessarily involve makeup in the first place.' At anti-Vietnam demos in the States – Lou was exempt from the draft due to being homosexual – gays sloganed 'Bring the Beautiful Boys Home' and 'Suck Cock and Beat the Draft'.

While *Transformer* was a much more subtle artistic statement, addressing Lou's sensitively informed type – no matter his sideline Bettye, whom he ignominiously referred to as an improvised secretary – the confused sexuality of the early seventies, straights in revolt against machos, the spearhead of the women's movement, provided gays for the first time with an identity that was an absorbent for the disaffected politicos who realised aspects of themselves in the minoritorised movement towards gay liberation. An immediate slow-burn success, *Transformer* reached number 13 in the UK and 29 on *Billboard*'s Top 100, completely reversing Lou's marginal cult status with the Velvet Underground and launching him into an unexpected mainstream market, no matter his lugubrious sexual identity and association with drugs and the Factory's sleazy underbelly.

At the same time that Reed was working on *Transformer* in Soho, his junkie hero William Burroughs was operating a psychic attack on the Moka coffee bar at 29 Frith Street, just round the corner from Trident,

71

using recorded weaponry that on a weird tangential plane would feed into Lou's altered reality methods when he came to record the anti-social feedback loops comprising *Metal Machine Music* in 1975. The Moka, London's first espresso bar with a Gaggia coffee machine, was opened by the actress Gina Lollobrigida in 1953, and had become part of Soho's dominant youth culture, so popular with teenagers it sold over 1,000 cups of coffee a day in glass cups with dusted chocolate cappuccino hoods. The bar became the focus of Burroughs' para-psychic campaign due to what he described as 'outrageous and unprovoked discourtesy and poisonous cheesecake'. It's been suggested that Burroughs was ejected from the premises for making sexual approaches to a youth but whatever the cause of the hostility, Burroughs as occult warrior had already perfected his technique on a previous attack on Scientology's London headquarters at 37, Fitzroy Street, repeatedly taking photographs and making street recordings to be played back the following day in situ as a means of tampering with reality and leading, as he put it, to 'accidents, fires or removals', in this case obliging the Scientologists to relocate to some way north in Tottenham Court Road.

Beginning his operation on August 3, 1972, accidentally contemporaneous with Reed beginning the *Transformer* sessions, Burroughs, coolly dressed in a fedora and bespoke suit, positioned himself outside the café, making random recordings of street life and repeatedly taking photographs of the Moka. 'They are seething in here,' he reported, 'the horrible old proprietor, his frizzy-haired wife and slack-jawed son, the snarling counter man. I have them and they know it.' Returning six times to spook the bar's daily functions and play back his recordings, and looking every bit an inscrutably occult agent, Burroughs' concerted strategy was so malevolently intense that the Moka bar closed on October 30, 1972, with the premises re-opening as Queen's Snack Bar, the new name with its queer connotations bringing additional satisfaction to Burroughs' successful psychic strike.

4

Help Me New York Stars

LOU's neurochemical obsession with methamphetamine, speed or crystal meth, a drug he maintained until 1977, was typically coloured by ambiguity in his 1973 admission, 'I still do shoot speed. My doctor gives it to me. Well, no, actually they're just shots of meth mixed with vitamins. Well, no, actually just Vitamin C injections.' Rather like his junkie mentor, William Burroughs, Reed's conversion of his body into an experimental drugs lab to induce altered states was an alternative to booze tolerance. 'I drink constantly,' he told the outspoken US rock writer Lester Bangs in their ambivalent chewing at each other's sensibilities. 'It destroys the nervous system. I'm getting tired of liquor because there's just nothing strong enough.'

Amphetamine, the active ingredient behind 1975's chemicalised drone attack, *Metal Machine Music*, 'for those who use the needle like a tooth-brush', propelled Lou's butch faggot 1973 tour like the mix of hydrogen and helium in rocket fuel. Amphetamine, or in Lou's case Methamphet-amine, comes as a powder, crystals known as ice, crystal meth, or in a tablet form prepared for injection.

Additives include lithium metal, iodine, red phosphorous, hydrochloric acid and sulphuric acid. The initial rush of large amounts of dopamine and serotonin chemicals in the brain, after a shot involves an intense surge of euphoria that can last from five to 30 minutes, with a feel good afterglow that may continue for another twelve hours. The drug's propulsion would sometimes keep Lou up for three days at a time, the subject of his song 'How Do You Think It Feels' on his *Transformer* follow up *Berlin*.

A potent central nervous stimulant, through activation of trace amine receptors (Lou's Amine B Ring in the liner notes to *Metal Machine Music*) meth increases biogenic amine and excitatory neurotransmitter activity in the brain, while very high doses of the kind Lou was taking in the seventies can result in drug-induced psychosis, delusions and paranoia, as the damaged brain cells lose their ability to secrete normal amounts of dopamine chemicals, resulting in depression, anxiety and delusional states. Sixties London mods often suffered from speed psychosis due to abusing Smith, French & Klein blues, including the archetypal Face, Pete Meaden, often credited as the prototypical mod fashionista, burnt out on amphetamine before finally taking his life in July 1978 at his family home in Edmonton from a barbiturate overdose.

During the *Transformer* '72 tour, a much deeper resonance disturbed not only Reed's psyche but also the degenerately partying Factory crowd, and that was the suicide of Andrea Feldman, a Factory intern who'd starred in three of Warhol's films, *Imitation Of Christ*, *Trash* and *Heat*. Andrea, a speed addicted wild child who'd pioneered a performance called Showtime in the backroom of Max's Kansas City that incorporated a striptease on the round table at the centre of the room, entered misguidedly into what she called her 'final starring role'. Leaving a note that said, 'I'm headed for the big time, I'm on my way up there with James Dean and Marilyn Monroe', and holding a bible in one hand and a crucifix in the other, she jumped from the 14th floor of 51 Fifth Avenue at 4.30 p.m. on August 8, 1972, having made dates that afternoon with a number of ex-boyfriends, including Jim Carroll, who were all waiting down on the sidewalk when she flew out of the skyscraper window.

Lou's confused sexuality still surfaced in interviews as he disbanded the Tots, and took on the gay self-destruct, Billie Holiday bruised makeup look of the 'Rock'n'Roll Animal'. Simultaneously Lou refreshed his sound with a new band dominated by the crunching power chords of Steve Hunter and Dick Wagner, abetted by an ensemble of Ray Colcord, Pentii Glan and Pete Walsh, who revamped Velvet Underground classics into rocky metal reconstructions that referenced the past only by shattering its contents into the present as familiar new. Hunter and Wagner were hired-gun metal guitarists recruited by Bob Ezrin for the *Berlin* sessions, and both, Hunter from Illinois and Wagner from Michigan, had appeared on Alice Cooper albums before joining Lou on his 1973 *Rock'n'Roll Animal* tour as stratospheric duellists adding a heavy wall of sound to Lou's camp front as a throwaway singer in gated Raybans turned psychotic on speed. After leaving Lou in 1974, both were integrated into the Alice Cooper 1975 live show, with Dick Wagner becoming Cooper's principal co-writer, lead guitarist and band director.

> 'You can't fake being gay, because gay means you're going to have to suck cock or get fucked. I think there's a very basic thing in a guy if he's straight where he's going to say no: "I'll act gay, I'll do this and I'll do that, but I can't do that."'

Lou spoke with authority now that his homosexuality had intersected with a pop cult wanting to be identified as bi or questionable gay tourist. In June 1973, Reed with Bob Ezrin as producer, returned to Morgan Studios, Willesden, London, to work on Lou's third album, *Berlin*, a black slab of unmitigatingly depressive domestic violence, involving Jim and Caroline as abusive protagonists, although aspects of their emotionally messed relationship clearly reflect the deterioration of Lou's incongruous marriage to Bettye Kronsdat: 'I'm gonna stop working my time/somebody else would have broken both of her arms.' Lou sings with a vicious contempt that you could take for real.

The inherent death wish in so much of Reed's songwriting was finally compounded into an intensely morbid focus on *Berlin*, with Lou again overestimating the project – 'I'm thinking of *A Streetcar Named Desire, Death Of A Salesman*' – but it wasn't anything correlating theatre, but a conceptual rock album, intimately and dispassionately telling a fragmented story about a relationship between a vulnerable American woman, Caroline, and Jim, a nefarious German speed dealer, with Caroline's suicide her only liberation from endless abuse. What makes *Berlin* so disturbing a concept is the total indifference and callousness of Reed's tone, his alcoholic drugginess colouring his absence of feeling, as though suicide is no big event, but a catharsis for Jim as a casual observer of the ruin he's created. The story is compelling for being worked on so cold, in the chilling way that in 'Sister Ray,' when Cecil shoots a queen, Lou's glacial response is 'don't you know you'll stain the carpet?' Reed's attraction to death by suicide as an excitingly dangerous impulse was related to Michael Watts for *Melody Make*, as a signposting of his thematic preoccupation along the way.

> 'Have you ever stood at a window and seen the pavement, and thought, "Just what would happen if I leaned forward a foot?" Then you'd find out if there was a heaven and a hell. Sometimes you get things out of people by writing and performing a song about them . . .'

Reed as a leather-jacketed, made-up, notorious edge-walker with the weird genealogy of Factory transvestites and casualties catalogued in his hippocampus, and drinking ferociously to compensate for what? – his closeted sexuality, abortive marriage, and partial lack of recognition – was to his British and European fans a New York cult faggot who'd done everything they were hoping to get into, and to which they lacked access in the time lag behind New York lowlife. It's the tone of lived-in dissipation from a foggy sensibility that gives *Berlin* its reputation as one of the most auto-destructively depressing records in history, and one admired for its rock bottom account of contentious sex between a fractured couple that Lou extended as a metaphor for contemporary Berlin, and its division between East and West, although no physical expression of geography ever enters the lyric input. *Berlin*, a hit off the back of *Transformer* in the UK, where it charted at number seven, while just scraping the *Billboard* Top 100, has more than anything the speed-vamped psychotic flavour of Reed's mind at the time, and the turbulent muddle of his sexuality filtered through a marriage turned sour from whiskey and beatings, as Lou's apparently vindictive misogyny took over. With Bob Ezrin persuading his two sons, David and Joshua, to scream for him on 'The Kids' as part of the melodramatic atmospherics of the nihilistic song, Reed again fires up his anger towards women, or in this case Caroline, with 'that miserable rotten slut wouldn't turn anyone away', as a savage put down of a promiscuity his type created in relations, without any means of appeasing the cause.

For all Lou's intellectual claims that *Berlin* was the rock extension of his reading at the time, Burroughs, Ginsberg and Selby Jnr, the record is thin on lyrics and charged by remorseless, indifferent cruelty towards its suicide themed subject, with Lou clearly alluding to his own life in 'How Do You Think It Feels', in the lines, 'How do you think it feels/when you've been up for three days speeding,' and 'how do you think it feels/to always make love by proxy'. Lou's emotionally damaged cycle is the key to the album's sustained moroseness – the interlocked outrage of his criminalised sexuality – and the superficial compromise of marrying so as to avoid 'making love by proxy'. An eyewitness account of the hard-drinking inception of *Berlin* comes from Bettye Kronsdat's recollection of waking up one morning to find Lou had demolished a bottle of Johnnie Walker Red overnight in the process of writing the album. Questioned as to his prematurely smashed state – Lou never usually started drinking until the afternoon – Bettye recalls:

> 'He told me he had written the album overnight, that RCA would finally have the album they had been pressurising him to complete for many months. He could hold on to his contract as the next album after *Transformer* was part of the package to keep him on the RCA label, and at the time, *Transformer* hadn't made that much money for RCA, so they were holding him to his contractual obligations. Then he gave me his notebook and told me to read the lyrics, picked up his guitar and began to sing.'

Whatever happened then, happened spontaneously, Lou's acoustic croak and Bettye's incredulous response to a whiskey-raw blueprint of *Berlin* delivered in a blue fog of spiralling Marlboro Lite smoke. Imagine it, *Berlin* at 8.30 a.m. as a sozzled tracking of depleted energies? An endgame, like you'd never hear it again – zero targeting minus zero.

But as symptomatic of alcohol and meth partially killing Reed's creativity in the seventies, very little of the material on *Berlin* was new, but rather re-workings of unused demos cut with the Velvet Underground. The title track 'Berlin' first appeared in a slightly more splintered version on his first solo album *Lou Reed* while 'Oh Jim' is a remake of the Velvet Underground outtake 'Oh, Gin', 'Caroline II' is a rewrite of 'Stephanie Says' from *VU*, while 'Sad Song' is another Velvet Underground alternate demo, and 'Men Of Good Fortune' was written as early as 1966, when it featured in the band's first live set. But live, before the Hunter/Wagner power-sourced guitar shattering figures band disintegrated, a mobile unit was on hand to record a seminal gig at Howard Stein's New York Academy of Music on December 21, 1973, with Lou now in the process of divorcing Bettye, and his cropped hair dyed piano black, his emaciated body on speed overdrive, his Biba black lipstick and fingernails, blue denim jean jacket and jeans, having him appear reconstructed butch, as he danced incongruously, flapping his hands to the guitarists ramped up power surges.

Even if Reed did risk looking like a disorientated casualty in the cyclonic riffs laid down by Hunter/Wagner, the set list – Steve Hunter's virtuoso 'Intro', 'Sweet Jane', 'How Do You Think It Feels', 'Caroline Says', 'Waiting For The Man', 'Lady Day', 'Heroin', 'Vicious', 'Satellite Of Love', 'Walk On The Wild Side', 'Oh Jim', 'Sad Song', 'White Light/White Heat' and 'Rock'n'Roll' – was the subject of two live albums, *Rock'n'Roll Animal* (1974) and *Lou Reed Live* (1975), that re-invented Reed on the moment as a bridge between his first three solo albums and classics from his reconfigured Velvet Underground repertoire that fitted with his dissolute *l'enfant terrible* image at the time.

Reed was effectively at something of a creative hiatus, lacking both the time and the impetus to write, and drawing heavily on his Velvets legacy to sustain his newly won commercial profile. There's every reason to argue for Reed being generically alien to audiences at this time, compared to Bowie's wardrobe-managed affectation of being a bisexual spaceboy, a sort of manufactured androgyny that interfaced the poppy-red haired persona he was projecting live as dystopian rock god.

Reed was much more dangerous in his cool black shades, Times Square bondage jeans and studded, zippered leather jacket as he appeared the experiential extension of his lyrics, a gay dude in his early thirties, who'd lived a very different life from an audience pulled into what seemed like a genuinely terminal lifestyle. I would argue Bowie was a brilliantly shape-shifting act and Reed indisputably the real thing, with little or no separation between the life and the work. The pyrotechnic guitar thrust of Hunter and Wagner, forensically riff perfect and annihilatingly loud, succeeded in desensitising Reed's lyrics in the interests of brutal metal, and in projecting him upfront as a cropped black or blond Jean Genet lawless copy, mincing on stage as a parodic, gestural queen, holding up while surviving his own excessive poisons.

Of the *Rock'n'Roll Animal* material and its metalised execution, Reed riding high on its commercial success, noted, 'It's the way those things should be done and hadn't been done correctly,' and even if Reed purists denigrate the album as a riff-heavy, repurposed travesty of the originals, Steve Hunter and Dick Wagner should be credited for gunning some of the most exciting, inimitable climb out guitar figures in the history of rock, as the blazing soundtrack to Lou's tachycardia-driven, frenetic disintegration onstage. Steve Hunter's unforgettable 'Intro', as a virtuoso solo building up sound before Lou came onstage, remains a one-off masterpiece of guitar induction. But Reed was not only in a danger zone, mentally and physically – he was still trading off the success of *Transformer*, and more significantly his only hit single 'Walk On The Wild Side' – more importantly he lacked new songs and seemed unable to address the glitch in his creativity. With RCA contractually pushing for a new studio album, a bottle-blond Reed, who'd experimented with having Maltese crosses stamped in his hair and tying up onstage with the microphone cord before injecting with speed, came off the road to cut an album at New York's Electric Lady studio album in a state of optimal speed psychosis.

The symptoms of amphetamine psychosis are similar to those of paranoid schizophrenia, and may include visual and auditory hallucinations, paranoid delusions of reference concurrent with both clear consciousness and uncontrollable, often violent, agitation. Schizophrenia spectrum disorder and amphetamine-induced psychosis are further linked by several susceptibility genes common to both conditions. In shooting up (Lou's preferred method), the amphetamine molecule consists of a phenethylamine core with a methyl group attached to the alpha carbon: the substituted amphetamines consist of the same structure with one or more

substitutions. Recovery rate is usually within 10 to 30 days after methamphetamine cessation. Steve Katz:

> 'The studio album *Sally Can't Dance* was in Lou's speed-period. We
> would start early in the afternoon and by 4 a.m. we'd all be dead tired
> and Lou would come out of the bathroom after shooting up and say,
> "Well, what's next?" We'd say. "Oh no, you gotta be kidding."'

When Hunter and Wagner defected to Alice Cooper's pseudo-gothic
roadshow, Reed's management pulled in Danny Weis on guitar and
Michael Fonfara on keyboards, both formerly members of the late sixties
band Rhinoceros, Paul Fleisher on saxophone, Prakash John on bass,
Whitey Glan on drums, while Doug Yule was brought in to play bass on
'Billy', a reunion that would have Yule integrated into Reed's 1975 touring band, as well as initially contribute to the *Coney Island Baby* sessions
produced by Godfrey Diamond. With Steve Katz, the brother of Lou's
manager Dennis Katz, and the guitarist from Blood, Sweat & Tears,
brought in for production purposes, Lou – no matter his self-disparaging
denigration of *Sally Can't Dance*, and his derisory dismissal of the album as
'cheap and nasty' – incongruously cut his most commercial record to date,
charting at number 10 in both the US and the UK, despite the unanimous
critical vote that *Sally Can't Dance* exercised only a modicum of Reed's
artistic potential, and was a manufactured product at the expense of the
artist. Certainly, Lou didn't help adjust negative opinion by claiming in
1976, 'I slept through *Sally Can't Dance*. They'd make a suggestion and I'd
say "Oh alright." I'd do the vocals in one take, in 20 minutes, and then it
was goodbye.'

True, or part of Reed's perpetual self-mythology? For all his disdain and
apparent lack of conviction in the record's trashy soul struts, I find it
intrinsically more interesting than its three studio predecessors, for being
so skewed, off-centre, and the document of sleazy crystal meth that had
Lou back to writing about his New York underworld coterie in terms that
are as referentially interesting as his Velvet Underground hardcore lyrics
about psychotic Factory superstars living in a delusional Warhol mirage of
vicarious fame. Songs like 'New York Stars', 'Ennui', 'Kill Your Sons',

'Ride Sally Side' and the unreleased 'Good Taste', as a CD reissue extra, perfectly capture Lou's disillusioned, depressive tone of having been a scene tourist to almost everything, while still in search of the ultimate optimised high, that in this case sounded like a navigable pathway into death. Critics tend to confuse Lou's anorexic speed loop, and Giacommeti physique with the album's contents, without seriously reviewing the differentials, having Lou believe negative criticism had rights of priority over his own low self-esteem. Even one of the most intuitively intelligent rock critics, Nick Kent, in reviewing *Sally Can't Dance* for *NME* gave the album no justifiable credibility. 'Reed is such a zombie, he can't even feel compassion for his subject victims. He just drones on into his Jack Daniels, staring dolefully around him spilling out dulled observation signifying nothing beyond a kind of terminal meepishness.'

In retrospect, that really doesn't do the album justice, any more than Allan Jones' similar complaint of the album's lack of vitaminised kill. 'I don't think Reed does care anymore. It's as simple as that. He's content to slide through his usual territory with both eyes closed, existing purely in a state of half-life.' But half-light, or Lou's piloting gateways through foggy alcoholic penumbra into his subject matter, is precisely the album's strength, as Lou negotiates a way of converting seriously altered states into their rock music equivalent. The album, too, as we know it, comprises original music with only the scorching, vituperative 'Kill You Sons', Lou's experience of electro-shock treatment, as reparative therapy for homosexuality retrieved from his inexhaustible horde of Velvet Underground demos.

Sally Can't Dance is Lou's cryogenic cool soundtrack to personal alienation and what he considered to be spurious fame, and his nonchalant phrasing often appears to make light of songs that are malevolently, punkishly nasty, or just whiskey-furred soporific in their Jack Daniels measured drawl. Andrea Feldman's drug-induced suicide is obliquely referenced in 'Ennui': 'All of the things that your old lover said/Look at them, they jump out of windows/And now they're just dead/It's the truth don't you realise?' In the elegiac 'NY Stars', Reed's recapitulative tone of assessing his recent past and present in one sweep, takes on modern abstract definition in the way of the New York school of poets, John

81

Ashbery, Frank O'Hara and James Schuyler. Reed, always at his best writing about New York, metabolises the emptiness of fame in a neon city underwritten by high unemployment, poor social welfare, decaying schools, the rampant spread of illegal drugs that create illicit street economies, hustling and urban gangs. Lou's cool meets the ethos he describes, 'Like new buildings, square, tall and the same/Sorry Miss Stupid, didn't know it was a game/I'm just waiting for them to hurry up and die/It's really getting crowded here/Help me N.Y. stars.'

The album's title *Sally Can't Dance* most probably comes from Sally, manager of the infamous 220 Club, located at 220 West Houston Street, one of the most famous of the transgender/gay nightclubs of the early seventies, a location descended directly from the Stonewall Inn by extension of the riots. The 220 Club, one of Lou's drinking tranny locales, was the principal venue for the transgender crowd, a distinction later shared by its upgrades, the Greenwich Pub, Sally's Hideaway and later Sally's II. Sally's partner, Jesse Torres, a femme queen also, was a significant glam attraction at the 220 Club, dragging it up as hostess manager. Times Square, the hub of Lou's sexual activities and in part inspirational source to his music, was in contrast to the Village, the site where black and Latin drag queens congregated and sold sex. The Village, with the exception of a drag/femme queen hustling strip along 14th Street and 9th Avenue, stretching over to the Hudson River, was more Caucasian, middle class, educated and generally more privileged.

In Lou's pick up radius of New York in the early seventies, there was also the Hay Market on Times Square, where hustlers hung out selling sex for $20; the Deuce on 42nd Street populated by hustlers, lowlife and johns, where sex by numbers took place 24 hours; and Tenth Floor Disco West 28th Street, across from the Everhard Baths, New York's first true private gay disco that catered to a sassier chic crowd into glamour and given the name Twelfth Floor in Andrew Holleran's quintessential *The Dancer From The Dance* (1978), New York's seminal seventies gay novel, and where Lou hung out, leaving his drink untouched for attitude.

On a lower social scale, as part of the gay meat factory, there was Grand Central Terminal (T-Room) at 42nd Street and Lexington. The men's room was located downstairs through the upstairs waiting room. As you descended the stairs there was a long line of urinals, always crowded with men openly cruising. Bruce Benderson, who wrote *User* out of his hustling reference frame, writes:

'As for me, I probably wouldn't have written a good sentence if I hadn't discovered Times Square and the hot Puerto Rican hustlers who came down from the South Bronx to frequent its mostly Mafia owned bars. In those days a lot of hustlers were poor white kids. Since the minimum drinking age in those days was 18, there was some very young trade in there.'

The Mafia allegedly dominated the saturated neon precinct of Times Square in the seventies, fronting most of its porn shops, strip joints, massage parlours and gay bars, acquisitively getting in on the emergent pink economy. The location had been a predominantly gay enclave since the twenties, largely because its theatres and recreation amusements attracted large numbers of gay workers with jobs as waiters and performers in restaurants and clubs, as busboys in hotels, and as chorus boys, actors, stagehands and costume designers. But by 1974, when Reed autopsied the place for queens, Times Square, with its notorious gay Terminal Bar opposite the Port Authority, had reached a nadir of profiteering sleaze.

Lou met Rachel, aka Tommy Humphries, the transvestite queen who was to be his inseparable, sympathetically detached live-in partner for the next four years in Club 82, bordering the Bowery and East Village, a basement venue with a history of trans and gender variant performers, and also an underground rock club and early hangout for the Max's Kansas City/Mercer Arts Centre glitter crowd. In 1974 it was hosting gigs by the New York Dolls, Television and pre-Blondie Debbie Harry as one third of the girl trio the Stilettoes. Lou's own account was given to his friend and photographer Mick Rock:

'It was in a late night club in Greenwich Village, I'd been up for days as usual, and everything was at that super-real glowing stage. I walked in and there was this amazing person, this incredible head, kind of vibrating out of it all. Rachel was wearing this amazing make-up and dress and was obviously in a different world to anyone else in the place. Eventually I spoke and she came home with me. I rapped for hours and hours, Rachel just sat there looking at me, saying nothing. At the time I was living with a girl, a crazy blonde lady, and I kind of wanted us all three to live together, but somehow it was too heavy for her. Rachel just stayed on and the girl moved out. Rachel was completely disinterested in who I was and what I did. Nothing could impress her. He'd hardly heard my music and didn't like it all that much when he did.'

Lou's typical gender morph from she to he, in mutating Tommy as same sex basics, is again consistent with his reparative therapy in which (shocked) male is converted into safe female substitute, he as a she, without (shock) for diagnostic deviation. For arguably the first time in his sexually scrambled life, Lou had met his polarised ideal, a woman who could out-glamorise glamour, as a man upstaging women, while remaining genitally a man. Rachel was for Lou the apotheosis of a Times Square queen transmuted into manageably shockable gay alchemical gold.

Rachel Humphries, a hairdresser from Philadelphia, came to New York to be part of Max's Kansas City drag queen milieu in 1970, a stunning half Mexican-Indian transvestite who identified as female, but was a man, and one resistant to gender reassignment surgery, although Rachel may have been on hormones as he is described several times as having breasts in contrast to stubble penetrating over-compensatory makeup. Rachel mostly wore women's tops and shoes, sometimes dresses and had waist length black hair, worn in a feminine style, shaped her eyebrows and stood out in the way transgender look often affronts and disturbs the straight by incorporating both sexes into a single focus. Like most drag queen hustlers, Rachel was looking to be elevated to stardom by meeting a facilitator to that pathway and found it in Lou Reed. According to Eddie McNeil's account in *Please Kill Me*, an oral history of punk, Rachel told him, 'I've met Lou Reed. I've made it. That's it. I knew this was gonna happen to me, and this is it and I'm in love.'

Steve Katz, who produced *Sally Can't Dance*, explained the Rachel phenomena as 'imagine a woman in a man's body getting by as a juvenile delinquent', while the photographer Eileen Polk recalls the taciturn Rachel as getting blasted one night at Club 82, and complaining on exposure that her cock was too miniscule to qualify as masculine. When Polk agreed on size limitations, and that it was unduly small, Rachel responded, 'Well it better be, because I make a better woman than a man.'

Rachel arrived at a paradoxical apogee and nadir of Lou's career, with *Sally Can't Dance* a confirmed commercial success, but with Reed, either as a symptom of speed psychosis or because he was preparing an investigative lawsuit against his manager Dennis Katz for what he alleged to be fraud and mismanagement of finances. This coming from the son of senior tax accountants was serious stuff, Lou no matter his car-chase speed habit, was too intellectually focussed to be subjected to what he claimed was financial malfeasance.

Whether the implied malpractice was fuelled by methamphetamine delusions or real, Reed was to split from Dennis Katz in late 1975 and to appoint the capricious entrepreneur and big time rock booking agent Jonny Podell as his mentor. Podell's principal base for social networking was Ashley's, the music biz bar and restaurant on Fifth Avenue at 13th Street managed by former Alice Cooper PR Ashley Pandell and his brother Carl, where Lou also hung out recreationally. Their brief partnership was termed 'a marriage made in an emergency award', given Podell's propensity for drugs which was on a par with Lou.

Reed's decision to take Rachel on tour with him for the autumn surge of his *Sally Can't Dance* album made a very clear statement of their same-sex liaison, with Rachel acting in his part as Lou's minder, her possessiveness making apparent he was off-limits to the druggy disaffected entourage, and his emaciated, twitchily uncoordinated stage presence attracted a pathological following. Reed's autumn US tour peaked with two intensely dramatic nights at New York's Felt Forum arena, a venue with a capacity of 4,000, and included in its itinerary Kickstart, at Cleveland Ohio, on September 9, 1974, where the set list comprised 'Ride Sally Side', 'Heroin', 'Kill Your Sons', 'New York Stars', 'Animal Language',

'Sally Can't Dance', 'Walk On The Wild Side', 'White Light/White Heat', 'New York Telephone Conversation', 'Good Night Ladies' and 'Rock'n'Roll' as an encore. It was additionally declared 'Lou Reed Day' in Cleveland, as it was in New York when Lou performed there. The tour took in 24 dates crossing from the East coast to the West, and winding up with shows on November 23 at Winterland in San Francisco and November 24 at the Civic Auditorium in Santa Monica, California, with Reed no longer a platinum blonde, but now a Biba black Rachel clone, borrowing her tops and personifying Raybanned made-up androgyny.

Enthused by the emotional stability Rachel provided, and with the two living in Lou's Upper East Side apartment, kitschly furnished in red velvet with a pair of antelope horns fixed on the wall, together with Lou's gold records and a faux-zebra rug slung on the floor as a gesture of decadence, Lou started writing again, while the two periodically fought, took drugs and liberated themselves into a Lou/Rachel personalised bubble. Inspired by his protective transgender partner, Lou entered New York's Electric Lady Studios in January 1975 to begin work on the album *Coney Island Baby*, demoing the title track, a nostalgic resume of identity dedicated to Rachel, before the sessions were interrupted by commitments to tour. The album was discontinued until October when Reed, by then broke, ended up recording the LP uptown at Mediasound, the little church under Godfrey Diamond's mood-sensitive directions to drenching the songs in Lou's favourite doo-wop harmonies.

To capitalise on Reed's cultish death–exhibit live attraction, RCA released *Rock'n'Roll Animal* Part 2 as *Lou Reed Live*, as another five extended metallised tracks pulled from Lou's Howard Stein's Academy of Music gig on December 21, 1973, featuring another time-slip Mick Rock photo of a sexless Lou totally blanked out by optimal fractured sunglasses, obfuscated by a grey on grey hat, a clone's rather than a rock star's studded leather jacket collar pulled up vertically as postmodernised alien androgyny. The brilliantly morphed, manipulative image confirmed audience expectation of Lou OD'ing onstage as a drug casualty, assuring the album hit 62 on *Billboard* as an occult fanbase attempted to beam up the past into the present as chemicalised time travel. While welcoming the reanimated

Velvets material given Hunter and Wagner's turbo riff drive, Robert Christgau, doyen of rock reviewers for the weekly *Village Voice*, noted the disdainful delivery of the solo material, 'invested with the kind of contempt that Lou seems to think goes naturally with having a real audience', presumably after having years of the Velvet Underground being a marginalised cult playing to college audiences and with repeat partisan residencies at the Boston Tea Party and Max's Kansas City.

Back in New York, and with an assiduous reading of *The Physicians Desk Reference* – a commercially published compilation of manufacturers' prescribing information on prescription drugs, updated annually, and Reed's most commonly consulted reference manual – Reed was experimenting with making his own customised speed. The brain child of amphetamine, as he worked at home on the modulated guitar feedback and noise terrorism, was the double album *Metal Machine Music*, a literal sonic repellent of post-modernised sound distortion, either intended as career suicide after the commercial success of *Sally Can't Dance*, or initiated to facilitate a definitive split with his 'kike' manager, Dennis Katz. Then again, it might also have been a genuinely self-deluded attempt to compete with modern minimalist composers like La Monte Young, using guitar loops as facilitators of rock avant-garde experimentation.

Whatever the album's defiant motivation, and speed psychosis has to be an ingredient, the controversy surrounding its anti-commercial hostility and radically solipsistic self-indulgence has resonated through the decades as a freak anomaly, an insanely delusional slice of weird, or a record that is continually ahead of its time, its subtle changes of tempo and tone the coding to idiosyncratic genius. Lou was, of course, *Metal Machine Music*'s chief proselytising advocate, theorising the record's vocal free contents as clean constructive noise.

> 'The record is the closest I've ever come to perfection. It's the only record I know that attacks the listener. It's impossible to think when the thing is on. It destroys you. You can't complete a thought. You can't even comprehend what it's doing to you. You're literally driven to take the miserable thing off. You can't control that record.'

Lou conceded that not even he had listened to its four vinyl sides in entirety, and yet his highly eloquent exoneration of the record's apparently intricate modalities was nothing less than impressive. Intellectualising the record's affinities with classical music, Lou in cerebral speed mode hyped his project into inimitable guitar ballistics.

> 'I could have sold it as electronic classical music, except it's heavy metal, no kidding around. I could take Hendrix. Hendrix was one of the great guitar players, but I was better. But that's only because I wanted to do a certain thing and the thing I wanted to do that blew his mind is the thing I've finally got done that I'll stick on RCA when the rock'n'roll shit gets taken care of. Now most people can take five minutes of it.'

Amphetamine delusional monomania, or qualifiable truth, as disruptive electronics inspired by LaMonte Young's Dream Symphonies, Lou was pitched between paranoid schizophrenia and a quirky neural pathway into the future.

> 'The thing is, that it's a fun trip. Not for most people because they get scared off, and I set it up that way. There are frequencies in there that are against FCC Law to use, they use them in surgery. But, if you put certain combinations of tones together, and if you keep building on them harmonically . . . there's seven thousand melodies. Like Sibelius will go gliding by, whoosh. It's all really speed, to say the least. I don't say that facetiously.'

Released in an art house gatefold sleeve, with a Mick Rock photo of a Lou personalised in blackout Raybans, his studded leather jacket sloganeering gay speed-freak outlaw, and with the liner notes referencing the *British Pharmacopoeia* and the molecular composition of speed, with the telling disclaimer 'my week beats your year', the whole construct was cryogenic in its moon-cold exemption from human, physical or emotional contact. It was noise for deconstructive zombies who hadn't yet earthed or responded to gravity as a stabilising force. And although the album sold 100,000 copies on release, RCA – realising its potential damage to an artist they were attempting to break (into pop?) – withdrew it from circulation after deeming it a rogue retroviral gene in Lou's career, in need of rapid correction. But Lou remained adamant in his defence of guitar symphony tonal oscillation:

'First of all, the only way to listen to it is on headphones. Hearing it on speakers is ridiculous, and you don't listen to it by yourself. And the thing is, each side (there are four) is more dense than the one before it, and it's in a different perspective. That's what the combinations and permutations are. It's not me standing in front of a microphone, it's not a rock'n'roll album. It's a machine in front of a machine.'

Given Lou's pharmaceutical dissociation at the time, machines substituted for humans, drugs for bodies, in his state of dopamine orgasm through mephamphetamines with *Metal Machine Music* the guitar organiser of chemical synthesis. There was no intervention, no intermediary – just Lou equals Lou equals Lou. 'They should be grateful I put that fucking thing out, and if they don't like it, they can go eat rat shit. I make records for me.' Lou's indignant, unapologetic solipsism was a hard defence to break, his defiant, isolationist edge walker angle savaging critics who almost unanimously discredited the album as unlistenable, obstructive noise. At a high point in his emotional life, Lou chose to intentionally suicide his emergent pop profile, intimating that *Metal Machine Music* was intended, anyhow, as a final record, a terminal postscript to a misunderstood career in music.

'A lot of people got turned off, and I am so happy to lose the people who got turned off – you have no idea. It just clears the air. That's the end of it. *Metal Machine Music* was going to be my last record.'

But it wasn't and Lou's facility to physically and musically morph in the accelerated seventies, with the artist on unedited hyperactive overdrive, allowed him, through RCA's Ken Glancy, the option to redeem his fuckedness quotient by recording a pop-friendly album as corrective to occult feedback frequencies. One literary source of input into *Metal*

Machine Music, and Lou's laterally quirky mind-set at the time of recording it, was Alice Bailey, born Alice LaTrobe Bateman in Manchester, who moved to the US in 1907, devoting her life as a writer to occult, esoteric psychology and astrological works. Bailey claimed her work was telepathically dictated to her by her Tibetan master, D.K. or Djwal Khul, as un-mediated contact, and the idea of psychic senders, or autonomous transmission from an extra-terrestrial source, played directly not only to the infrastructure of *Metal Machine Music*, but also into William Burroughs' resourcefully random cut up method. Her five-volume *Treatise On The Seven Rays*, volume three of which concentrates on esoteric astrology, was vital to confirming Reed's own belief in synchronistic accidental patterns of sourcing the sort of simulated intergalactic noise coded into *Metal Machine Music* for those who could navigate its directives.

Despite posters advertising a peroxided, sunglassed 'Wanted Lou Reed Dead or Alive' (what's the difference?), by the time of his summer and autumn 1975 tours Lou had reverted to his black, naturally curly hair, increased his weight marginally and was playing guitar again, contrary to the terminal drug image promoted on the sleeve of *Metal Machine Music*'s fabulous Mick Rock gatefold sleeve. With a tight unit of Doug Yule on guitar and keyboards, Bruce Yaw on bass, Marty Fogel on saxophone, Michael Suchorsky drums, Reed personally appeared re-energised and referred to his band as 'playing like bandits' on the summer leg of their intensely tight European tour, with something of Reed's anger over the vilification of *Metal Machine Music* fuelling his defiant energy quotient onstage. Lou was now playing with nothing to lose after the catastrophic nihilism of his imploded excursion into electronics.

By the time his 1975 European tour shifted to America, new songs had been added to his repertoire. Playing at the Felt Forum in April, he risked 'I Wanna Be Black', the minor lyric 'You Can Really Dance' and a stunning version of 'Dirt' (as it was to be printed as a poem and not the grainy revamped version which was to appear on *Street Hassle*). He also included 'He Must Take His Bow', 'Work With Me Annie', 'Coney Island Baby' and 'Kicks'. The audience, particularly at New York's Felt Forum, were vehement and often tetchily uncontrolled, with Reed telling them several times to shut up and fuck off, his own condescending manner to his admirers going so far as to emphasise 'psychologically' in 'Dirt' as a big word and clearly beneath their comprehension.

'Dirt' is unquestionably the great song from this show. Reed recorded it with Godfrey Diamond, but sadly it never got on to *Coney Island Baby* though it was included as a bonus track on the 30th anniversary CD reissue of the album in 2006. Reed admirers will know the lyric as it appeared in the limited edition of four poems comprising the final pages of Reed's intended collection *All The Pretty People*. He made various attempts at recording 'Dirt' on January 3, 5 & 6, 1975, in what were the original and abruptly terminated sessions for *Coney Island Baby*. The version recorded on January 6 and produced by him is a nonchalant, masterfully understated rendition that keeps close to the original poem, but Reed alters lines for the sake of economy and sounds convincingly decadent as a street creep. The song was given another try-out in October of the same year when Reed resumed sessions for *Coney Island Baby* under Godfrey Diamond's direction, but to date this outtake still hasn't surfaced: when Reed came to record the song for *Street Hassle* (1978) it was a completely different version, a virulent character assassination of his former manager, and shared nothing in common with the original other than the word 'dirt' itself.

The version of the poem or lyric he was singing in 1975 had made an earlier appearance in the *Coldspring Journal*. It was a confirmation that Reed's concerns were still primarily lyrical, after the unverbalised statement that *Metal Machine Music* represented, and it typifies Reed's writing at its notoriously sleazy best. Sex on the docks, uptown women who slum for downtown sex with 'dirt', added to the viscous depraved aura which hangs over the song like smudged harbour fog. And there was 'Kicks', in which Fogel's sax took the song into a disturbed murder medley, the number's powerful blood-tempo sounding pathologically deranged. It was Reed at his most menacing and this minatory narrative – the murderer kills the man he's seduced, 'far better than sex' – demonstrated that Reed had lost none of his abilities to write songs just as apocalyptically chilling as 'Heroin'. 'Kicks' was sung deprived of the gothic overtones it had assumed in the bleached skeletal tour the preceding year, sounding closer to a reading of the nerves, the slow acoustic lead into the last part proving sympathetic to Reed's voice with its reliance on syllabic count. 'And different people have peculiar tastes', seemed the perfect message in the other new song introduced that night, 'Coney Island Baby'. It was also uplifting to hear Reed singing about 'the glory of love' after the depression which had raged through his heavy metal assaults on Europe's stadiums in 1974.

Undoubtedly, Reed's more agreeable stage presence had something to do with the security of his relationship with Rachel. Godfrey Diamond, who was to produce *Coney Island Baby* thought Rachel 'was stunning . . . Mexican and gorgeous', But not so Lester Bangs, who was still pouring undiluted vitriol on someone he took to be a brainless mutant. With a lacerating insensitivity to transsexuals, Bangs proceeded to register his surprise at the apparent contradiction between Rachel's stubble and tits:

> 'If the album *Berlin* was melted down in a vat and reshaped in human form, it would be this creature. It was like the physical externalisation of all that fat Lou must have lost when he shot all those vitamins last winter. Strange as a yeti from the cosy brown snow of the east. Later I noticed it midway in the interview, turning the pages of a book. But from the way it did it, it was obvious that it was not reading, it was merely turning pages . . . At first glance I thought it was some big, dark swarthy European woman with long rank thick hair falling about the shoulders. Then I noticed that it had a beard, the bearded lady with Lou Reed, that fits. But now I was closer and it was almost unmistakeably a guy. Except that behind its see-thru blouse, it seems to have tits. Or something.'

'She's a he,' Lou snapped at him. Godfrey Diamond got to know her during the recording of *Coney Island Baby* and describes her in a very different manner from Bang's antagonistic, prejudicial viewpoint:

> 'I always got off talking to Rachel . . . she/he was so amazing. She would talk to my girlfriend for hours about nail polish and style. I must say, hands down, that she's the best hair-cutter I've ever met. She cut

my hair twice and it was gorgeous. And if she is doing anything else with her life at the moment. That's a big mistake. The way they got along . . . she was always there. Then out on the street, Rachel would walk about four yards in front of us as if to act as Lou's bodyguard.'

Speaking to Mick Rock in a *Penthouse* interview in early 1977, Reed said of their relationship:

'I enjoy being around Rachel. That's all there is to it. Whatever it is I need, Rachel seems to supply it. At least we're equal. No to so long ago, I was still afraid I'd got into one of those Pygmalion situations where you can get into somebody and get them into good enough shape and then they go and leave you. But Rachel's also helped me get together. I mean, I have a real reason now for not letting myself get fucked over like I have so often. Rachel can help me . . . There's someone hustling around for me I can totally trust. It's a lot of responsibility but that's the way Rachel wanted it and it's been a job well done.'

In Blake's Hotel, London, before his Hammersmith Odeon, 1975, Lou is screened by dark green shades and beginning to adopt the clothes which symbolised his relationship with Rachel; the black vinyl zipper gloves, the floppy beret angled over one eye, the transparent outer sleeves floating over zip-shouldered tops. In Gerard Malanga's portrait taken over that summer in New York, Reed addresses a baroque mirror, his lipstick carefully articulated, nails painted black, and it's apparent that he had adopted a far more feminine appearance than in his *Transformer* glitter period. He had become the incarnation of one of his transvestite songs: the perfect complement to his transsexual lover.

Reed was in England in March 1975 to play Bristol's Colston Hall on the 24th and two scorching nights in the Hammersmith Odeon on the 25th and 26th, the second date added by popular demand. The illuminated sign outside the Hammersmith Odeon read: IT'S ALL TOO MUCH. LOU REED IN CONCERT. His previous year's concerts had seen a wasted drug ennui push Reed to perform often monotonously and with an air of total detachment. Something of this legacy seems to have been anticipated by Reed's fans anxious to perpetuate the myth of Lou Reed as OD anti-hero. But the sign proved false and the new Reed was apparent as he took the stage without even his customary shades to screen him from his audience. Dressed in a simple dark shirt over his black T-shirt and jeans, he looked like the epitome of New York cool, demonstrating yet again his extraordinary ability to physically mutate and correct his metabolism. Max Bell, reporting one of the shows in *NME*, commented:

> 'Firstly, Lou's forsaken his greaseball look and is back to vintage '68 mid-length curly. Secondly, if he doesn't seem exactly happy at least he isn't about to break anything, and it isn't actively painful to watch him.'

More important were the new songs. 'Coney Island Baby' and 'Kicks' were introduced to Reed's English fans for the first time and Velvets numbers like 'Pale Blue Eyes', sung into a blue spotlight, and 'New Age' and 'Some Kinda Love' finding newly constructed, jazzy inclusion in the dynamic repertoire of songs, were all enthusiastically received.

Reed's most intelligent and sympathetic critic, Allan Jones, writing in *Melody Maker*, reported:

> 'The music, like Reed, is stripped down to its essentials, cutting through to the bone, with a rhythm section that knows enough to keep out of the way but unobtrusively brilliant, a sax player to add colour, and Doug Yule's vicious lead guitar, spine-tingling memories of the Velvets as he and Lou crawl through the subway on 'Waiting for the Man' and a stunning 'New Age', with Lou, legs slightly apart and sagging at the knees, spinning the insults fast off the lip.'

Particularly stunning in the Hammersmith Odeon show was a version of 'Kicks' that was menacingly different from a later recorded version of *Coney Island Baby*. The song was dramatically performed over a heart-beat drum, with Lou strumming his guitar and Doug Yule beating the strings with a drumstick, the awesome vocal delivery accentuating the psycho-sexual kicks.

With RCA permitting Reed a last chance option to make a rock album successor to *Sally Can't Dance*, and attempting to mask *Metal Machine Music*'s controversy by releasing *Lou Reed Live*, Reed, perhaps sniffing renewed antagonism compromised on the album's original title *I Wanna Be Black*, used the more benign *Coney Island Baby*, undoubtedly lifted from the Excellents' 1962 doo wop single of the same name. He entered New York's media sound studios in October 1975, hot off a year of devastating, acutely professional touring that had reinvented Reed as a supremely audacious cult performer, legislating over audiences not only with formidable contempt, but also wired punkish musicianship.

5

Gimme Some Kicks

BEFORE he took up the *Coney Island Baby* project again, in an unmanageable state of speed-mania Lou told his most confrontationally sympathetic interviewer, Lester Bangs, a rock journalist for *Creem*, 'Fuck this Steve Katz bullshit of, "Oh, yeah sorry kids, the next album'll be songs you like."'

The mood of the album was to be roughed up doo wop, given explicit pop expression by Godfrey Diamond's fluent and euphoric production, and Lou tentatively listed potential song titles for the album as 'Kicks', 'Dirt', 'Glory Of Love', 'I Wanna Be Black', 'Leave Me Alone (Street Hasslin')' and 'Nowhere At All'. In the aborted January sessions he'd laid down versions of 'Kicks', 'Coney Island Baby', 'Crazy Feeling', 'She's My Best Friend' and 'Dirt'. Reed also told Bangs that 'Born To Be Loved' and 'You Don't Know What It's Like', both outtakes from the *Sally Can't Dance* sessions, were to be included, together with a reggae-based version of 'A Sheltered Life'.

With Steve Katz initially slated as producer, an intractably defiant Reed resisted all remonstrations to co-operate. Talking to Diana Clapton, Katz recounts familiar symptoms of what can only be termed Lou's recurrent speed psychosis:

> 'Each day was a new head trip. Finally, I said to him, right in front of all the musicians who'd gone through this — "I give up." The drugs had taken over and things were completely crazy. I felt that Lou was, at the time, out of his mind. So I had to stop the sessions. I had someone in authority from RCA come to the studio and verify that I could not make an album with the artist — that was that.'

Lou's high school year photo from 1959, from Freeport High School, Freeport, NY. The citation read, in part: "Tall, dark haired Lou likes basketball, music and, naturally, girls.... He is one of Freeport's great contributors to the recording world."
SETH POPPEL/YEARBOOK LIBRARY

Lou in his senior year at Freeport High School, singing at a school assembly, second from the right playing guitar.
SETH POPPEL/YEARBOOK LIBRARY

Lou, performing on stage with the Velvet Underground in 1966. ADAM RITCHIE/REDFERNS

Lou (centre right) with members of the Velvets and Warhol Factory crowd. Warhol is in the centre of the shot, obscured as ever, and Nico is in the foreground. EVERETT COLLECTION/REX FEATURES

Lou (left) with Sterling Morrison, John Cale and Mo Tucker in 1969, proudly presenting the new Velvet Underground album *White Light/White Heat*.
MICHAEL OCHS ARCHIVES/GETTY IMAGES

Lou joins Nico on stage at the Batalcan in Paris in January 1972. They and John Cale performed songs from *The Velvet Underground And Nico*.
MICK GOLD/REDFERNS

Lou and David Bowie on stage at London's Royal Festival Hall, July 8, 1972. GUS STEWART/REDFERNS

ans wade in the water to get close to Lou at London's Crystal Place Bowl, September 15, 1973. DAVID WARNER ELLIS/REDFERNS

ou with Rachel, aka Tommy Humphries, the transvestite queen, his inseparable live-in partner for four years during the seventies. CAMERA PRESS

Lou on stage with John Cale and David Byrne at New York's Ocean Club, July 21, 1976. ROBERTA BAYLEY/REDFERNS

Lou with Patti Smith in New York, 1976. RICHARD E. AARON/REDFERNS

Lou with Andy Warhol and Arista Records President Clive Davis at a party in New York, December 11, 1976. ALLAN TANNENBAUM/POLARIS/EYEVINE

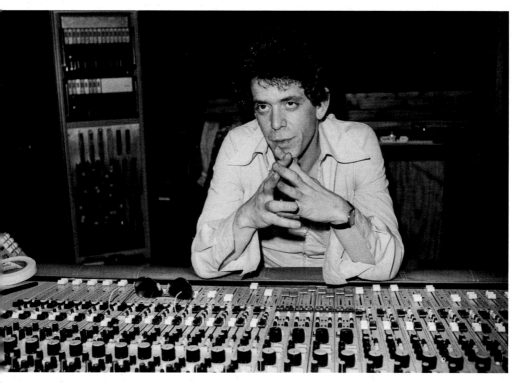

t the controls, where Lou most liked to be. LYNN GOLDSMITH/REX FEATURES

The Transformer on stage: Copenhagen, Denmark, August 19, 1973. JORGEN ANGEL/REDFERNS

Reed, meanwhile, was living a retainer of $15 a day, and living with Rachel at the Gramercy Park Hotel. He talked to Bangs about his life at the time in an interview later published as *How To Succeed in Torture Without Really Trying*:

> 'I've never made any bones about the fact that I take amphetamines. Any sane person would every chance they get. But I'm not in favour of legislation because I don't want all those idiots running around grinding their teeth at me. I only take methedrine which most people don't realise is a vitamin, Vitamin M. If people don't realise how much fun it is listening to *Metal Machine Music*, let 'em go smoke their fucking marijuana which is just bad acid anyway. And we've already been through that and forgotten it. I don't make records for fucking flower children.'

As a typical remake, Reed pulled himself back from the edge, working out and drinking carrot juice in a self-regulated plan of detoxification. In September 1975 at Ashley's on Lower Fifth Avenue he propitiously encountered the young upcoming producer Godfrey Diamond, an engineer at Media Sound, a meeting reinforced by Lou having known Diamond's brother from the Factory days. Back at the Gramercy Park Hotel Lou played Godfrey Diamond eight of his new songs using his Telecaster plugged into a tape-deck. Enthused by what he heard and willing to produce the fractiously outlawed artist, Diamond negotiated a budget with RCA and set about trying to re-establish Reed's commercial credibility without sacrificing his artistic integrity:

> 'We did have something of a discussion on 'Street Hassle' and 'I Wanna Be Black'. I felt both were excellent, but they did not belong to this album. I thought at this point in his career, the idea was to get the most commercial product possible, but without selling out to his fans. To make it playable on WNEW and (the old) WABC (AM and FM New York Radio). 'Street Hassle' was brilliant, but it wasn't hooky and it was far too heavy.'

It's possible that the new version of 'Street Hassle' to which Godfrey Diamond refers is the lyric 'Street Hasslin', written for Reed's projected book of poetry, *All The Pretty People*, to be published by Stonehill in 1976. In fact eight of Reed's poems, subtitled *Attitudes*, 'Kicks', 'Games', 'Dirt', 'It's Just Like In the Movies', 'The Slide', 'The Man', 'The Leader' and 'Street Hassling', appeared in the *Coldspring Journal* in January 1976, guest edited by NY culture critic Victor Bockris, and offer some of the most viciously psychosexual extremes of his lyricism. In 'Street Hassling' transgender queens are brutally exploited by the law. 'Patrolman #4/Picks up Renee thinks that she is a whore/Tries to cop a feel/Find out he's a boy not a girl/He's too hot/All the hormone shots/ Make policeman a bit too hot/Renee says she is so pleased/To see patrolmen on their knees.'

These brutally pathological poems belong as much to the frontiers of violent erotic geometry explored by J.G. Ballard in *The Atrocity Exhibition* and *Crash*, as they do to urban underbellies navigated by William Burroughs and Hubert Selby Jnr in their extrapolation of hardcore sleaze as urban motivator. Lou explained that the progression of his intended book followed an extreme trajectory: 'From the start they get rougher and harder and tougher until it's just out and out vicious, doesn't rhyme, has no punctuation, it's just vicious and vulgar.' All lack of personal involvement in *Attitudes* gives them a totally objectified, unemotional coldness, as though amorality is the unconditional substitute for feeling or community.

Under Diamond's tutelage, a constructively minded Reed entered the studios on 18 October 1975, optimally charged to redeem his rock cult status as New York's premier street poet.

> 'We started last Saturday. Everybody's been fabulous. It's a very small group of people, just me, Bruce, Michael, Bob, and Godfrey Diamond, our engineer. Period. Ken Glancy, the president of RCA, he's just incredible. I can't think of many presidents of record companies who would go along with this. This is coming out just totally the way I want it, from top to bottom. Which means just totally the way the other guys want it too because we all want the same thing. I love this album, and I love the people who are involved in it.'

Right from the album's opening track 'Crazy Feeling', a song recording Reed's Club 82 meeting with Rachel, 'You really are a queen/such a queen/ and I know cause I've made the same scene', as optimal endorsement of gay, the album's layered doo wop submerged romanticism adopts Rachel as inspired focus. Given a New York sunshine lift by Diamond's fluently superlative production, while retaining a nocturnal soundtrack – Reed is writing about his specific coterie – and using audio-tape collage to generate atmospheric tension on 'Kicks', the album never falls short of exemplary pop. In between sessions, Lou and Rachel walked their newly acquired dachshunds, The Baron and The Duke, in Washington Square Park, both skinnily dressed in black with Rachel walking protectively in front of Lou like a streetwise vigilante minder.

'Charley's Girl' – Reed cut a different version for the single release, but it's the same song – is seminal punk with a storyline of a band being busted for drugs and Charley's girl acting as informer. It is intimately conversational, but with a typically misogynistic undertow: 'If I ever see Sharon again/I'm gonna punch her face in' as ebullient punkish threat. 'She's My Best Friend', a retread of an old demo, is similarly confiding, asserting that gay or bisexual men need women friends as confidants, but it's 'Kicks', sung over a backing tape of cool, witty or referential partyers, and introduced as 'the morning of the show' that compounds Reed's speed-induced homicidal fantasies in which killing for kicks is conceived of as better than sex. In live performances Reed, more aggressively, called the slashed victim 'some motherfucker little cocksucker', the song's lyric content finding correlations with 'Sister Ray' in its concerns with pathological violence, and to a lesser extent with the Rolling Stones' 'Midnight Rambler,' with its ripper end, 'I'll stick a knife a right through your throat.'

By contrast, 'A Gift' is dulcet, satiric, a tongue-in-the-cheek salute to the gay world with Reed considering himself a gift to the women of the world by reason of his inaccessibility, contemplating how 'like a good wine I get better as I grow older'. The song's mellow tempo as a throwback to *Transformer*, sung over a whispered backing chorus, is Lou at his most nonchalantly casual, as though it's all too much to bother and too easy to do cool.

'Ooohhh Baby' as uptempo commentary on sleaze, signposts similar territory to the lowlife explorations on *Sally Can't Dance*, dealers, hookers, transvestites and after-hours bar aficionados who hang out in New York's scene are characterised with caustic wit and unshockable diffidence, with hints of Warhol's backroom crowd at Max's Kansas City, growing old and mitochondrial in the light.

'Nobody's Business' again finds Reed's sexual coding implying a subcultural exclusivity – an underworld knowledge that gives him fascinating legislation over the listener, an experiential authority that's a private affair, rather like the sort of sexual preference to which Reed alluded when interviewing drag queens about deviancy and how far they would go for money.

Coney Island Baby's centrepiece and title song is a celebratory and surprisingly nostalgic homage to Rachel, saturated in the intensity of Lou's feelings for his new partner and the realisation that the redemptive 'glory of love' is a transcendent thing that gets above suffering, and even if the city is 'something like a circus or a sewer', it's made possible by the feel good glow love brings to ordinary daily experience. Even Reed's fadeout declaration, 'I swear I'd give the whole thing up for you Rachel' sounds genuine, of the moment: on Lou's speeded up pulses. Here we catch him in a state of reflective vulnerability – in live performances of the song he would improvise the line 'Hey Lou Reed, you ain't ever gonna be a human being,' as a pointer to his usual inscrutable refusal to display emotion, but 'Coney Island Baby', a rare concession to humanity in Reed's mid-seventies songwriting, succeeds in romanticising Rachel or Tommy Humphries as his personalised apotheosis or queen.

His most commercially polished album since *Transformer, Coney Island Baby* reactivated Lou Reed's ability to write pop songs with effortless facility, a gift he navigated with singularly unquestionable arrogance at the expense of contemporaries who were almost unanimously derided. It brought Lou back in the *Billboard* Top 20, but reviews were inevitably mixed, given that Reed was invariably measured against his work with the Velvet Underground, uncredited at the time, and future-forwarded into the criterion against which his solo work was unfairly to be judged. Bill Henderson, reviewing the album for *Street Life*, considered it better than the lazy compromises informing *Sally Can't Dance*, but still short of what was expected of a Lou Reed album, as though undelivered potential was always going to be superior to recorded product:

> 'The short summation is that *Coney Island Baby* is nowhere near as bad as *Sally Can't Dance* and in fact is maybe his next best studio album after *Berlin* – but with competition that isn't saying a lot. And it primarily gets my vote because the best here is excellent. The best are perhaps typical Lou Reed songs – none of them disastrous but stuff that I'm sure he can crank out with one cortex tied behind his head. And if he can't, if this is all his best (and in his latest interview he suggests that he thinks this is so), then he is in worse shape than I thought.'

Lester Bangs – closer to Reed's music than any other critic, despite his slippery sycophancy and often deprecatory reportage – elicited more from Reed than any other journalist in a series of sensational *Creem* interviews, but he too was tepid in his praise, and cautious of the album's gay content, but came out in favour of Lou's reinvented pop gift:

> 'Lou's favourite old Velvet songs were always the ballads, and he's got a right to be sweet on himself. Love is silt. Anyone who has ever taken Quaaludes and wound up loving the rest of the human race so much they ended up in bed with a turnip knows that. The lyrics are better than any Lou-nee Tunes in a while, but note that not since *Transformer* have so many of them been so explicitly preoccupied with the, er, ah . . . 'gay' scene.'

British reviews were mostly uniformly disparaging, with Charles Shaar Murray headlining his review in *NME* 'The Impotence of Being Lou', as though his relatively unacclaimed past with the Velvet Underground represented an infallible criterion to which he could never again aspire. What was Murray looking for, waiting for, from Reed that he didn't satisfy, given that *Transformer, Berlin,* and *Sally Can't Dance* had each successfully recreated the artist as subcultural anti-hero to a new compulsively fascinated fan base and live audience?

'Yep, from the man who brought you *Sally Can't Dance* and *Methe-drine Machine Music* is yet another bunch of lame jokes and disastrous return visits to the sites of former triumphs, all overlaid into a set of backing tracks whose only connections with the vocal tracks are the tempi, the keys (most of the time, anyway), and the chord changes.'

Having trashed the whole upbeat recharged creative energies in Reed's directive that led to the making of *Coney Island Baby*, Murray proceeded to devalue his entire solo career as an inept, artistically flawed aberration:

'Having found an audience (or, more accurately, having one frog-marched in his direction), he belaboured them with a series of remorselessly flabby, perverse and trivial albums, each one more and more of a caricature than the last, each one depicting him with less and less dignity, each one carving a greater slice from his legend, each one, finally, devaluing him more than the last.'

Paul Nelson, writing for *Rolling Stone*, was more directly on the moment in considering the album affirmatively as 'timeless terrific rock'n'roll', an optimally poppy execution of songs inspired by Rachel as psychic sender, in which Lou reaffirmed his smart pop incentive:

'The songs themselves – as structured and melodic as any Reed has written – are timeless, terrific rock'n'roll. And the strength of the genre is accentuated by the simplicity and logic of crisp, tactile pro-duction (by Reed and Godfrey Diamond) and careful, resourceful arrangements which emphasize both electric and acoustic guitars and inventive background vocals.'

The making of the album, too, was an unstoppable triumph of resistant creativity over managerial litigation on the part of the angrily deposed Dennis Katz. Lou was resolutely upfront about fighting his patch:

'I made *Coney Island Baby* and was served three times with separate subpoenas [by Dennis Katz]. One before, one during and one after. It was just two weeks ago that the last injunction against it was denied. If it had not been denied the record would have been recalled.'

Reed was $700,000 in the red to RCA in October 1975, and simultaneously considered archetypal godfather of punk to a new straightforward guitar-driven music evolving in New York as punk. In the final weekend in November 1975, Lou and Rachel went to the downtown venue CBGBs to catch the hyperactive brattish Ramones, aggressively dressed as Lou clones in leather biker jackets and skinny jeans, returning to see them again a day later, taping them from his seat with his Sony portable cassette recorder. He'd recorded Television there too, weeks earlier, much to Tom Verlaine's annoyance, refusing to hand over the tape and clearing out of the club with typical indignant Lou 'fuck you' hauteur.

Having parted amicably from RCA in the summer of 1976, Lou was temporarily without a record label and, lacking any integral band with which to tour, he made a guest spot at Mickey Ruskin's Lower Manhattan Ocean Club in July 1976. In addition, he ventured onstage with John Cale at St Mark's Church in the Bowery to debut an acoustic 'Coney Island Baby', joined David Byrne of Talking Heads in supporting Cale's 'A Close Watch' and then combined with Cale for a ripping garage version of 'Waiting For The Man', by now the seminal cover theming the new aggressive punk at Max's Kansas City and CBGBs. Ostracised by the music industry but acclaimed by New York's new wave, Lou sat it out waiting for a deal that seemed an impossibly long time coming.

As the newly cryogenically acclaimed Godfather of Punk, a cartoon of Lou Reed as Frankenstein fronted the premiere cover of *Punk*, a magazine produced out of 356 Tenth Avenue, an office space called 'The Pink Dump' by three Connecticut kids living in a Chelsea storefront. It contained a spontaneous interview done with Reed at a CBGBs Ramones gig. Conscious of the age differential – Reed was now 34 – he took to adopting the signature role Uncle Lou as his resilient epithet. Incongruously alienated by age from a punk genre of which he was subversive prototype, Reed's love/hate relationship with punk simmered with dualistic tensions. Reviewing his solo career to date, and situating his work in the present, which is already the future, Lou pronounced:

> 'All the albums I put out after this are going to be things I want to put out. No more bullshit, no more dyed hair faggot junkie trip. I mimic me better than anyone else, so if everyone else is making money ripping me off, I figure maybe I better get in on it. Why not? I created Lou Reed. I have nothing even faintly in common with that guy, but I can play him well – really well.'

Lou's summation of his subcultural influence on the whole Patti Smith, Ramones, Television, Talking Heads partial rip off of his superior artistry was an authoritatively subtle putdown of an aggressive cognoscenti, inspired by his attitude and indomitable cool, but lacking his lyrical facility to impose an ownership on New York as street laureate. 'I'm too literate to be into punk rock. The new bands are cute, but I really don't know anything about punk at all.'

Lou's distancing of himself from a progeny anxious to win his notice was typical of his essential isolationism and refusal to be categorised, as though rock somehow didn't accommodate his talents, but at the same time was his inexorable choice of artistic expression. In reality, Reed was broke, uncompromisingly alienated, and naturally deeply insecure about his future in music:

> 'There was just me and Rachel living on 15 dollars a day, while the lawyers were trying to figure out what to do with me. Then I got a call from Clive Davis and he said, "Hey, how ya doing? Haven't seen you for a while." He knew how I was doing. He said, "Why don't we have lunch?" I felt like saying, "You mean you want to be seen with me in public?" If Clive could be seen with me, I knew I had turned the corner. I grabbed Rachel and said, "Do you know who just called?" I knew I had won.'

Reed though, remained attached to his obsession with Times Square/ Tenth Avenue drag queens, assembling a large collection of taped recordings detailing their often coprophiliac practices as sex workers and eliciting for money the full extent to which they were prepared to go. Now living with Rachel in an Upper East Side apartment, with his pile of stereo gear, his video cassette player, his Andy Warhol books and weighty volumes of British and American pharmacopoeia, Lou wearing his customary disarming black Raybans and a black studded leather jacket, proceeded in an interview with *Rolling Stone* to play extracts from a recent recording of a Times Square queen that clearly interfaced Lou's own repertoire of transgender fetishes:

> Queen: Arman is a glass coffee-table queen.
>
> Reed: He's a what?
>
> Queen: He has this lovely apartment.
>
> Reed: Oh, that's where you lie under the table?
>
> Queen: He lies under the glass coffee-table on a little velvet cushion and you gap yourself over the coffee-table while his face is pressed up against it. And then afterward you can make him eat the shit off.
>
> Reed: You did that?
>
> Queen: Yeah, I commanded him to. I dipped lunch meat in it and had him eat the lunch meat.'

Reed's deregulated catalogue of same sex agenda provides something of a psychological mapping of his mind at the time (not the pathological result of speed psychosis) in which from the earliest age men substituting for women, as more glamorous than their female counterparts, while remaining male identified, were his predominant sexual attraction, with Rachel aka Tommy his idealised partner. By way of compromise, he also played a voice and piano only demo of 'Senselessly Cruel', which was to go on to his next album, given the working title *Nomad*, crediting an Andy Warhol designed sleeve that ended up as *Rock'n'Roll Heart*, with a fantastic moody blue Mick Rock photo as cover design.

It was Clive Davis, president of Columbia Records from 1967–1973, and recently fired for allegedly using company funds to bankroll his son's bar mitzvah, who signed Reed to the company he founded in 1975, Arista Records, named after New York City's secondary school honour society of which he was a member. In short order he also brought to the label prestigious acts like Barry Manilow, Dionne Warwick and the newly re-energised Kinks. Seeing the commercially dipped Reed as a potential spearhead of his Arista roster, Lou's signing was announced on the August 14, 1976, with both Lou and Arista anxious to emphasise in the accompanying press release that his poetry had been published in such literary periodicals as the *Paris Review, Harvard Advocate, Fusion, Another World Poetry Anthology, Ox, Cold River Review, Transatlantic Quarterly*, etc, as a clear pointer to Reed's literacy, thus setting his lyrics apart from most mainstream pop. John Morthland, reporting in *Rolling Stone* in September, wrote of 'an unusually healthy looking Lou Reed' who gave a press conference at the rehearsal studio for his upcoming album. But according to Morthland, Reed's speed state was soon evident in the liberated depravity of his methedrine stuttered conversation:

> 'But when he sat down with a pair of reporters during a short break, he spaced out, as if on cue. Reed free-associated, touching on such topics as giving cabbies the finger, Doberman Pinchers mating with German Shepherds, Dorothy Parker at the Algonquin, dwarfs, Freemasons, Sean Connery going bald, and the merits of amphetamines over liquor.'

What Clive Davis hadn't counted on was signing an artist without an album, and one so enthusiastic to get into the studio and outstrip his younger contemporaries that two of the songs, 'Banging On My Drum' and 'Follow The Leader' were so minimally skeletal as to contain one line only, repeated in a frenetic speed rush, while 'Chooser And The Chosen One' was solely instrumental for lack of lyrics. The album, its title changed from *Nomad* to the more punchy *Rock'n'Roll Heart*, is fuelled by methedrine molecules, with Reed tripping over syllables in his urgency to translate dopamine hyperactivity into music.

Reed described his emergent album as 'very danceable, the kind of thing that if you were sitting in a bar and either wanted to punch somebody or fuck, you'd probably play it on the jukebox. Our single will probably be 'Banging On My Drum'. That's what the Ramones should do.

Three chords is three chords, but there is a finesse to it.' The scheduled tour for *Rock'n'Roll Heart*, from October to December, would be 'a fully fledged attack, a seething assault. I call it germ warfare. I like to think of us as the Clearasil in the face of the nation. Jim Morrison would have said that if he was smart, but he's dead.' With Godfrey Diamond too exhausted, or declining to produce the album, and with Lou once again threatening to rename it to *I Wanna Be Black*, it was obvious that Clive Davis had lost control of his artist from the start. Disdainfully, politically incorrect and incurably controversial, Reed spelled out the lyrics of his song to an interviewer: 'I want to be black/have natural rhythm/shoot twenty feet of jissom too/and fuck up the Jews/I wanna be black/I wanna be a panther/have a girlfriend called Samantha/and have a stable of foxy whores.'

Produced by Reed, who played all of the guitars on the album, and with a personnel of Michael Fonfara on piano, organ and harp, Bruce Yaw on bass, Michael Suchorsky on drums and Marty Fogel on sax, and with a jazz feel adding a blue flavoured texture to the album, as a throwback to Reed's fifties admiration for the likes of Ornette Coleman, John Coltrane and Don Cherry, *Rock'n'Roll Heart* is drenched in self-indulgent mania to maximise on minimal material, and at its worst self-parodic and meaningless in its contents. While the flyby tempo and mood of the album perfectly rivals the punk genre with which he was in contention, and with a sophisticated edge on three chords, few of the songs other than 'Ladies Pay', 'Temporary Thing', 'You Wear It Well' and the Velvets' old demo 'Sheltered Life' have any sense of finish. With much of the material written hurriedly in the studio, the songs are attacked with manic surges of vocal energy that are nothing short of an achievement in themselves for what must rate as the ultimate in amphetamine delivery of the punk mid-seventies guitar-driven raucousness. The album's opener, 'I Believe In Love', typifies rush, an unlikely theme, doubtless inspired by Rachel, of whom Lou commented: 'He's hardly heard my music and didn't like it much when he did. Still isn't all that enthusiastic. Rachel loves disco music and Diana Ross.'

Rock'n'Roll Heart, the subject of an extensive advertising campaign aimed at Reed's pop rejuvenation, sold moderately well, but was essentially the ghostbrand of an underwritten album flawed by a needlessly impetuous attempt to beat the New Wave antagonists he'd been stalking: the Ramones, Pere Ubu, Television, Richard Hell and Patti Smith. Reed's indisputable cool was unlikely ever to be threatened or upclassed, and its arguable that he downgraded his talents by hurrying into an album without a producer and lacking crafted lyrics for constructive songs that only scratch the surface and lack any narrative development. Minimal, punkish, 'fuck you, I'm Lou Reed', they tore up the moment to no great effect. Reviewing the album for *Rolling Stone*, Frank Rose found it at best superficial, as though speed overtook meaning:

> '*Rock'n'Roll Heart* is a replay of every snarl he ever put on wax. On its twelve songs he contemplates a variety of typical Lou Reed subjects – love, hate, good times, bad times, fame, hipness – in a manner that's deceptively perfunctory. He seems to have reduced his work to a series of skeletal phrases which he fleshes out with music that's lean and raw. The key phrases are all refrains: 'I'm banging on my drum'; 'You wear it so well'; 'You're caught in a vicious circle'; 'It's just a temporary thing', Reed chants them like mantras, until they're almost stripped of meaning. He has scooped out their depth – and given us nothing but surface.'

The album's rapid burn-up minimalism seemed an empty gesture, a psychotic abuse of talent or a depredating send-up of voracious Lou clones, all frenetically working his old space, Max's Kansas City. If Lou was the metaphoric death's head insignia of his copyist epigone, rock's Great Beast with the numerical designation 666 in Crowley's system, then he was that by default, and urgently in need of new songs to sugar his scandalous leftfield reputation.

Nick Kent in reviewing the album for *NME* under the heading 'Reed Commits Gross Banditry' discerned, 'Just that same old 3 a.m. Vermouth and Mogadon hangover of a voice droning out these vapidly pathetic lyrics which end up signifying precisely nothing . . .' The album was never that bad and in the 21st century sounds postmodern in its refusal to commit to feelings or concretise subject matter, instead speeding into an abstract vanishing point that is the never arrived at future. The album is a whiteout, blackout, blueout, greyout sonic surface over which Lou arrogates with gated Raybans. A commonplace sight in guitar stores talking intense tech to sales guys, discussing the guitar in his hand or the amp that guitar was going through, Lou was now living with Rachel in a block of luxury apartments in East 52nd Street that dead-ended at the FDR Drive, overlooking the East River, on the proceeds of his Arista signing. The following year he would move to a six-room apartment above a bagel shop on Christopher Street, the gay hub of New York's West Village life.

After Lou attended a poetry reading by Camille in a Reade Street loft, the walls decorated with Camille's paintings of giant Tarot cards, a fan invited back to discuss long-term amphetamine abuse with Lou, remembered the apartment on East 52nd Street as minimally furnished, marble floored, with a big futon on a low platform, and rows of new hardcover books all relating to Warhol and the Beats on the shelves. There was a bookcase full of random papers, a rare-for-the-time digital clock, a tripod with a new RCA video camera and an RCA TV and VCR stereo. Accompanying Rachel into a pristine kitchen, the fan was to discover the fridge empty except for a packet of bacon, a quart of milk and a quart of Tropicana, as though food had been dispensed with for drugs.

Chris Charlesworth, *Melody Maker's* New York correspondent, 1973–77: 'In 1976 Lou gave me two television sets. By this time we'd met socially a few times but I'd never attempted to interview him as I knew his reputation. It was better being casual friends with Lou. That was the way to stay friendly. I remember a party where he and my old *MM* pal Roy Hollingworth jammed for 20 minutes on the same chord. He'd used about 50 TVs as a backdrop at a show I saw at the Academy of Music on 14th Street and when I bumped into him at Ashley's a few weeks later I asked him what happened to them. "They're at my apartment," he said.

' "I don't have a TV," I said.

' "How many do you want?"

' "How many you got?"

' "Fifty."

'Lou gave me his address, an apartment block on 2^(nd) Avenue in the fifties, and next day I turned up there. Sure enough TVs were piled high. I took two. They were b&w, ex-hospital Lou told me. They worked, too, just. I rigged one up in the living room at my place on 78^(th) Street and another in the bedroom, and used bent coat hangers as aerials. Thanks Lou.'

With the same speed attack of assumed guitar heroism Reed had manifested in interviews exonerating *Metal Machine Music*, he continued to promote his guitar playing on *Rock'n'Roll Heart*, tripping journalists into confused speechlessness by the rapidity of his transitioning fire:

> 'I play all the guitars. I'm also the background voices too, except for one song. I play a Gibson SG. I've got a '56 Fender Strat. All my life I've waited for the right Strat and I finally found it. It was about a year and a half ago; I saw it and felt it, I didn't even have to play it – I just knew. Me! The laziest person in the world, right. I took the finish off the whole thing and varnished it natural wood, the whole trip. Then I thought for the studio I ought to have a different sound so I got a Firebird, but I couldn't handle it, just too big and clumsy and heavy. I had a Les Paul Jnr which I liked because it had only one volume control and one tone, but it wasn't loud enough and the neck was too big. Les Paul Custom is too heavy and the Melody Maker isn't loud enough so that leaves you with the Gibson SG. I heard it and said, 'Oh my God, there is that sound,' and onstage it sounds like a bank of Marshals. It's only a small amp and two twelve-inch speakers, though no fancy stuff.'

Reed's unstoppable megalomania sounded remotely hollow in view of the comparatively lightweight album he was promoting with such aggrandised bulleting conviction. With his motor neurons operating at different chemicalised speed to his interviewers and record company, Lou now entered the studio to produce the album *Wild Angel* for Nelson Slater, a survivor of one of Lou's short-lived Syracuse Street bands, oddly enough for his old label RCA. Lou contributed guitar, piano and backing vocals to an unnotable, slightly funky album having incorporated one of Slater's songs 'Complete The Story Now' into his 1975 live sets. This may have been the motivation behind Reed producing *Wild Angel*, an anomaly redeemed only by Mick Rock's sensational artwork, with a bondage photo of a manacled woman, her head shaved and a black chain slicing her red-lipsticked mouth, as another pointer to Reed's transgender propensities.

There was no studio album from an apparently uninterested Lou Reed in 1977, although there was news in the autumn that he was in the studio mixing *Street Hassle*. Taking advantage of the recording hiatus, RCA issued the compilation *Walk On The Wild Side – The Best of Lou Reed*, the Mick Rock designed sleeve depicting Polaroids of Lou and Rachel, Lou in a camp black beret and customary aviators and Rachel looking typically ambiguously sexed. As an incentive to fans, the album made available the *Coney Island Baby* outtake 'Nowhere At All', an angrily guitar licked, lyrically minimal scorcher that was originally the B-side to the single 'Charley's Girl', itself a different mix from the album version.

Lou, at his most impromptu vitriolic in interviews, was again in a strange head space, clearly unable to write new material and impotent to affirm continuity at a time when he was in direct competition with his volatilely wired young progeny, the New York punk scene that was brimming with ratty streetwise hormones. Neither Lou's anger nor his bored indifference, both masking his temporary inability to write, ever got attached to his creative songwriter's resources. He appeared burnt-out and possibly back on heroin. While London kids rushed on speed, New York's drug was Mexican brown heroin, 50–60 per cent pure, as opposed to heavier cut White Asian, and cheap, three to five dollars a bag, or $20 for a rock. Addicts proliferated, both on and in detox. The situation was so acute that an organised nucleus of recovering junkies established a tent city near the state capital in Albany to protest against the defunding of residential rehab facilities, a demonstration mobilised by Julio Martinez, a South Bronx Puerto Rican ex-junkie who was co-founder of the Phoenix House treatment centre.

Reed was 35 and lacking either the creative or commercial renaissance that should have been initialised by his move to Arista, although speaking to Mick Rock in *Penthouse*, he once again had only praise for Clive Davis:

> 'He was everything I hoped he would be. He genuinely cares. He more or less backed me right in the middle of litigation proceedings with my old manager. I mean, at the time no one would touch me with a twenty-foot pole . . .'

Presumptively returning to the working title, *I Wanna Be Black*, Reed raided his *Coney Island Baby* outtakes, Velvet Underground demos and impromptu two and three liners to begin work on an obliquely occult, muddy, binaural album, liberated into literate punk only by its title track, 'Street Hassle'.

6

Uptown Dirt

WITH Godfrey Diamond again announced as producer but declining the offer, Lou brought in his old friend Richard Robinson, typically controversially, given that Robinson's production of his first solo album *Lou Reed* had met with unanimous negative criticism. The album was part live recordings, part studio. '*Street Hassle* was recorded live in Germany,' Lou announced. 'They didn't understand a word of English – like most of my audiences. They're fucked up assholes, what difference does it make? Can they count from one to ten?'

Both on his German 1977 tour and his three nights at London's New Victoria Theatre in April 1977, Reed, without introducing them, had included with deliberately slurred, fractured diction five new fragmented songs, 'Shooting Star', 'Leave Me Alone', 'Pretty Face', 'Get Up And Dance' and 'Real Good Time Together' in a laconic slovenly drawl as though incoherent bits were all the audience merited. The numbers sounded like anti-songs delivered by an edgily truculent anti-hero. With the attitude of a disaffected rock Jean Genet, mixing baroque language with gutter obscenities, the Lou who recorded *Street Hassle* was either iconoclastic punk by default despite the disclaimers, or avuncular junkie too speed-wiped to bother. That Reed had done fast energy a decade earlier and was now selling attitude rather than content didn't help. For all their timeless originality the Velvet Underground were a sixties phenomenon and New Wave with their abrasive helium licks in a way Reed wasn't. Style and literacy weren't punk, and Reed, in attempting to dictate over it, was an awkward renegade fit, admired for songs largely written in the previous decade.

Released in the US in February 1978, by virtue of its title track *Street*

Hassle was conceived as a dramatic return to form, a critically acclaimed restoration of Lou as New York's nefarious prince of sleaze, with first issue copies of the album stickered with a *Rolling Stone* commendation: 'A stunning incandescent triumph. A masterpiece.' In truth, it both is and isn't a product of that expectation.

Recorded binaurally for tech-heads with a system developed by Manfred Schunke, credited as an engineer on *Street Hassle*, the technique involved placing two microphones in the studio in an attempt to mimic the stereo sound and loud volume of actually being in the studio with the performers, with the engineers employing a mannequin head with a microphone implanted in each ear, the full binaural facility, though, being effective, as Lou admitted, only on headphones. The overall sound to the listener is muddy, grainy and self-indulgently obscure, and Lou was to extend its use for two further albums, *Take No Prisoners* (1979) and *The Bells* (1979). *Street Hassle*'s title accurately describes its mean, gutter-infested, compassionless ethos, with Reed's trashy put-down of his former manager Dennis Katz in 'Dirt' extending to the insultingly abject depravity of 'You'd eat shit and say it tasted good/if there was some money in it for you.'

Reed's remake of an old Velvet's demo, 'Gimme Some Good Times' as the album's self-parodying opener with its direct references to 'Sweet Jane' and himself as the 'rock'n'roll faggot junkie', now sung as a jaded, disillusioned hedonist, his voice coated with urban grime, evaluates all experience as equal: 'No matter how ugly you are/to me it always is the same'. The album's amoral tone in which good and bad can't be differentiated is its film noir strength, although its unrelieved monochrome lack of emotional colouring is often claustrophobic, as though Lou's down is the only subterranean level. The deterioration of Lou's relationship with Rachel is the submerged subtext to the despondency signalled by an album I find flatly depressive, and more so than *Berlin*; and which originally was a live set, rejected by Clive Davis at Arista, who initially wanted 'Street Hassle' reduced to its compacted first two minutes rather than developed into epic confessional of a gay breakup. In interviews Reed made it very clear that his songs were addressed to men and not women. This was made emphatic in the opening lines of the elegiac three-part 'Street Hassle', 'Waltzing Mathilda whipped out her wallet/ Sexy boys smiled in dismay/She took out four twenties caused she liked round figures/Everybody's queen for a day.' Rachel, Lou's celebratory queen in the upbeat doo-wop heady 'Crazy Feeling', is now the discarded warred with reject.

> 'They're not heterosexual concerns running through that song,' Lou emphasised, 'I don't make a deal of it, but when I mention a pronoun, its gender is all important. It's just that my gay people don't lisp. They're not any more affected than the straight world. They just are. That's important to me. I'm one of them, and I'm right there, just like anybody else. It's not made anything other than what it is. But if you take me, you've got to take the whole thing.'

Reed had never sounded more affirmative about being gay, or less likely to be electro-shocked for owning up to his identity than in the late seventies when he committed to his same sex orientation. He was additionally eloquent about the studio recording of 'Street Hassle' and its expansion into a three-bit song at Clive Davis' suggestion.

> '"Street Hassle" is basically a two-minute odd tape loop. The basic track's all the same, but with different overdubs put over it. It shows how many ways you can look at the same thing. What I did was record a whole string section, but I only used part of it – the cello. I only brought in the whole string section for one part, so it kind of sweeps in real panoramic. I had three vignettes, so I thought the perfect thing here was to dissolve, like in a movie-shift, one set of music past another set, sort of pan them and BOOM, you're into the second world.'

'Street Hassle' belongs in the same lawless, taboo-busting tradition as 'Heroin', 'Sister Ray' and 'Kicks' in Reed's cataloguing of rogue sub-cultures, only the exhaustion and desperation in his monotonal voice bring the emotional storyline right up front like a pathological hit and run. A decade's deregulated abuse of stimulants coats his voice in narrating raw street poetry as compassionless as it is brutally real. Managed with shockingly unmodified cool, only Reed could have conceived of confiding, 'When someone turns that blue it's a universal truth/and you just know that bitch will never fuck again/so why don't you grab your old lady by the feet/and just lay her out in the darkest street/and in the morning she's just another hit and run.'

If Lou had wanted to assert his ruthless punk supremacy over a genre of three-chord dissidents citing him as subversive archetype, then 'Street Hassle' restored his dignity as rock's premier street poet who dissolved all boundaries of the fuckedness quotient of his outlaw milieu. That the song involves disruptive personal issues and the disintegration of his relationship with Rachel adds harrowing authenticity to the sense of separation and loss on which it pivots. In his *Diaries*, Andy Warhol noted that 'He's sort of separated from Rachel the drag queen, but not completely, they have separate apartments.'

> 'Let me propose something to you. Take the guy who's singing in the second part of 'Street Hassle'. Now, he may come off as a little cruel, but let's say he's also singing the last part about losing love. He's already lost the one for him. He's not unaware of those feelings, he's just handling the situation, that's all.'

The private and dispassionate public Lou, do the two match, is simply dealing with the situation of breakup, the only criterion of survival, the reality of Rachel's continuous transgender dilemma as to whether to lose genital identity as Tommy or become reassigned Rachel? According to a third party friend of the couple:

> '[he] sat with Rachel on suicide watch one night when she was distraught over Lou's rejection. She'd been scheduled again to begin gender reassignment surgery until Lou changed his mind about it yet again. Later, around 3 a.m., I met Lou to go to the ATM to get cash to pay Rachel's hotel bill. A friend at the time and I took Rachel shopping for butch clothes, khakis and a plaid shirt, that he wore with his high-heeled boots. And one of those last times I saw him he

was shouting a proposal of marriage to me across the street in the East fifties.'

Rachel, or Tommy Humphries, died at 29 of Aids related cancer.

The only other song sufficiently developed on *Street Hassle* to have any lyrical merit is 'Dirt', not the much superior 'Downtown Dirt', an outtake from *Coney Island Baby*, but a thuggish hit job done on his former manager, incorporating rather than sampling the Bobby Fuller refrain 'I fought the law and the law won' as strangulated chorus. Binaurally infected with fogged vocals, Lou nonetheless executes a killer riff that churns with whiskey and animosity. Allan Jones in *Melody Maker* reviewed it as,

> '[a] compelling tirade constructed around the hellslammer riff that introduced Bowie's "Station to Station" (don't ask me who got there first), that lurches with an exaggerated stagger through a vindictive landscape. You wouldn't argue with this slurred street cameo of simmering lowlife threat, or necessarily want to play it twice, unless you had a target in mind.'

The rest of the album, mostly recorded live, is instantly forgettable, unmelodic and rough, with live versions of the inane mantra 'Leave Me Alone' and street tough 'I Wanna Be Black' falling short of their studio recorded counterparts as *Coney Island Baby* outtakes, suggesting Lou's empty gestures of contempt didn't so much rival punk as reduce his version of New Wave to no-colour absent songs, improvised redundant scrambles like 'Pretty Face' and 'Shooting Star' as abuse of his songwriting facilities. In treating punk as intellectually moronic, Reed downsized his talent by attempting to clone it.

The album's critical acclaim in the US didn't translate into sales, giving it a chart placing of 89, while in Britain, even at the height of New Wave, it failed to make the Top 100, but sold well in Europe, peaking in at number 12 in France. And Reed was always tirelessly defensive of his superiority over what he imagined or dismissed as puerile opposition.

'I'm so tired of the theory of the noble savage. I'd like to hear punks who weren't at the mercy of their own rage and who could put together a coherent sentence. I mean they can get away with "Anarchy In The UK" and that bullshit, but it hasn't an eighth of the heart or the intelligence of something like Garland Jeffreys' "Wild In The Streets".'

The song 'Street Hassle' defined Reed more than the ethos, the two colliding accidentally so that his personal fragmentation ripped into punk assault without being a part of it, like a dirty smudge on a gunked bathroom tile. There's no redemption offered in any phrase of the lyric, with Lou affirming his remorseless psychopathic cold in the same diction he employed for his group of poems *Attitudes*, intended for the unpublished collection *All The Pretty People* in which amorality glowers like a black diamond.

British critics weren't so kind and Julie Burchill, reviewing *Street Hassle* for *NME*, trashed both the album and Lou's diffident complaints of not being properly acknowledged as the unrivalled Sadean progenitor of anarchic punk.

'Maybe Arista should stop Lou making records and make him write to a problem page instead. He seems quite frustrated, and very ungrateful for his good fortune. All this stupid extolling of vileness when millions of people would give their eyes for an easy life in an affluent band . . . He's such a tired old boy, so flabby and numb in his New York City cocoon that he hasn't even caught on yet that positive thought/action is the only way. Lou Reed is apathetic, empty and defeated like ninety-nine per cent of rock these days.'

Redundant to a new generation peaking in the late seventies, Reed fed off isolation to self-mythologise his street-bandit status: New York wasn't London, and the separationist genres of gay and music subcultures suited Reed's mystique of having done it all, been in it all, in ways of degradation the kids could never follow. Lou was assumed to have out-gayed gays and out-punked punks and out-drugged druggies as an infamous intellectualised

Judy Garland of the gutter. But musically he was pushed and, like Bowie's attempt to sideline punk through his collaboration with Brian Eno on the ambiently disarranged *Low*, *Heroes* and *Lodger* as deliberate art-house, non-competitive escapes into cultivated obscurity, Lou's sustained anti-commercialism forced him out to the peripheries of chart incentive towards a place in which he felt safe from invasive teens forcing attention with distraught three-chord rants.

On the back of *Street Hassle* and the resurgent credibility the title song gave him as a bad boy, Reed toured the States in spring 1978, his outright punk hostility of the previous year replaced by a new anecdotal talkative-ness, a boozed self-referential commentary in deconstructing the lyric, while the melody line was buried in a lurching blues, with Lou's indomi-table authority and newly adopted Roland guitar synthesiser smothering audiences unprepared for this new transitional phase of his unpredictable seventies career.

Lou was effusive about the merits of the Roland synthesiser guitar and how it incomparably enhanced his playing. Backstage at the Tower Theatre, Philadelphia, he enthused about its annihilated killer energies to Allan Jones, attributing his new aggressive playing and the shattering of set pieces into bluesy textured extensions, to the capacity for optimal distor-tion provided by the instrument.

> 'Oh, oh, I still know I'm the best man. Who else is there? Kansas? Mel Tormé? Come on, I'm Dante with a beat, man. When I get onstage with this fucking monster, I'm like Bach, Bartok and Little Richard. I'm so hot at the moment, I burn myself every time I touch a guitar . . . This thing is the invention of the age. I haven't been this excited since the first record I made . . . This is the sound I heard in my head at the time of 'Sister Ray'. I've done nothing but track this one sound down. It's been frustrating, 'cos I always approached the guitar as if it was an orchestra – am I not the King of Flash? That's what distortion was all about.'

The *Street Hassle* tour, unlike the album's falling off the edge noncha-lance, found a wired combative Reed not only confidently consolidating his guitar skills, but revving up his vocal delivery into rock blues and soul intonations. The live recordings of Lou's standout shows at the Old Waldorf Theatre, San Francisco (March 23), Cleveland Music Hall (March 26) and the Masonic Temple, Detroit (April 25), where his arrangement of 'Heroin' to accommodate his girl chorus Angela Howells and Chrissy Faith is superbly improvised, are all outstanding instances of reinvention, as are the New York Bottom Live shows from which the live album *Take No Prisoners* was recorded, and issued originally as alternate red and blue vinyls in a gatefold sleeve.

John Rockwell in the *New York Times* noted the new musical feel:

> 'His musical gifts manifest themselves in his work with a band, and much of the time Friday [The Bottom Line, March 11] was spent in crunching, textually dense instrumentals with multiple opportunities for solos that never wandered off into the too loosely-structured or the self-indulgent. The result was curiously akin to the neo-Roxy Music style of pounding progressiveness that David Bowie had been espousing of late, and that's fitting, Mr Reed has many parallels with Mr Bowie, and that's meant as a compliment to both of them.'

A Reed 1978 set usually comprised 'Gimme Some Good Times', 'Satellite Of Love', 'Leave Me Alone', 'I Wanna Be Black', 'Walk On The Wild Side', 'Coney Island Baby', 'Dirt', and 'Street Hassle' with the encores including 'Sweet Jane', 'Sister Ray', 'Heroin' and 'Rock'n'Roll'.

Reed had returned as an innovative experimentalist, repurposing his material into a reckless fusion of rock, blues and soul, sunglassed, lipsticked, battered and leather jacketed, but this time round confident of a real or illusory mastery. Coolly smoking onstage, and often drunk, his extempore self-appraisals of Lou, as smart neglected musical genius, both challenged and irritated audiences hoping for straight delivery.

Take No Prisoners, as the manifestation of Reed as camp comedian noir, and unmitigated expositor of sleaze, and pulled from a week of live recordings at New York's Bottom Line in May 1978, came with Uncle Lou's unconditional endorsement, while also serving as the album Reed contractually owed his old label RCA.

'I wanted to make a record that wouldn't give an inch. If anything, it would push the world back just an inch or two. If *Metal Machine Music* was just a hello note, *Take No Prisoners* is the letter that should've gone with it. You may find this funny, but I think of it as a contemporary urban-blues album. After all, that's what I write – tales of the city. And if I dropped dead tomorrow, this is the record I'd choose for posterity. It's not only the smartest thing I've ever done, it's also as close to Lou Reed as you're probably going to get, for better or for worse.'

The record also threw a new light on Reed as garrulous raconteur of bitchy gossip, adept at camp repartee and spontaneous stand up one-liners, demythicising in the process standards like 'Sweet Jane' and 'Waiting For The Man', through irreverent put downs of the music industry that payrolled Reed's scandal making. It also suggested Reed's gay identity off-stage, and his effusively camp figures of expression masked by his usually uncommunicative role with audiences. In that sense *Take No Prisoners* strips the man bare like no other album in letting the audience in on sub-culture aspects of his private identity.

Wearing a black T-shirt sloganed with his own *Street Hassle* logo, skinny jeans or black leather trousers, and blackout reflective Raybans, Reed seemed never so grittily sure of being Reed as he lashed audiences verbally and electronically. On its release *Take No Prisoners* was issued with a stocker: WARNING: THIS ALBUM IS OFFENSIVE and this admonition at the height of street-wrangling punk was controversially correct. On top form Reed was more abusive than ever. Dictionary definition: Verb: use something to bad effect or for bad purpose, misuse: Synonym: Treat with cruelty or violence, especially regularly or repeatedly: Synonym: Make excessive and habitual use of (alcohol or drugs, especially illegal ones).

Onstage at the Bottom Line, Reed defiantly not only ripped up his own songs into disassembled blues, their backstories and the front row rock critics like Robert Christgau of the *Village Voice*, described as toefucker, and John Rockwell of the *New York Times*, but reaffirmed his dubious status as rock's most formidable historian of its transitioning decades. You could argue legitimately from Lou's expensively intellectualised diction in interviews that no one emerged as his equal in terms of acute knowledge of the pop/rock genres he so resolutely explored. In evaluating his own talents he arrives there through critical assessment of others, and is arguably, invariably, right on the point.

Right from the confrontational bravura of 'Sweet Jane', the album's opener, a scorchingly improvised whack of misregulated black humour, dragging Vietnam politics into the unlikely plot, 'Are you political Lou?/political about what?/give me an issue/I'll give you a tissue/wipe my ass with it', the set is a loquacious platform for Lou to shape-shift familiar songs into a verbal collage of fuck you motivation. The album's five star track, or depressing bore, however you frame it, is Lou's 17-minute trawl through 'Walk On The Wild Side' in which the song's cast of Factory drag queens is updated into Candy Darling, 'putting silicone in her tit', and Joe Dellesandro being sub-literate, and Reed taking credit for writing the song after he was approached originally to write a musical adaptation of Nelson Algren's novel of the same name for Broadway. Unnervingly uncomfortable in his role as stand-up comedian Reed displayed an effortless facility at dipping in and out of spoken asides to focus on loud predatory rock noise as his real business at the Bottom Line.

Andy Warhol, Truman Capote, Tennessee Williams, Reed's punk clones are all dished dirt through his in-joke invective. The binaural recording, together with the mix of monologue, rap, blues and Lenny Bruce/Benny Youngman-style comedy, upends the linear progression of songs, or blasts them into stratospheric noise and rant, as with 'Leave Me Alone' and 'I Wanna Be Black', while a return to the Velvet Underground's 'Pale Blue Eyes', originally a fragile ballad, is shattered into bits of sonic space junk. An unpredictably drug-croaked 'Waiting For The Man' is directed into revised storylines with Lou sounding rock bottom and indomitably mean.

The album is best viewed as autobiography; it's Lou's anecdotal evaluation of a life in music recapitulated in public, or more importantly to his New York public; and Mikal Gilmore writing in *Rolling Stone* caught the album's bandit flavour and Lou's anti-hero attitude:

'Lou Reed doesn't just write about squalid characters, he allows them to leer and breathe in their own voices, and he colours familiar landscapes through their own eyes. In the process, Reed has created a body of music that comes as close to disclosing the parameters of human loss and recovery as we're likely to find. That qualifies him, in my opinion, as one of the few real heroes rock'n'roll has raised.'

Reed's savage cameos of street life leave the listener fascinated by his deviated journey away from his parent's identity as affluent tax accountants into an underworld in which survival is regulated by drugs, transgender and smart and dodgy mind games to keep ahead of annihilation on the street. 'I do Lou Reed better than anybody,' he tells us menacingly at the Bottom Line and 'You want to know the real Lou Reed? Turn around. Now bend over.'

Take No Prisoners is as raw, uncompromising and intrepidly outrageous as any rock artist has ever dared live, and inventively superior as an album to *Street Hassle*, both issued in 1978. If *Street Hassle* sounded like an avoidance of competing with frontline New Wave energies, then *Take No Prisoners* was full on war with street rats that left them a long way behind by virtue of Lou's inimitable, style. In an interview with *Creem* magazine in December 1978, Lou was unconditionally upfront about being gay and the guilt and distress his lifestyle brought him.

'I have such a heavy resentment thing because of all the prejudices against me being gay. How can anybody gay keep their sanity? I just wouldn't want listeners to be under a false impression. I want them to know, if they're liking a man, that it's a gay one – from top to bottom.'

Assimilated into the openly gay identity of living on Christopher Street, Reed's angularity as an artist seemed sharpened by his sexual orientation and integral to his writing sensibility in characterising unrepentant urban outlaws. The idea of a straight Lou simply wasn't compatible with his body of work, as it isn't with most creative edge-walkers liberated by same-sex attraction into a less constrained social conditioning and marital framework than their straight contemporaries. Lou told Mikhal Gilmore of *Rolling Stone*:

> 'Being gay, I have found so many women, deluded creatures that they are – are attracted to you because you're not interested in them. I'm Lou Reed and have all this access, but even before I was Lou Reed it happened that way. I could walk in and just because I wasn't interested, it came across as the ultimate cool. "Hey, he really doesn't give a shit." It never dawns on anybody that he doesn't give a shit because he couldn't.'

Maintaining his misogynistic, lethally ant-feminist beliefs, Lou in keeping with his *Berlin* sensibility, 'somebody should have beaten both of her arms', warmed to expansion in providing *Creem* with his singularly negative views on women:

> 'I'm a chauvinist down to my toes. I think women admire force all the more for not having it. It's axiomatic that a woman is all the more impressed that you could kill her. A woman can get turned off if you're appreciative of her when what she really wants is to be smacked across the mouth.'

But is Lou arguably confusing women here with a certain type of self-punitively resentful Times Square drag queen, the sort who like Arman the coffee table queen were humiliated into eating shit as retribution for their deviant sex?

In 1978, reviewing years of abuse and self-imposed injury, Reed purchased an escape from New York by buying a sizeable farmhouse in Blairstown, New Jersey, where he could fish, hustle a motorbike down the country roads and, like Burroughs, shoot hoops in his backyard and pursue a restorative diet of fruit juice and pistachio nuts as his latest nutritional discipline. After playing a short European tour in August 1978, Reed returned to America to begin work on the recording of his third binaural album, *The Bells*, set for release in April 1979. 'This is the kind of day,' he told Mikal Gilmore in interview, 'if you were in the village in New York, you might go down to some gay bar and see if you can make a new friend'. Reed was referring to a rainy, drizzly day when the Village seemed an opportune pick-up place.

But in late 1978, again contradicting his ambivalent sexuality, the modalities punished and rewarded by reparative shock therapy, at an S/M gay men's club in New York Lou met Sylvia Morales, there out of curiosity with Anya Philipps a Chinese-American impresario, as a buffer against the club's hostile policy to women. We know why Lou was there but why Sylvia, a 22-year-old ex-stripper, dominatrix, a habituee of CBGSs and unlike Rachel a fan of Lou's music and presumably with sufficient sexual boundaries to allow for Lou's inherent homosexuality? In 1978 gay pride impacted with the rainbow flag designed by Gilbert Baker, first used as a symbol of solidarity with banners carrying the slogan: 'In a world full of Caterpillars it takes balls to be a Butterfly' signifying the differential. That Lou was at the Eulenspiegel, largely a place where gay men met for conversation, rather than Xenon, the Loft, the Paradise Garage, Aux Puces, Half-Breed, Le Directoire/Twinkle Zone, etc, suggests he was probably a regular there, as part of his mapping of New York's gay recreational facilities.

If Reed's art up to this point had been a partial attempt to resolve complex psychological issues through his music, acting out private in public, then he was prepared to assess the conflict between how close the work was to being the real man, in an interview with Mikal Gilmore.

> 'I guess the real Lou Reed character is pretty close to the real Lou Reed, to the point, maybe, where there's really no heavy difference between the two, except maybe a piece of vinyl. I keep hedging my bet, instead of saying that's really me, but that is me, as much as you can get on record.'

Reed's continuous awareness of his personal life as the public image with which his fans identified was a recurrent theme throughout his seventies interviews, and it is the sensitive criterion by which most artists assess whether they are personally accountable for how the work affects their public, or whether creativity is a universalised expression that adopts its own autonomy according to individual interpretation. Again, attempting to dissolve his medium of rock into literary parallels, Reed was as always perceptively eloquent with Gilmore.

> 'I have songs about killing people, but Dostoyevsky killed people, too. In reality, I might not do what a character in my songs would, if only because I'd be jailed . . . In my own writing, for instance, I'm very good at the glib remark that may not mean something if you examine it closely, but it still sounds great. It's like a person who can argue either side of a question with equal passion, but what do they really think? They might not think anything, so you might not get to know them.'

Like Morrissey, Reed's intelligent theory about his writing is often more interesting than the actual lyric, due to the often overrated attention words attract in their attachment to music when on the page they lack a corresponding charge. I mention this because the dilemma was central to Reed throughout his career, in dismissing rock as a moronic, trivial genre, and yet often exaggerating his own literary claims, not in proportion to literature, but to pop itself. There's the constant feeling with Lou, particularly oppressive in the seventies, that he was wasting his intelligence on what he perceived to be illiterate audiences, and that he was altogether too smart for his profession, but addicted to the fame and money, and in his case notoriety, that it brought. Self-identifying as a 'faggot', he'd also chosen an industry in which his sexuality was not only endorsed, but advantageous in terms of actually enhancing mystique.

Reed didn't make public the nature of his relationship with Sylvia Morales, or stop going to gay clubs, and between March 21 and April 12, 1979, undertook a European tour, a drunk and belligerent one on his part, playing Stockholm, Copenhagen, Hamburg, Berlin, Dusseldorf, Paris, Mannheim, Stuttgart, Offenbach, Basel, Munich, London and Dublin. With Chuck Hammer ostensibly incorporated into Lou's band, so that he could feature songs from the morosely confessional *Berlin*, Lou's hostile, desensitised vocals and churning guitar solos contributed little more than raucous density to a stage presence thickened by alcohol. Months earlier he had provided Allan Jones with perhaps the real account of *Berlin*'s origins, trashing Bettye Kronsdat as a neurotic casualty and para-suicide who he'd ejected as an impediment to his life and career.

> 'If only they KNEW . . . Like during my recording session, my old lady – who was an asshole, but I needed a female asshole around to bolster me up; I needed a sycophant who I could bounce around and she fit the bill, but she called it love, ha! Anyway, my old lady, during a recording session, she tried to commit suicide in a bathtub in the hotel . . . cut her wrists. She lived. But we had to leave a roadie with her from then on. It's funny, another girlfriend of mine told her, "Look – if you're going to do it for real, slice THIS way – and not THAT, darling." '

This compounded misogyny coming at a time when Lou was to meet his future wife, Sylvia, is totally consistent with Reed's deregulated psychology and sexuality. Who was Sylvia to Lou, a man with a woman's body? An opposite that was the same?

Reed's 1979 set, usually extended to two and a half hours, and best heard on the bootleg recording *Come Back Lou*, from Eissporthalle, Berlin, again pivots on a rework of familiar favourites, 'Sweet Jane', 'Waiting For The Man', 'Heroin', 'Pale Blue Eyes', with a consolidated suite of songs from *Berlin* delivered in variant moods of anger, sentimentality or full on debauch, and with little of the despondent fragility as to the mood on which the originals depend. It's hard to ascertain the source of anger and frustration behind Lou's 1979 tours, other than the audience is invariably his target, but the more amiable extempore stand-up comedian of the previous year was replaced by a truculent Reed looking for a fight with anyone and everyone. Rounding on a heckler at his April 10 Hammersmith Odeon show, Reed spat out, 'Eat shit you fucking asshole,' having already warned the front row, 'I hate journalists, I hate photographers.' Reed's mood of glowering alcoholic rage fuelled shows that if they were a retrospective of his career to date, fell a long way short of the originals.

At the time of releasing *The Bells* in April 1979, a jazz-inflected, unremarkable affair without apparent focus or commercial appeal, Lou again hiked up an aspiring literary talent that wasn't in evidence in his new album. Reed said he had expectations . . .

> '. . . to be the greatest writer on God's Earth . . . in other words I'm talking about Shakespeare . . . Dostoyevsky . . . I want to do a rock'n'roll thing that's on the level of the Brothers Karamazov . . . starting to build up a body of work, y'know, I could come off sounding very pretentious about this, which is why I usually don't say anything, I prefer not to . . .'

Perhaps the key passage to *The Bells* comes in a song 'All Through The Night' in which the buried subtext of partying voices, an effect Reed had used to brilliant effect on 'Kicks', is answered by his own desperation of the moment, 'With a daytime of sin and a night time of hell/everybody's gonna look for a bell to ring/all through the night/I'm feeling mighty ill myself/it happens all the time/it ain't so much when a man's gotta cry/to get a little loving and some piece of mind.' The lack of lyrical purpose in songs like 'Disco Mystic' and the Dion DiMucci influenced 'I Want To Boogie With You' and generally on an album that like 'Street Hassle' dispenses with language for shattering sound collage, suggests the parameters of Lou's art had shifted to cataloguing discordant sounds. If the album singularly lacks pop hooks or memorable tunes, then its success lies in creating the sort of dystopian textured soundscapes Bowie had explored in his *Berlin* trilogy as oppressive, menacing music snapshots of the times. Lou's turbulent Roland synthesiser guitar and Don Cherry's haunted, siren–like sax succeeded in creating solid menace, an obsidian wall on which to use sound like graffiti-tags pointing up not only to distressed listening, but a questionably discontinuous future.

The album's title track, a stultifying slab of dissonant drone over which Don Cherry's sax wails like a fugitive hostage is like a dense aural smog until Lou's broken voice emerges from the deadening mix to narrate the suicidal jump of an actor from a Broadway ledge into traffic, as a poignant fragment verbalising menace that sounds like a tainted soundtrack to World War III. Surprisingly, it was Lou's inveterate antagonist, Lester Bangs, who critically championed the album, the same man Lou had demoted to 'an insect, because he should be writing about sports, which I hope he's doing. He should get out of rock'n'roll. He's just a big schlub from Detroit, he's fat and he's got a moustache. I wouldn't shit in Lester's nose.'

As one of the few critics sufficiently intrepid to trade insults with Lou, Bangs having denounced most of Lou's solo career as inferior to his pioneering work with the Velvet Underground, perversely took up with *The Bells* as a deviated step-change away from Lou's affiliation to what he conceived as mainstream pop. With the suitably weird attracting the weird, Lou's currently oblique, but aggressively arresting sound attracted Lester back into the contentious arena of their differences. Lester was drawn right in, clearly encouraged by the fact that *The Bells* was one of Lou's albums without an overtly gay theme, as the pursuit he'd resisted in reviewing *Coney Island Baby* as faggot alpha waves for same sex people, in other words Lou's chosen queer retinue.

That *The Bells* wasn't a pro-gay album in Lester's terms promoted generosity on his part in assessing its merits. Lester was additionally pleased with the album's cover art, missing the point that a heavily made up Lou, now the Dorian Gray of *Transformer*, and holding up a girl's mirror that he studiously avoids looking into, is framed as a dissolute ageing queen, a Lou in transitional late thirties still relying on makeup to enhance his image, not as Sister Ray, but Sister Lou. It was a point lost on Lester, anxious to come clean about his disparaged icon's sexual transitioning through the seventies, not to a resting point, but an agitated increase in unrest.

The first indication that we've got something very different here is the no-bullshit cover art; the second, a cursory listening to the lyrics. Immediately one notes the absence of mirror shades and S&M. Lou Reed is walking naked for once in a way that invites comparison with the Van Morrison of *T.B. Sheets* and *Astral Weeks* and the Rolling Stones of *Exile On Main Street*. *The Bells* is by turns exhilarating ('Disco Mystic' an exercise in churning R&B that should have been a hit single if there was any justice), almost unbearably poignant (all of the lyrics) and as vertiginous as a slow dark whirlpool (the title opus).

Lou's musical achievements on *The Bells* aren't lyrical, they're aggressively sonic as though his wall of guitar hostility is a weaponised affect used to advantage like a missile shield against intended opposition, which at the time was Camden or CBGB's unqualified teens, who imposed only a delinquent threat on his uncontested hard-core status as rock's criminally questing drug mafia. Lou's wholly paranoid reaction, dictated partly by age, to a new emergent youth culture, appeared disproportionate to the threat, as though his current insecurity was in part the product of lack of commercial sales, and a perceived lack of recognition for his prototypical cool.

Cantankerous and formidably drunk, Reed ran into headlining skirmishes with the law on his volatile spring tour, and this at a time when Reed had just begun his relationship with Sylvia Morales and seemed explosive with incandescent rage. At Offenbach Reed took particular dislike to a GI in the audience, focussing his anger on this individual, shouting at him from the stage, demanding his removal and leading the band back to the dressing room by way of protest. Returning to the stage, and molested by a girl who'd just jumped on it, Reed furiously knocked her down, breaking her arm in the process and kicked her off the stage. German riot police arrested Reed for assault and charged him with inciting a riot. 'They took me to jail alone,' Lou recounted later. 'How would you like to get into a van with twelve goose steppers saying they're going to test your blood?' And according to Chuck Hammer, 'They really wanted to search him and seize drugs so they could claim the capture of Lou Reed, the famous heroin freak . . . He had nothing, but they made him stay the night.'

Insensitive to the girl's injuries, Lou denied any responsibility for assault and riot. 'The problem was a bunch of drunken American soldiers. They wanted to have a riot and they had one.' Over $17,000 of damage was caused, but Reed remained resolute he was in the right. The verbal abuse and vitriolic threats delivered from the stage in previous years were now becoming physicalised, and were to culminate that month in Reed repeatedly punching David Bowie on April 10 at the Chelsea Rendezvous restaurant in Sydney Street, South Kensington, where Lou and Bowie and their respective entourages met after Lou's show at the Hammersmith Odeon, where in an effort to unnerve the audience Reed had on caprice played the whole gig with the house lights full on and invited his bass player to render a 45-minute version of 'You Keep Me Hanging On', the 1966 hit by the Supremes.

Reed's subsequent physical assaults on Bowie were witnessed by Allan Jones of *Melody Maker* who reported gleefully on the incident in the following week's paper. They seem to have been precipitated by Reed suggesting to his smart producer of *Transformer* that he produce his new album *Growing Up In Public*, only to be met by the response of 'clean up your act', a remark that prompted Reed to repeatedly beat Bowie round the head screaming, 'Don't you ever say that to me'. After an attempted reconciliation, Bowie evidently rephrased the remark, only to be hit again by Reed bellowing, 'I told you NEVER to say that' with Lou storming out of the shocked Chelsea Rendezvous, littering glasses as he exited. Lou was again defiantly unrepentant about his use of physical violence.

> 'Yes, I hit him more than once. It was a private dispute. It had nothing to do with sex, politics or rock'n'roll. I have a New York code of ethics. Speak unto others as you would have them speak unto you. In other words, watch your mouth.'

Reed's ugly, turbulent spring European tour was not only a worrying manifestation of his unchecked chronic alcoholism, but also indicative of his musical sensibility in dishing contempt and often demeaning performances to his audience. Still projecting as legitimate bar room brawler, apparently exacerbated by every aspect of his personal life, Reed hiked up his anger quotient at New York's Bottom Line on June 3, 4, 5 and 6, for some reason using the stage as a therapy room for his violent inner conflicts, smashing microphones together, mauling hecklers and savaging his Arista boss, Clive Davis, who was in the audience on June 4. With 'Heroin' demoted to a stumbling soul ballad, Lou rounded on the audience, stating: 'How do you think it feels when I hear you calling for a pop song called 'Heroin'? The evil of that drug – you don't know. When I say it's my wife and it's my life, do you think I'm kidding?'

In the second set, ignoring musical boundaries, Reed issued into an hour-long medley of 'Sweet Jane' and 'Sister Ray' as an uninterpretable

stormy affront to a partisan New York audience dragged into Reed's paranoid scoping of musical espionage undermining his reputation as the best.
Telling the audience he wouldn't have 'Arista lick my asshole', Lou proceeded to attack his patron Clive Davis, supportively occupying a front
row seat, giving him the finger before shouting out 'Here, this is for you,
Clive. Where's the money Clive? How come I don't hear my album on
the radio?' This act of savage rudeness was one of the few Reed was forced
to retract through a press statement made on Arista's request.

> 'I've always loved Clive and he happens to be one of my best friends.
> I just felt like having a business discussion from the stage. Sometimes
> out of frustration you yell at those you love the most. I have a mouth
> that never sleeps and I suppose that's why I make rock'n'roll records.
> Trying to read anything deeper into all of this is pointless.'

But the damage was done and the fault wasn't Clive Davis' it was
Reed's, whose Arista output was careless, negligent, wilfully obscure and
indomitably self-indulgent. *Rock'n'Roll Heart*, the best of them, was a
casual throwaway and neither *Street Hassle* nor *The Bells* were in any
instance radio-friendly, or likely to hack into the mainstream, as Reed
lurched irately and drunkenly through the late seventies, maintaining a
popular cult status with which he was perversely and signally dissatisfied.

As the tour progressed, so Reed grew more raucously self-parodying.
With an enthusiastically supportive crowd behind him he played Columbia University on September 21, again disseminating the word 'fucking' as
though he'd invented it. Halfway into an apathetic 'Waiting For The
Man', Lou launched into the first of his distempered aphoristic digressions.
'When I was a tot I thought about going to a school of journalists as I
wanted to be a writer, so I just wanted you to know there's still hope.'
Aborting another Velvet's remake 'I'll Be Your Mirror', Reed pulverised
the song's fragile beauty, torturing the lyrics and throwing in 'fucking'
everywhere. Reed then proceeded to carve up a monotonal 'Leave Me
Alone' thrash by vicious asides about sexuality. 'You know, there's a
difference between the way you talk to a man and a woman.' And then in
response to a heckler, 'Because I fucked your mother, you asshole.' And

then, pointing to his ambivalent sexuality, 'Wait a minute, it's Lou Reed, wait a minute I got very confused, I should say I fucked your father. How about if I fucked you?'

Lou's denigration of 'the fucking Fords', surged into 'Men Of Good Fortune', as though he was on a personal mission to expose corporate corruption. Working up the brutal street snapshots of 'Street Hassle' and slapping the microphone during the spoken passage, 'Hey that cunt's not breathing', Reed referenced the song's lyrics, telling the audience derisively that they had a voice, but that 'some fuckers didn't have either a voice or a dick to call their own.' Phone in callers to WPIX New York Radio, where Reed was hosting a show, largely thought that Columbia University was 'fantastic', although Lou was quick to block any adverse criticism.

In October a burnt-out Reed returned to Europe as part of the unstoppable live assassination of his repertoire, in which all sensitivities were overwritten by loud pub-rock vocals, a tour that took in three nights at London's Hammersmith Odeon on October 17, 18 and 19 as part of Lou's European itinerary. Ironically, building on the height of his seventies notoriety as disaffected rock dissident, Reed's music failed to match his reputation as literary punk, and devolved into antagonistic chaos rather than the constructive angle of an artist ahead of his contemporaries. And Lou was too drunk after Rachel's departure to care: too dysfunctional to do anything but drink. British critics, though, didn't spare Lou his shambolic, wrecked performances, and rightly pulled him up for failing expectations.

Robbi Miller writing for *Sounds* complained of Lou's shot, destroyed vocals and that 'though the back-up band was near faultless, Lou Reed sounded more like Jimmy Pursey doing Frank Sinatra than the bloke on *Transformer*. And he ruined the peaceful colour of "Perfect Day" with his mangled yelling, turning it into a glib piece of self-gratification.' And Ian Penman writing for *NME* was unsparingly derogatory:

'He ruled out the multiplicity of rock'n'roll performance and sketched in a tired and tiresome caricature, a bar room bore figure whose every gesture and intimation fell on stony ground, floored arrogance and bathos.'

133

So much had happened in Reed's first decade as a solo performer that the drunken hoodlum onstage in 1979 was hardly recognisable from the energised Lou who had shocked audiences into alert recognition of the flawless manipulation of his work in 1976, the undeniable apogee of his touring. Reed's excesses had visibly sunk him, and brought with it not only a total disrespect for his audiences, band and musical direction, but for himself as a performing artist. Chuck Hammer, Lou's guitarist, tells of the humiliation he underwent when Lou came onstage drunk at Kansas City, crashed into an amplifier, and in the process knocked his guitar out of tune and pulled the band offstage.

> 'He bears down on me with his alcohol breath and screams, "How could you fucking do that to me? I could send you home right now" . . . Meanwhile outside the whole audience is going crazy. He made me go out there all alone and re-tune his guitars. I came back and said, "Your guitars are now in tune."'

His voice no longer an instrument of sensitively inflected phrasing, but of loud declamation, Reed finished off the year on December 24, 25 & 26, by playing his home territory, The Bottom Line, where he continued drunk and disruptively skewed, adding an improbable 'White Christmas' to the set and delivering a superbly offbeat 'Heroin', accompanied only by piano and acoustic guitar, proving once again his genius as an improvisational artist by transforming the song right on the threshold of a new decade. Introducing the song with 'I'm gonna try for the Kingdom, if I can,' and keeping to spoken word Reed punched in asides: 'If I had my way I would shoot every deal' he told an adulatory audience. 'Jesus didn't have a son, he was a son,' adding 'you guys, I don't know if you can shoot up right . . . it kills you even if it does clean your teeth.'

After launching into an unmemorable new number, 'Love Is Here To Stay', Reed announced his engagement to Sylvia Morales to his audience, who sceptically treated it as a drunken joke. His faggot years suddenly and incongruously reversed to straight, this was his outrageously ebullient exit from the seventies as a maverick with a questionable future.

7

I've Always Been That Way

ON February 14, 1980, Lou Reed and Sylvia Morales were married in Lou's Greenwich Village apartment on Christopher Street, the gay capital of New York, by New York State Supreme Justice Ernest Rosenberger. Reed himself wrote the two short vows from poems by Delmore Schwartz, before the invited guests went off with Lou to play pinball in Playland on Times Square, a notorious pick-up site for hustlers. The irony of the marriage wasn't lost on *NME*'s Teazers columnist:

> 'Lou "Kiss My Ass" Reed announced his betrothal to Sylvia Morales, self-styled mixed media artist, whatever that means. Lou and his bride have bought a 148-acre farm in New Jersey with the money he saved from giving up drugs. How absolutely tedious it must be to be Lou Reed these days . . .'

A decade and a half younger than Reed, Morales was a tough-minded business woman who came to monitor his press statements, kept his life private, forced him into Alcoholics Anonymous in 1981 and cleaned up his act as the undisputed spokesman of drugs, deviated sex and decadence. Reed fans remain divided as to whether Morales was his redemption or the moralist instrumental in killing off his edge-walking groove of living out his personal aberrations through the direct physicalisation of his art. Effectively the marriage put an end to Reed as public figure, the drunken contestant alternately shocking and thrilling incredulous interviewers with gay disclosures, and the man using the authority of his stage presence to vilify his fans. The complete turnaround of image, consonant with approaching 40, wasn't easy to effect, and did nothing to elevate Reed's musical profile as he struggled with an attempt to go mainstream in the eighties without any convincingly fired-up creative impulse, simultaneously dragged into concessions that seriously compromised his music.

It's apparent from his seventies' set lists that Reed not only couldn't escape his Velvets legacy, but that the trio of songs 'Sweet Jane', 'I'm Waiting For The Man' and 'Heroin' were seminal to his personal and artistic identity, and together with 'Walk On The Wild Side' comprised the consistently popular landmarks in his songwriting career. Before firing his jazz-funk band and going into self-imposed retirement from touring, Reed on the back of the release of *Growing Up In Public* in June 1980, his final album for Arista, capitalised on his live popularity by playing four US dates, Chicago, Cleveland and two at New York's Bottom Line on June 1 and 2, before kicking into a lucrative European tour that took in Genoa, Bologna, Avellino, Barcelona, Madrid, Paris and Lyon, perpetuating the unmistakeably inebriated sound of the previous year, in which full on bombast substituted for artistry. Chuck Hammer was adamant that the tour was singularly motivated by Lou's profiteering designs for money:

> 'That summer we did our most wildly successful tour – he really made money. In our European tour the summer before, he had carefully played a whole lot of medium venues, working very hard and staying away from the capital cities. This summer he made the real killing; 60,000 seats instead of 3,000. Sometimes 80,000 people would show up . . . We were driven to and from the stadium in police cars. It had been a brilliant strategy on Lou's part, but that's when the crunch started to come down with his band.'

The tour was highly successful financially. In the fall Reed played Don Krishner's television show and a number of dates in California, including the old Waldorf and the Roxy Theatre September 6 and 14 respectively. Returning to New York he had the band put down some tracks for an animation film with MGM, but bad feeling had set in and the split was inevitable. According to Chuck Hammer:

> 'Lou was getting more and more annoyed – he has a very short tolerance for other people's complaints. Maybe he also felt guilty about

having all that money in his pocket and finding reasons why no one else should have it. By the time we got back here, to go into the studio and put down some tracks for an animation film, he started to pull away. This one was always asking for more money, this one was always getting stoned, this one was always eating constantly and always asking if we could order in. My personal obsession was becoming a guitar hero, but Lou could go along with that . . .'

It was to prove the end of an era for Reed. By early 1981 he left or was forced to leave Arista which had sold out to the German Ariola organisation. It was no longer the beneficent Clive Davis empire of 1976, sympathetic to quality irrespective of its commercial potential, but a company which could not afford to float financial liabilities.

Having re-signed to his old label, Reed was interviewed by the French journalist Bruno Blum at RCA's offices in New York in December 1981:

'I'm not touring again. I'm not appearing any more. I don't have a band . . . I might imagine a one shot at the Bottom Line, but it would be an odd thing. I'm certainly not going to any place outside New York.'

Lou was also sufficiently reflective as to be able to insight the deficiencies of the band he'd let go, and how his desire to return to a four-piece, two guitars, bass and drums, was at variance with the multitasking ensemble he'd assembled in the seventies, and one into which he didn't as a guitarist fit.

'For the last few years, I was working with musicians who were into jazz and funk. I was playing guitar on my records because I really couldn't play with those guys, being a simple rock'n'roll player. I thought it would be interesting to explore that direction, but there was a gap between me and them. You can hear it on the records. So I said, "You've carried this experiment far enough. It's not working. The ideas are there and then they disappear, the music isn't consistent, you seem isolated, there's a certain confidence that's not there because you're not really in control." So I dissolved the band.'

Nor was *Growing Up In Public* Shakespeare or Dostoyevsky, although the better-crafted lyrics appeared to have been worked on before going into the studio rather than improvised on the spot. Confessional, lubed with whiskey and without hooks, the album proposed moments of lyrical calm, like 'Teach The Gifted Children', a copy of Al Green's 'Take Me To The River', 'My Old Man', a hammered home recollection of his father beating his mother as an act of domestic violence, jokey cameos like 'The Power Of Positive Drinking' and unabashed banality like 'How Do You Speak To An Angel' with Lou's answer being 'You say, hello baby.'

Called by Lou 'one of the drinking records of all time' and recorded at George Martin's studio at Montserrat, the reflectively confessional songs like 'My Old Man', 'Growing Up In Public', 'Standing On Ceremony' and 'Smiles' seemed to indicate that the intensely private Reed felt the necessity to evaluate his past, and in particular his troubled adolescence, all cast in the lyrical vein that so distinguishes him as a songwriter. *Growing Up In Public* is essentially an album about survival, about consolidating some sort of platform from which to review the present and continue, and no matter the unmelodic, workmanlike expression of the material that mostly lacks inspired shimmer, the album is arguably the best constructed of his Arista years in its careful presentation of songs from the studio. Reed's guitarist Chuck Hammer thought the album flawed from the start.

> 'There were many things wrong with this album. Personally, I don't think Lou was sure he wanted a hit record out of Arista; he wanted to do something quiet and meaningful. He was caught, again, between being Lou Reed and being successful. But he did come out with some beautiful pieces – 'Teach The Gifted Children', which he borrowed from Al Green's 'Take Me To The River', especially was fantastic.'

A stripped down album of basic emotions, in which lyrics counted as the building blocks of a song, Reed had virtually abandoned language on *Street Hassle* and *The Bells*. *Growing Up In Public* suggested a sufficient change in direction to have Reed survive the seventies, not as a burnt out speed kamikaze, but as a resilient, combative maverick, still capable of reshaping his talent into the ultimate Lou Reed album.

Growing Up In Public slipped under the radar without any commercial impact, picked up only by Reed's loyal fanbase, inevitably buying into past reputation in the hope that something of that quotient (i.e. the Velvet Underground) would resurface on a new Reed album. There was also the radical dichotomy between Reed live and studio, the one fortified by reworking Velvet's classics, and the other recording songs that were rarely incorporated into live sets, making it abundantly clear to Reed himself, that he'd let his talent lapse into something strictly identified by his groundbreaking sixties origins with the Velvet Underground, a fact made glaringly apparent when he was asked to perform at the Rock and Roll Hall of Fame 25th Anniversary celebrations and chose to play 'Sweet Jane' and 'White Light/White Heat' as his representative numbers.

Growing Up In Public is an interim affair, neither inspired nor featureless, but just there as an addition if you like the artist. The album photo of a slightly ravaged Lou, minus shades or eye makeup for the first time on any of his solo albums, is in part the transitional clue to his facing a new decade without artifice or association with transgender references. The pensively natural shot with Lou wearing a casual green jumper is like the album, unpretentiously naked.

Reed spent the eighties astutely getting rich at the expense of artistic credibility, and if marriage helped stabilise and curtail his excesses, then it also contributed to a series of careerist albums – *The Blue Mask*, *Legendary Hearts*, *Live In Italy*, *Mistrial* and *New Sensations* – that were awkward, mediocre, lacking in conviction and without any apparent theme, other than Reed's attempt to reconstruct his image as a middle-aged conservative advocating domesticity as a way of staying out of trouble, and playing live as strictly business, rather than as a proponent of integrating his personal crises into a music that plotted his attitude, and wonky dissolution, note by note to the edge.

Re-signed to his old label RCA, the best of these albums is the rehabilitatory *The Blue Mask* (1982), the scorchingly shocking title track sounding as forcibly perverse as anything Lou had done since the Velvet Underground, and fuelled by unmediated rage: directed at what – his past, his parents, electro-shock, Rachel, the whole annihilating experience of being gay in an anti-gay USA, or at everyone and no one? Reed's lyric impacts like a grenade. Evoking images of military torture or extreme S&M, his index of rage never lets up throughout the title track, as Reed and Robert Quine slash savage chords over a victim scenario prescient of reported Guantanamo atrocities. Burning up on rage Reed stokes his violent delivery to criminal imaginings: 'I've made love to my mother/ Killed my father and my brother/what am I to do?/Take the blue mask down from my face and look me in the eye/I get a thrill from punishment/ I've always been that way . . .'

More pathologically extreme than 'Venus In Furs', 'The Blue Mask' was renewed evidence that Reed could still structure songs from the sort of extreme subject matter excluded by mainstream pop, and erupt into explosively creative violence. Victim and torturer are inseparably bonded in a pact of degradation that Reed controls with suitably deviated vocals. 'I loathe and despise repentance/you are permanently stained/your weakness buys indifference/and indiscretion in the streets/dirty's what you are and clean is what you're not/you deserve to be soundly beat.'

Not since the epic 'Street Hassle' had Lou engaged with street poetry on this level, extrapolating his anger as an uncompromising weapon, and with rage that culminates in an image of brutal castration: 'Cut the stallion at his mount/and stuff it in his mouth.' Emasculation here is the final severance to end all others, with his own cock stuffed into the victim's mouth. Part of Lou's revival must be attributed to his working with Robert Quine (1942–2004), whose angular guitar playing, and discordant shortcuts, had been picked up by extensively watching Lou's technique with the Velvet Underground, as a devoted fanboy: his cassette recordings of the Velvet Underground live in 1969, eventually finding official release in 2001 by Polydor Records, as *Bootleg Series Volume I: The Quine Tapes*, probably the best audio documentation of the band playing a college circuit.

The nephew of the philosopher W.V. Quine, Robert's colourfully individual technique, picked up from rock, jazz and most blues, led to collaborations with amongst others, Richard Hell & the Voidoids, Brian

Eno, Lloyd Cole and Tom Waits, but most significantly with Reed. Commenting on his guitar education through watching the Velvet Underground, Quine wrote: 'I got a lot of pleasure and inspiration from these performances. As a guitar player, they were an important element in shaping what direction I wanted to take.' Quine was to partner two albums with Reed, *The Blue Mask* and *Legendary Hearts*, before tensions with Reed forced him to quit, although he rejoined the band for Lou's 1984 world tour for a financial incentive. In part, it was Quine's instrumentation that got Reed back on track with *The Blue Mask*, although other than the title track the album again fell short of memorable songs, lacked stand out singles and seemed a leisurely compromise, as though divested of a shocking past, Reed had settled for a professionalism that marked time in the New Jersey countryside.

The album's opening track, 'My House', dedicated to Reed's mentor Delmore Schwartz, is serenely thoughtful, mature pop that manifests all his new-found stability, with self-congratulatory images ('I've got a really lucky life/my writing, my motorcycle and my wife'), and the realisation of Schwartz as 'the image of the poet on the breeze', a conception that came to Lou after believing he'd contacted Schwartz via a oiuja board sitting in his farmhouse. One could argue that *The Blue Mask* is the beginnings of Reed's attempt to construct an acceptable public image, and the title track apart, the album settles for an uncomfortable conformity with 'Women', flagrantly contradicting Reed's unrelenting misogyny voiced in seventies interviews, as either an essay in apology or disinterested irony. One of the artificialities of rock music, something from which Reed is usually exempt, is the belief that anything that affects the artist is of vital significance to the record buying public, in itself the assumption of unmediated self-indulgence. The subject of Lou's marriage was negative sensibility on the *Blue Mask*; songs like 'Heavenly Arms' and 'The Heroine' are drenched in bad taste sentimentality, rather than honest emotional responses to the conflicting energies of marriage. Hatched against Lou's American poet contemporaries, Robert Lowell, Sylvia Plath, Anne Sexton, Marilyn Hacker, James Schuyler, Ted Berrigan, etc, his attempted love lyrics bottom out as redundant cliché, still further enforcing the separation in his work between literary aspiration and its execution in his songwriting.

Apart from the scorching ante of the title track, two songs start out as legitimate Lou. 'Underneath The Bottle' and 'The Gun', both opening pathways into mining self-destructive aspects of himself that extend into others as shared psychic dilemma. 'Underneath The Bottle' is Lou's squaring up to lowered creative impetus without booze: 'Liquor set me free/I can't do no work/the shakes inside me.' For Lou, withdrawal from alcohol and substances wasn't just neurochemical detox, it was dis-identification from his artistic selling point as drunken butch faggot endorsing the same deviated reality in his audience. Reflecting on his chronic lapses, he sings 'Seven days a week/on two of them I sleep/I can't remember what the heck I was doing/I got bruises on my leg/from I can't remember when/I fell down some stairs/I was lying underneath the bottle.'

At the time of writing the song, Lou was still drinking heavily and a casualty of alcohol. And although his seventies work was fuelled by alcohol, most notably whiskey, there was no song specifically addressing the subject, partly because there was no break in his abusive cycle to permit reflection on its effects. Robert Quine's sinister guitar riff underling 'The Gun' highlights the only other song on *The Blue Mask* to carry a sniff of the real Lou. On December 8, 1980, the delusionally fixated Mark Chapman, inspired by a personally decoded reading of J.D. Salinger's novel *The Catcher In The Rye*, fired five shots from a .38 special revolver at John Lennon as he was returning from a recording session at Record Plant Studios. Accompanied by Yoko Ono, Lennon was walking towards the arched entrance of the Dakota apartment building on Central Park West in New York and hit four times in the back, causing multiple injuries to the left shoulder and chest, left lung and subclavian artery. Ten minutes later, at 11.07 p.m., Lennon was pronounced dead by Dr Stephan Lyn at St Luke's-Roosevelt Hospital Center. An unrepentant Mark Chapman justified the killing on the grounds that Lennon lived a lie, that the idealism and pacifism expressed in his music was totally inconsistent with his capitalist lifestyle. 'He told us to imagine no possessions,' Chapman stated, 'and there he was, with millions of dollars and yachts and farms and country estates laughing at people like me who had believed the lies and bought the records and built a big part of their lives around the music.'

Lennon's abrupt, premeditated murder not only generated global shockwaves but impacted on the elevated status of rock star as unmediated cultural avatar, and like the rest of rock's self-appointed aristocracy Reed must have felt threatened by Chapman's exposure of the fundamental contradiction between public image and private individual, professed empathy with the people and personal acquisition of wealth at their expense. Lou's highly controversial interviews, bad boy persona, and verbal abuse of his audience, certainly qualified him as a potential hit for a psycho, and its arguable 'The Gun' was written in response to Lennon's pitiless assassination.

The killer in Lou's song 'The Gun' carries a nine millimetre Browning, and his kick is in subjecting a man to watching the slow exacting execution of his wife. 'I'll put a hole in your face/if you even breathe a word/tell the lady to lie down/I want you to be sure to see this/I wouldn't want you to miss a second/watch your wife.' Delivered with the same psychopathic, cold, unreasoning tone as 'The Blue Mask', 'The Gun' is its companion piece in optimal sadistic terror.

Lou's attempt to remake his image through *The Blue Mask* appealed neither to fans nor the record buying public, with the album making a disappointing number 159 on the *Billboard* Top 200. Chris Buckham, reviewing the album for *Sounds*, was totally dismissive of Reed's evident loss of inspiration:

> 'Lou Reed can now be considered a walking disaster area. This is not due to any of his personal habits, or the state of his physical health, but to the fact that he can no longer write a halfway decent song.'

Burkham was equally cynical about Reed's sympathetic portrayal of Kennedy in 'The Day John Kennedy Died', one of the album's major embarrassments.

> 'The JFK adulation schtick is a last-ditch attempt by Reed to gain favour with the upper echelons of US society. Take me, he screams,

my star is descending. Lou Reed is the drunken bum propped up at the bar next to you who will mumble and splutter about what a good guy he is . . . the sad truth, though, is that he is just another has-been.'

For all the unnecessary vindictiveness of Burkham's liquidation, he had again touched on Lou's open nerve, that he was still largely living off his sixties' reputation with the Velvet Underground, as the criterion by which each subsequent album was measured. As an act of bravura Reed had claimed, 'My new album is like a Velvet Underground record', but it wasn't of course, and its real energies come only from the abrasive interaction of Reed's and Quine's equally distressed and provocative guitars. Mark Cordy assessing the album for *NME* was only fractionally more sympathetic:

'It's not that Lou Reed has written more of my favourite songs than anyone else since, like "I'll be Your Mirror" and "Heroin", it's that he's translated what sounds like his happiest times into a creative nadir and banished himself to the suburbs of imagination; a thoroughly silly crime and punishment. The music is insipid and lifeless, there is nothing outstanding, no 'Temporary Thing', to turn your head around; and a clutch of canny couplets do not a poet make. Neither do they compensate for a lazy, undignified disgrace.'

Lou's remake, and conscious programme of coming to terms with ageing, did nothing to restore his creative talents, any more than the three ineffectual albums that were to follow in the same vein of eclectic misfits with mainstream music, transcended by occasional songs that hinted at partial successes restrained by Lou keeping well inside the edge.

Legendary Hearts (1983), the second and last of Reed's collaborations with Robert Quine, is no better and no worse than *The Blue Mask*, only the material intimates at disillusionment with marriage and the rockiness of persistent detoxification. To compensate, Lou had taken up the inner discipline of Wu-syle Tai Chi Chuan, or Chinese boxing, as an exercise uniting physical and psychic energies, saying of his newly chosen union of conflicting actions, 'It's an aesthetic and physical discipline that I find exquisite. The discipline is in the ability to relax. It's very beautiful to watch.'

Tai Chi Chuan, an internal Chinese martial art practised for both its defence training and its health benefits, was Reed's first choice of hard and soft martial technique, aimed at focussing the mind solely on the movements of the form to help promote tranquillity and clarity. The practice described in the Tai Chi classics is characterised by the use of leverage through the joints based on co-ordination and relaxation, rather than muscular tension, and helps open the internal circulation, breath, body heat, blood, lymph, peristalsis, etc. If the meditative and martial aspects of Tai Chi Chuan seemed an unlikely function for Lou as necessary for maintaining optimum health, then he was to stick with its disciplines for the rest of his life as integral to his inner resources.

As attempted self-therapy Lou had taken up burning out his anger, as part of withdrawal, by bulleting a Kawasaki GP2 through the New Jersey countryside, and *Legendary Hearts* is partly a bike influenced album, most notably on 'Bottoming Out', one of its few stand out tracks. The banality of the album's cover, featuring a silver and black biker's helmet, with Reed in his new biker boy phase at a total remove from Mick Rock's acutely lyrical focus on image as Reed's selling point in the seventies, was all packaged into another undistinguished Reed album, as though the artist had temporarily lost direction, and was dangerously in denial of his past, and still restrained by an awkward need to conform. For Reed fans the compromises were disappointing, as the artist progressively distanced himself from the subject matter of his songs, suggesting by the album's title that he was already a legend belonging to a past decade and inoperative in the present.

The title track does contain some half-good lines by Reed's standards, in a song in which ordinary human love is measured against the impossibility of aspiring to transcendent, or legendary love, and seems to point to marital discord as one of the album's recurrent themes. 'Legendary hearts/tearing us apart/with stories of their love/their great transcendent love/while we stand here and fight/and lose another night/of legendary love.' When Reed sides with emotion, and the best of his songs exist without it, he tends to be either sadistic or sentimental. 'Legendary Hearts' is neither, and finds Reed writing nervously from median territory, passionate about his need to fight for the higher concept of love in which idealistically he believes, but is ill-fitted to achieve it.

Like *The Blue Mask*, *Legendary Hearts* is essentially a three-song album, the title track, 'The Last Shot' and 'Bottoming Out', all instances of rising above politically correct yet spurious patriotism, and tritely conceived domestic situations that mediocritise the record's subject matter. 'The Last Shot' documenting Lou's painful withdrawal from substances, and alcohol, and all the conflicting personal issues it brings up, is the one song linking his past to the present, as an authentic symbiosis of divisive tensions that ring true to character as autobiography: 'The last shot should have killed me/pour another drink/let's drink to the last shot/and the blood on the dishes in the sink/blood inside the coffee cup/blood on the table top.' Lou was understandably reluctant to admit the song's biographical associations, drawing attention to the fact that sometimes empathy substituted for truth.

> 'One of my goals has always been, if you listen to it, it sounds 100 per cent true, and you wouldn't doubt me for a second. And it is one hundred per cent true, but it's not always about me though, a lot of it is, but you can't ask me which ones . . . if I go after a subject, I know it well. I know it well enough to taste it. This is the right that every artist has to protect his inner space, to make it his imaginative house.'

However we imagine it, Lou's transitioning from a gay relationship to straight, the neurochemical flattening of being without drugs, and gradual withdrawal from alcohol, must have thrown him into oscillating states of depression and anger. 'I shot a vein in my neck and coughed up a quaalude,' Lou confesses, like a cameo from a Burroughs novel, and totally done in by it all, only this time recollecting the act, rather than doing it. Reviewing the album for *NME*, Cynthia Rose picked it out:

> '[it is] as mature a piece of writing as the title track, but much more harrowing. The real knowledge behind music like this – double

edges as sharp as a Wilkinson blue blade – is worth a hundred "Heroin"'s or a thousand *Transformers*. It's conveyed so powerfully partly because here (in contrast to other cuts) Reed's had the technical smarts to leave most of the expression up to the song's melodic fabric – his vocals are appropriately, ambiguously flat-statement.'

If *Legendary Hearts* wasn't Reed by request of his fans, and risked sounding formulaically dated in the eighties, then 'Bottoming Out' impacted with invigorating Lou impetus, his narrative of blazing a trail with his GPz, as the physical extension of his incendiary chemistry, to avoid potential domestic violence, coming alive as one of the album's high points: 'But if I hadn't left I would have struck you dead/so I took a ride instead . . .' With Robert Quine gunning up firepower, Lou narrates a burn-out that could have ended in the perverse attraction of suicide. 'I'm tearing down the route 80 east/the sun's on my right side/I'm drunk but my vision's good/and I think of my child bride/and on the left side in shadows/I see something that makes me laugh/I aim the bike at that fat porthole/beyond the underpass.' *Legendary Hearts* won Reed no new fans, and tested the patience of the old, as he appeared a resolute survivor of his self-engineered crash, unable to find engaging subject matter outside his own personal life, and having little of interest to seriously report. Marriage to Sylvia wasn't a particularly exciting event to Reed fans, any more than his newly acquired patriotism on numbers like 'Martial Law', 'Home of the Brave' and 'Pow Wow', all equally redundant exercises in trying to win favour by a specious all-American sanctimoniousness that just wasn't Lou Reed.

Predictably, Lou returned to live performance, with shows at the Bottom Line in February and March 1983, implementing his tried four-piece, Reed, Quine, Saunders and Maher, with a routine show filmed for subsequent video release as *A Night With Lou Reed*, the mechanical set mining the Velvet Underground's history at the expense of new material. Drawing on his by now core Velvets' numbers, 'Sweet Jane', 'Waiting For The Man', 'White Light/White Heat' and 'Rock'n'Roll', together with other Velvets' songs like 'Sunday Morning' and 'New Age', Lou and

Quine's prankishly inventive guitar figures sound choppily meshed and superlative to vocals delivered without sensitivity of phrasing. The set sounded like the business it was, faultless but bleached of personal involvement. Andy Warhol, who was in the audience, noted, 'Lou's lyrics you can understand now, and the music was really loud. He did a lot of familiar songs, but you didn't recognise them, they sounded different.' For Reed fans it was hard to adjust to his new formal presentation of public image, his personal life rigidly off-limits, his avoidance of repartee with the audiences having him execute the show cold. The reinvented Reed sounded smart, professional, accomplished but dull, as though a slice of his brain had been reprogrammed to live in denial of his past. Reed's blank front was like a Dulux whitewash of his personality.

Reed's partial renaissance presented real problems for his critics, including David McCullough:

> 'A problem. Reed is not totally dead, he's twitching still slightly. The final effect is like one of those horror movies where someone is trying to kill off a body, sticking knives in here, there and everywhere, and it still keeps jerking back to life again and again. He won't go away and that's dreadful and somehow a gift.'

It was never as bad as that, but Lou's adopted cold war tactics weren't promising either. In September 1983 the Reed ensemble played stadium dates at Verona, Florence, Rome and Turin, with part of the deal being that RCA would tape the shows for a live album *Live In Italy*, a double set released in January 1984, but only in Europe. Again, consolidating past achievements with workmanlike skill, Reed acquitted himself with an uneventful, uninspired album that was essentially another career retrospective, and with the exception of kicking up a prowling guitar storm on the medley 'Some Kinda Love'/'Sister Ray', the album remains a dispensable item in Lou's discography. Impotent to hike up sales of his new releases, Lou was essentially living off old product, and while his clean-up act allowed him to be assimilated into the rock mainstream, he was without the commercial profile to capitalise on dubious admission. Still identified by his one transgressive commercial hit, 'Walk On The Wild Side', Reed hadn't cut it album-wise since the mid-seventies, with RCA patronising a prestige artist on the strength of his back catalogue. But insidiously, invasively, via doing commercials for Honda Elite scooters, and by participating at the request of Paul Simon in his movie *One Trick Pony*, and in the animated film *Rock And Rule*, Reed was demoralisingly passing through the industry's blood barrier into the sanitised pathways of mainstream legislation. Worse was to follow when Reed contributed the inane three-chord 'Hot Hips' to the John Travolta/Jamie Lee Curtis module *Perfect*, a song so throwaway as to seriously undermine his creative facilities. To his real fans Reed was in danger of prostituting his reputation, not to the advancement of his work but to its trivialised debasement. For the moment Lou appeared to have outlived himself creatively, and to be looking for acceptance rather than challenge as the dynamic from which to create.

After two failed albums for RCA, Reed returned to the studio in 1984, with Robert Quine absenting himself from sessions, to initialise a more commercial thrust in recording *New Sensations*, and desperate to find a hit. Lou explained his tech concessions in the process of recording and how he was benefitting from state-of-the-art studio technology to update his sound.

> '*New Sensations* is vastly different in sound and ideas from other records. There's drum-machines on this one because I discovered they were the key to the sound I was after. Luckily, my drummer Fred Maher, really loves drum-machines so he and the engineer spent days programming the different patterns. I also recorded with a click-track for the first time. Ten years ago if you'd punched up a click-track I'd have walked out, but now I can see they're useful in keeping time and letting you worry about where to put the feeling rather than always listening out for the drums.'

In his deliberate efforts to go commercial, Lou scored a minor hit with 'I Love You Suzanne', an unpretentious stab at superficial pop, and the album – co-produced by John Jansen – was purposely a showcasing for Lou of 'certain sounds that I heard on the radio': in other words, a collage of bass and drum tricks that Lou amalgamated into his sound as eighties modern, forensically schizoid. Again Lou sounds on sanitised remote, as though every questionably decadent aspect of his personality was sponged by anti-viral wipes to substantiate a claim for admission into the rock hierarchy.

Mostly the album feeds off small incidents and domestic cameos, every-day affairs realised through big city life, and the more serious excursions into how private and public worlds meet like 'Doin' The Things That We Want To', a song that namechecks Sam Sheppard and Martin Scorcese. 'What Becomes A Legend Most' and 'High In The City' are well crafted gestures, no matter how anodyne and ephemeral in terms of finding any trace of the real Lou in there. This time Reed had seriously gone missing from his album, and his constructed theme of adult rock, minus personally twisted confession, again pointed seriously to lack of engaging subject matter in Lou's employment of his music as still another process of rehab. The title song delivered no new addition to the sensory repertoire of new sensations, at least not as one would have anticipated from an artist who'd dedicated time to fine-tuning altered states for the better part of two decades, but who chose instead to write about the simple euphoria induced by biking across the state, heading for the mountains, document-ing a love affair with his bike as optimal projectile sensation.

Lou's mastery of guitar nuances, though, couldn't be faulted on the album, and as usual he was eloquently and analytically succinct about his methods:

> 'It's about getting into the tone of the guitar. For a while I was playing a plexiglass guitar and was into volume overload. Then I started getting interested in a lower volume, different kind of tones, and the experience of hearing a chord really clearly, and that's where it ended up with *New Sensations*. I spent a lot of time playing different guitars and amps looking for certain sounds that I wanted on the record.'

Maybe it's the album's lack of urgency, it's casual, modern directive, lacking rogue genes in its organism that threw Reed fans at the time of the album's release, as though the album was obligatory rather than necessary, a contractual product rather than a work of inspired creative urgency.

> 'I wanted to have fun with it, and there were certain sounds that I heard on the radio – a certain kind of bass and drum thing – for instance – that were really strong and exciting, and I wanted to hear that. In many ways, it's like an early Velvet Underground album because I played all the guitar parts in the early Velvet Underground. I generally told people exactly what they should be playing.'

But the seminal difference between *New Sensations* and an early Velvet Underground album was that one sets out to establish safe boundaries, while the other uncompromisingly smashed frontiers in the interests of cutting edge experimentation. Reed's redundant criterion of constantly measuring new against old was to his irremediable disadvantage in attempting to superimpose the past on the present.

Cleaned up, Reed was still slim, amazingly youthful given his drink and drug habits, and critics rarely remarked in the seventies on his unconventional good looks; the forcible shock of naturally wavy hair, sensual lips, elevated cheek bones and the widely spaced eyes, the left one lazily dipped, and most often screened by shades that gave Lou attractive gay sex appeal, his physical features submerged by layers of full-on cerebration.

On the strength of the video promoted single 'I Love You Suzanne', *New Sensations* got a chart placing of 92 on the *Billboard* 200, a minor advancement on its two predecessors, but confirming that Lou Reed was still dependent on a loyal and increasingly disillusioned fan base for record sales, and lacked reinvention to appeal to a new generation of record buyers. Reviewing the album for *NME*, Edwin Pouncey was cautiously positive about the album's merits.

> '"Whaddya do all last year Uncle Lou?" you could almost be asking, as the needle of your record-player begins to free the stories. Stories that are hardly extraordinary, but ones that hold a fascinating quality in the ways they are told. *New Sensations* does have the power to put an electric thrill down your spine and Lou Reed is still worth listening to even though he doesn't hit sideways anymore.'

After a four-year absence from touring, Reed revised his resolution to play only occasional dates in New York, and in 1984 underwent a rigorously extensive tour that took him across the States, and then on to Europe and the Far East. Reed's touring personnel, Robert Quine, re-conscripted on guitar, Fernando Saunders on bass, Fred Maheron drums and Peter Wood on keyboards, delivered an invariably circumscribed set, authoritatively executed and near faultless, with all the controversials, 'Heroin', 'Kicks', 'I Wanna Be Black', 'Sister Ray', banished from formulaic playing, directed by Reed and Quine's loud, spiky, guitar friction. The tour in itself was a public declaration that at 42 Lou had subscribed to a new lifestyle. Reviewing Lou's show at London's Brixton Academy, Don Watson in *NME* wrote:

> 'It's not that he was bad, in fact I often wished he'd trip headlong over his professionalism – anything to induce a little chaos. What was on show was the expected omnibus of a career, with the biggest cheer saved for 'Walk On The Wild Side'. The normally laconic Reed, sententious only when his intention is to abuse, talked politely to the audience between songs. The motif for Lou's 1984 shows seemed to be written into his song, 'Legendary Hearts', with his revocation of his former habits: "he's in the past and seems lost forever".'

Reed, however, was quick to argue that radical changes in his lifestyle, including marriage, need not imply that both he and his work were consigned to the past as historic facts in rock's endless cataloguing of casualties.

> 'I would hate to think the power of what I wrote about would be dependent on being happy or unhappy and that all I was, was a person who wrote songs about drugs and that is all I'll ever be – 'Heroin' is all I can do as a songwriter . . . I was just passing through, and I've been doing this on all my albums.

> 'As for domesticity, I don't know what the term means. I get the impression people have contempt for marriage, you're considered lame, some sort of putz who's content to sit at home swilling beer and going bowling Thursday nights. Not that there's anything wrong

with that, but I don't think of myself as someone who's got married and therefore severed all creative ability, aggressive hardness or flash.'

In effect, Reed was accentuating the qualities he'd temporarily lost in the interests of what he was denying, the outlaw street savvy that had fuelled his work as the recalcitrant drug toting Hubert Selby Jnr of rock, diarist of New York's downtown underbelly in which deviation was the primary rule of survival. Reed's career move in abandoning his role as degenerate spokesman for sexual outlaws, endorsed by the media but sniffed at disapprovingly by fans, was central to his mid-eighties drive for mainstream acceptance at the expense of artistic integrity. The unlikely notion of Reed selling out was substantiated by his marketing Honda scooters on TV, with Neil Leventhal, Honda's Motor Scooter Manager, proclaiming: 'Reed is an innovator – one of the pioneers of new music. His music is unique and experimental – much like scooters.' To a sound-track of 'Walk On The Wild Side' and slouched against his scooter outside the Bottom Line, the ad sloganed: 'Don't settle for walking. Who else could make a scooter hip?' The sell out was maximised when the follow-ing year Reed shamelessly signed a deal to advertise American Express cards. Lou Reed? It couldn't be? But it was.

Mistrial (1986), Reed's next studio album for RCA, was a synthesised, quickly dated affair that again lacked thematic focus, other than Lou's con-tinued rehabilitation demanding public approval. Using computerised percussion and synthesised bass, and with Lou's aggressively idiosyncratic guitar figures absent from the sound, the user-friendly MTV-sanctioned *Mistrial* was still another instalment in Lou's compromised career, and didn't in any way predict his startling and brilliantly unexpected return to hard urban energies with *New York* three years later. He commented:

> 'Weird, isn't it? I don't know why people give me record deals, I think it's because they at least break even, and I think they're making a few bucks while they're at it. I'm a cult figure. But I sell some records.'

A patchy attempt to find a more popular market, and lacking all evidence of the literary sensibility Reed tirelessly promoted as his distinguishing forte, *Mistrial* substituted sound for content, opportunism for conviction, with Reed miscast as aberrant moralist, appealing to the people of New York City to absolve him of his notorious past in the light of his reconstructed present. Reed had a go at his new love rap in his gauche offering 'The Original Wrapper', attempted to address the issue of video nasties in 'Video Violence', which again sounded like a misplaced homily aimed at sanitising his once subversive metier rock'n'roll. Bland throwaways like 'No Money Down', 'I Remember You' and 'Spit It Out' all unsuccessfully placed emulsive layers over Lou's hoodlum banditry, and advocacy of rock, as sonic smash and grab lawless entrant.

Although Reed undertook a successful tour of the States in 1986, his career as an innovative recording artist looked to have reached an impasse. And yet there was a fundamental contradiction in this, in that his use of studio facilities and guitar artistry were at their optimal best. What was manifestly lacking, though, as it was for the likes of David Bowie and the Rolling Stones, was any sniff of the real equated with survival and rebellion as the basic resources of rock, a lack contingent on wealth and exclusion from the coding of ordinary life. Lou was manifestly out of touch both with his dystopian city, and the urban commonalities that had inspired his writing of the sixties and early seventies. Music had become a purely cerebral occupation for him, an enjoyable rather than urgent sense of communicating with the world. Most of *Mistrial* is related from a comfortable domestic interior looking out at the world. *NME* for one had little time for these vapid compromises:

> 'Wife-beating, Aids, Madonna, and food fiddles are all pleasant enough dinner conversation, but really nothing to sing about, which makes it perfect for Lou Reed. The agoraphobic sensibility of 'Outside', which extols the virtues of staying at home, is just one of the neurotic postures Lou assumes behind the three-chord structure – a tribute to emotional and musical deprivation.'

Whether rock stars improve with age, or deleteriously grow into self-parodic clones, is a subject of ongoing debate, and while musicianship should arguably improve with experience, the energised visuals of youthful projection, and the social injustices that often fuel them, aren't usually consistent with ageing. Reed by the mid-eighties was clearly in there to stay, even if his lifestyle seemed radically divorced from the revamped expressionless sixties Velvet Underground numbers he was endlessly repeating as live repertoire. Probably not since *Street Hassle* had any Reed album generated excitement amongst his fans whose generosity extended to tolerating almost a decade of indifferent work on the reputation of past achievements on which Lou continued to sell tickets.

Mistrial, though, isn't all bad, and although handled with less temerity than *New York*, tolerant rather than vituperative, domestic rather than streetwise, *Mistrial* is in some of its directions the first draft of the consummately acquitted *New York* that followed three years later; only Reed lacked the edgy angle of incorporating his city's social inequalities into the equanimity he was experiencing at the time of recording *Mistrial*. Although Allan Jones in *Melody Maker* praised 'Video Violence' as manifesting a 'scalding venomously orchestrated disco whiplash' with Reed inveighing against 'moral turpitude, with men grabbing their crotches at the sight of the thirteenth decapitation, it's somehow the wrong singer to be talking grievance against so called sexual deviance.' Even if Reed, like the ageing Presley in the years before his death, was in danger of becoming an unlikely reactionary, the role decidedly didn't fit. Lou's sudden infatuation with being aggrandised by a mainstream altogether lacking in his pioneering one-off originality, but anxious to acclimatise him to their uneventful limitations, was central to his loafing through the eighties looking for celebrity attachments to endorse his seniority.

It's only with 'Tell It To Your Heart', which leans heavily on Reed's love of fifties girl groups and doo-wop, that something both durable and authentic evolves from *Mistrial*. Looking back to slow tender epics like 'Coney Island Baby', 'Tell It To Your Heart' succeeds in a genre of urban romanticism at which Reed is peculiarly adept. And it's the only lyric on *Mistrial* that holds up as street lyricism rather than reportage. There's something moving about Lou sitting up staring at the night sky above New York – and picking out a light in the sky which only turns out in the end to be the lighting fixtures used by a TV crew shooting a commercial

155

in the street. But the image of the singer running through the darkened streets to enquire, his leather jacket squeaking as he runs, lends a filmic quality to the small incidental narrative. And for those who care about words, Reed shows himself to be in best form. The song is an apposite gift to New York lovers, in the way that 'Coney Island Baby' was a more personalised declaration of love to Rachel, and more obliquely a sanctification of the gay community. 'Tell It To Your Heart' is redemptive without the need for self-recriminating apologies or appeal to have his past wiped clean of infamy.

Reed's reinvention, that is the trajectory started with *The Blue Mask* and extending right through the eighties, appeared opportunistically disintegral, as though his intended update was dated by compromise and manifestly not on the moment, and having temporarily abandoned his signature roots, Reed appeared to have lost it. It's arguable that without *New York*, coming three years later to restore Reed's artistic credibility, Lou would have lost out on the nineties, other than as a stadium survivor mechanically reworking his sixties centrepieces as ubiquitous crowd pleasers.

The death of Andy Warhol aged 58 at 6.32 a.m. on February 22, 1987, while undergoing recovery after a routine gall bladder operation, shocked Reed and the ex-Factory survivors into the fuller awareness not only of their own mortality, but their often unpaid indebtedness to the original pop svengali, who in Reed's case had patronised the wholly arty and uncommercial experimentation of the Velvet Underground's debut album. That Warhol had never received any money for its production, and been studiously ignored by Reed for a decade, not invited to design record sleeves, shoot videos, omitted from the guest list for his wedding, ignored at the MTV Awards, shocked Reed not only into an unnerving sense of guilt, but also into the incentive to reclaim his songwriter's craft and the need to 'work' that Warhol had imposed as a de rigueur Factory discipline. Recovering from a standard op at New York Hospital, Warhol had died in his sleep from a sudden post-operative cardiac arrhythmia, caused by improper care and water intoxication, with the Hospital duly sued by Warhol's brothers, who received an out-of-court settlement of $3 million.

Andy's body was transported back to Pittsburgh for an open-coffin cere-mony that Reed didn't attend. The coffin, designed for a superstar, was a solid bronze casket with gold plated rails and white satin upholstery. Dressed in a black cashmere suit, a paisley tie, a platinum ring and Raybans, Andy was posed holding a small prayer book and a red rose, and the funeral liturgy was conducted at the Holy Ghost Byzantine Catholic Church on Pittsburgh's north side. Before the coffin, covered with white roses and asparagus ferns was lowered, Paige Powell appropriately dropped a copy of *Interview* magazine, an *Interview* T-shirt and a bottle of Beautiful by Estee Lauder into the grave. Even if Warhol had effectively died in 1968, when he was repeatedly shot by the delusional Valerie Solanas after going cool on a play script she attempted to coerce him into agenting, his real death sent shockwaves through his New York coterie as it signalled the end of Andy's significantly branded popism.

After a string of indifferently received albums, RCA failed to renew Reed's option, and he chose to start a new career with the more adventur-ously independent Sire label, founded in 1966 as Sire Productions by Seymour Stein and Richard Gotteher, with each investing $10,000. In the sixties Sire had signed progressive acts like Climax Blues Band, Barclay James Harvest, Tomorrow, Matthews Southern Comfort and proto-punks the Deviants, a policy continued into the seventies when Seymour Stein had pioneered subversives like the Ramones, the Dead Boys, the Under-tones and Talking Heads, in the process switching distribution from Polydor Records to Warner Bros to consolidate the label's active, lively profile. Along the way Stein signed Madonna and the label mushroomed into the mainstream, attracting cool UK acts like Depeche Mode, the Smiths and the Cure.

Now in his mid-forties and with the Velvet Underground's achieve-ments 20 years behind him, Reed had to either turn his career around and find a creative renaissance, or risk becoming an ambassador of his past. As it was, he came up with the highly acclaimed *New York* (1989), a gritty, fired-up album about the inequalities of his own city, physicalised into his writing as organic space and resonant with mean, indomitable Reed atti-tude, as he worked issues of New York's critical lack of welfare and financial depression into an angry suite of songs that not only returned him to the Top Forty, but initialised a rejuvenation of alacritous creative energies that would extend over two further albums, *Songs For Drella* and *Magic And Loss*, as the mature realisation of novelistic rock that Lou had always promised but somehow failed to deliver.

8

Dirty Boulevard

A T 46 coming on 47, after a decade of mostly uninteresting and
uninspired music, and after leaving RCA for the second time, the
chances of Reed making it into the nineties as a regenerated and critically
respected artist seemed remote. Mainstream rock of the type that had
allowed U2 to assume a premier position was itself in contention with
urban genres like electro, techno, house and digital recording associated
with synthpop, as well as the reinvention of Michael Jackson, Prince's
superstardom, the emergence of Madonna, Whitney Houston and Janet
Jackson. And in conflict with Reed there was a late eighties American
alternative scene dominated by styles ranging from quirky alternative pop
(They Might Be Giants and Camper Van Beethoven), to noise rock influenced by the Velvet Underground (Sonic Youth, Big Black), to industrial
rock (Nine Inch Nails, Ministry), grunge emanating from Nirvana and
indie rock from R.E.M. and the Pixies.

Against this broad spectrum and eclectic range of styles, Lou went back
to the basic two-guitar, drums/bass dominated rock he knew so well and
invariably did best. And utilising this unit as his medium gave Reed two
distinct advantages. A new generation had discovered the Velvet Underground as prototypical de facto cool, and *New York* was inspired and perfectly timed in addressing the appalling social deprivations of the Reagan
administration, social policies also implemented by Margaret Thatcher in
the UK, with profiteering at all costs given forcibly unlegislated authority
over artistic and cultural domains. Racial tensions, urban poverty, Aids,
endemic drug problems, disruption of social services, street violence and
subway muggings were all part of the day-to-day agenda Lou addressed by
New York, on which he resolved to work his city's degenerative energies

into the focus of singularly adult rock. Autocratic oligarchs with zero tolerance for deprived minorities, Reagan and Thatcher brokered unprecedented power and wealth in the financial sector and a corresponding acute state of social unrest among the marginalised.

The rapid deterioration of Reed's New York ethos had been accelerating fast since 1985, when asked by the *New Yorker* to contribute to a series 'What I Like About New York' he'd affirmed:

> 'Freedom, endless opportunities in everything – films, Chinese culture, people, places, things – a city of wonderful, impossible mixtures and energies. The only city in the world deserving the name. What I don't like – crime, traffic, a criminal subway system, a city government that is oblivious to the plight and feelings of the poor, the minorities, the homeless. Antiquated criminal justice system and union rules, regulations and membership; second-rate public school system.'

Lou's personal observations on the ups and downs of New York do little more than highlight the continuing adventures of capitalist differentials creating rich and poor in unequal irremediable measures. If Reed, one of New York's wealthy penthouse capitalists, felt threatened by the increasingly demonstrative poor, then fear inspired in him the role of elegist to social decay on his new album. In an interview with Neil MacCormick for *Hot Press*, Reed once again confirmed his undeviating belief in rock'n'roll as a serious, redemptive phenomenon.

> 'Rock'n'roll – you can do so many things with it, but it doesn't seem like so many things are being done with it. But I thought, since I started the Velvet Underground, there's this very big area you can write about seriously, aiming at adults. So that when you listen to the record you didn't have to switch your mind off. Not just party music or crotch music. I'm a serious guy and I wanted to use that space for something other than what is generally available.'

Conceptualising his city allowed Reed to take up a cause other than himself, and write about the dispossessed junkies, crackheads, whores,

Lou as biker, in trademark black leather jacket and holding his motorcycle helmet, photographed in the mid-eighties.

Lou and Sylvia Morales cut the cake after their marriage on Valentine's Day, February 14, 1980, in New York. ROBERTA BAYLEY/REDFERNS

Lou with writer Jim Carroll in New York, February, 1984. EBET ROBERTS/REDFERNS

Lou poses for a portrait during a shoot for the 1988 album cover *New York*.

Lou alongside African music star Fela Kuti at Giants Stadium, New Jersey, June 1986, announcing Reed's involvement in the forthcoming Amnesty International Concert. EBET ROBERTS/REDFERNS

Lou with Bono on stage at the McNichols Sports Arena, Denver, June 8, 1986. U2 were among several artists taking part in the Amnesty International tour. EBET ROBERTS/REDFERNS

ou with John Cale in the late eighties, around the time they were working on *Songs For Drella*, their tribute album to Andy Warhol who died in 1987.

Lou performing with Sterling Morrison and John Cale at New York University, December 5, 1992. EBET ROBERTS/REDFERNS

The reformed Velvet Underground, photographed in 1993: Reed, Morrison, Cale and Tucker. CAMERA PRESS

ou with Mo Tucker and John Cale as the Velvet Underground are inducted into the Rock & Roll Hall of Fame at a ceremony in New York, January 5, 1996. As a tribute to Sterling Morrison, who died in the previous year, the band performed a new elegiac song, 'Last Night I Said Goodbye To My riend'. NEW YORK TIMES/REDUX/EYEVINE

ou and David Bowie at the premiere of the film *Basquiat* at the Paris Theater, New York, July 1996. In the film Bowie played the role of Andy Warhol, entor to painter Jean-Michel Basquiat. RICHARD CORKERY/NY DAILY NEWS ARCHIVE VIA GETTY IMAGES

Lou in London in 1998. MICK HUTSON/REDFERNS

urban revenants and humiliated poor, while at the same time capitalising on the process, in an artistic and career move that helped greatly to restore his seriously dipped artistry. There is no way round the essential paradox that in addressing the underclass rock music arguably exploits them further by having them buy the product to the artist's material gain. Blanking on the marvellously innovative achievements of the New York school of poets, John Ashbery, Frank O'Hara, Ted Berrigan, James Schuyler and Kenneth Koch, Lou set out his endlessly restated pitch as New York's major literary talent.

> 'Well Faulkner had the South, Joyce had Dublin, I've got New York
> – and its environs. It's just a big city. The reason I don't think the
> album's inhibited by topicality is because I travel around a lot. I talk
> to people, and it's just the same old stories over there. Different
> name, same situation.'

Whatever the self-mythologised confusion of genres, Reed was a rock lyricist, and a highly adept one, and *New York* is possibly the best crafted of his albums, the one with a composite subject to address, a capitalist exploitation that threatened the class creating it with civil violence by way of retaliation. Homeless children, PTDO Vietnam war veterans, the Halloween parade decimated by Aids casualties, themselves treated like plague carriers of a virus endangering straights, gang warfare over drugs, and a subway patrolled by psychos and muggers desperate for crack money, was the anarchic social ethos Reed addressed as a writing project, rather than a scrambled studio exercise in rock cliché.

Working as a sparse unit, Mike Rathke on guitar, Rob Wasserman on fretless electric bass and Fred Maher on drums, Reed's compressed, ruth-lessly streetwise sound took issue with his city in the most combative terms that rock music can influence disinterested ideologies in their bias towards unequal distribution of wealth. Reed's tone throughout the album is brutally realistic, sardonic, angry, but rarely compassionate: his method is what he does best, social commentary that lyricises the facts without any resolution. *New York* is in essence historic observation without altering any of the topics it addresses.

In 'Romeo Had Juliet', Reed's dystopian nihilism extends to imagining an apocalyptic end to his sick city. 'I'll take Manhattan in a garbage bag/with Latin written on it that says/It's hard to give a shit these days/Manhattan's sinking like a rock/into the filthy Hudson what a shock/they wrote a book about it/they said it was like ancient Rome.' It's this sort of flagrant, flameout indictment, done with casually sweeping condemnation that makes *New York* into the sort of rock fiction Reed had always envisaged, but never quite delivered; but it still remains commentary that doesn't alter anything other than professing the courage to say it. But in terms of realism Reed squares up to his subject like a hit and run. In a series of lyrical snapshots, Reed in the same song confronts drugs as illicit currency in his best take on the subject since writing 'Waiting For The Man' a quarter of a century earlier. 'Outside the streets were streaming the crack/dealers were dreaming/of an Uzi someone had scored/betcha I could hit that light/with my one good arm behind my back/says little Joey Diaz/brother give me another tote.'

This is such a massive improvement on Reed's clean-up therapy albums of the eighties, in his characterisation of songs, rather than recycling of strictly personal issues. The album *New York* is constructed out of language, its Manhattan towers are built out of words, its America out of the construction of myths as in 'Last Great American Whale', Lou's rock equivalent story of Melville's *Moby Dick*, where the whale is integrated into formative geography. It's always difficult to ascertain whether Reed entered rock because he realised he wasn't by nature a novelist, or whether his total involvement in rock since his teens prevented him from realising his literary ambitions. Reed has always wanted the values one way: take it or leave it on his terms. Asked whether *New York* was his way of saying he couldn't give a shit about his critics, Reed replied:

'It is. It's also about language. That's why I say maybe we shouldn't think of me making rock'n'roll records. I'm in this for the long haul. I feel I've just started to get a grip on it, what I can do with it, what I want to do with it. And who I'd like to take with me when I do it. It's really easy in a sense because the people who like it will go with me. And the people who don't will say I'm full of shit. And more power to them. They don't want me and I'm not interested in them either. That's OK. I have no problem with that.'

Again refusing to believe that there is anyone in any creative field greater than himself, Reed pioneered *New York* as rock's equivalent of great literary expression, likely to be lost on less discerning listeners.

On 'Dirty Boulevard', the song that best evokes squalid urban poverty and corrupt authorities, Reed focusses on New York's rampant depravity. Put through the deprived character of Pedro, Reed's angry slashing reportage of what was actually happening on the New York streets is good rock history put into fiction. 'Give 'em your hungry, your tired and your poor and I'll piss on 'em/that's what the Statue of Bigotry says/your poor huddled masses/let's club 'em to death/and get it over with and just dump 'em on the boulevard.' It's as vituperatively aggressive as you'll get, the restraint curtailing eruptive anger; but the equation is very clear in its targeting of the uncaring rich, the movie stars checking out of their limousines for an opera at the Lincoln Centre, with the traffic backed up to 39th Street, and transvestite whores giving blowjobs to cops by the Lincoln Tunnel. Reed as laureate of sleaze had finally arrived with an album of cohesive rather than splintered catch lines as lyrics. This is Lou taking on authority through the authority of being Lou Reed, rich tax accountants' kid challenging his home city to modify its plutocratic supremacy sufficient to get the poor and homeless off the street.

New York reaffirmed Reed's legacy as a bad guy, and that was the album's selling point, as someone dangerous like Burroughs, or Ginsberg, whose art could still point a handgun at political injustices. Here was the elder statesman of rock renewing his interests in themes conveniently expurgated from his eighties albums, in a partially sycophantic campaign to go mainstream, busy guitar gunning and spitting on the material ethos to which he belonged. Lou's artistic shedding of his own class won him both old and new fans in his effort to reconstruct his image as unabated enfant terrible, approaching 50, with the balls to piss all over his city's skyscraper facades. Eloquently conducive to talking of drug issues in relation to their social and economic context in New York's illicit economy, Lou was for legalisation at the expense of the rogue dealer trafficking impure additives in street drugs that mind-fucked with chronically dependent users. Speaking to Sean O'Hagan at *NME*, Lou presented his case for legalisation:

> 'I'm for legalisation. All this prohibition stuff. Think what you could do with all the money they spend trying to fight drugs. Legalize it, tax it, make it pure, stop the disease, the killing, the crime; I mean they can't stop it 'cause the market for it is so gigantic. That's the bottom line. We're tied to all these markets in the first place, all these countries. But, like, if they took the huge illegal profit out of it, that'd hurt them. Imagine it – big deal, there's a drug store. It'd be cheap too. OK some drugs I personally think you should only be able to get when you're over 50. If you live past 50, you can try Ecstasy or whatever the hell you want! But legalize the shit. Take the taboo and glamour out of it.'

This coming from the man who had propagated injectable methedrine as Vitamin M in the seventies, and simulated shooting up onstage, and made drugs into an inseparable part of his image, is a more intellectualised evaluation of how drugs could arguably be introduced into a utopian society to discredit illegal profiteering, cartels, drug mules and dealers. It's in other words, an important insight into Lou's mindset at the time of recording the brutally realistic *New York*.

The success of Reed's first Sire album – it went gold in the US, UK and France – wasn't only its compounded artistry, but its author's stepping out of class to attack his own. While in the past Reed had lyricised decadence as his subject, he was always the privileged rock star dropping in on sleaze for sensory gratification, but now stripped of defences, and affiliated to the wealthy sector under random threat, Reed turned furiously on the rich for leaving him vulnerable, a reaction that mistakenly identified him with the poor and helped restore his artistic credibility.

In 'Strawman' Reed constantly questions surfeit of riches, the superfluous need of the mega-rich to add private empire to empire, and how the quest is ultimately as meaningless as spitting in the wind. Instead, Reed places his trust in vision and the imagined occurrence of the poetically marvellous as a corrective to capitalist greed. 'Does anyone need yet another blank skyscraper? If you're like me I'm sure a minor miracle will do/a flaming sword or maybe a gold ark floating up the Hudson/when you spit in the wind it comes right back at you.' Reed's contempt for the Reagan administration is sustained with disgust throughout the album in much the same way as in the UK Morrissey ('Margaret On The Guillotine'), the Beat ('Stand Down Margaret') and Elvis Costello ('Tramp The Dirt Down' and, with greater subtlety, 'Shipbuilding') railed against the equally arrogant and avaricious Thatcher cabinet. 'Does anyone need yet another politician/caught with his pants down and money sticking in his hole!' is questionably as raw to the truth as you can get. Reed had nothing to lose, and speaks with assured solidarity of endemic political corruption with total disregard for the suffering. Talking to his sympathetic sparring partner Allan Jones in *Melody Maker*, Reed proved as snarlish and prickly as ever in talking core politics of his album. Lou was quick to validate the absolute realism of his themes:

> 'It's not anything I'm making up. This is not Lou being negative. Or picky. Or so terribly selective that I've focussed on this narrow corridor of negativism. I just write about the things that are happening to me. And it's just terrible what's happened to New York in eight years of Reagan being in the White House. It's just terrible. Especially when you realise it needn't be that way. Something could be done, and the fact that nothing's being done just makes me mad. You know the Reagan administration was the most corrupt American government in modern history. And now we've got Bush . . . The Reagan legacy is a three trillion dollar debt and a war he waged against people who can't fight back. Women. Children. The poor. People who are sick. People who are dying of Aids. The attitude of someone like Bush on Aids is somewhere along the lines of "Well, they deserve it . . ."'

What saves *New York* from being nihilistic in the manner of *Berlin* is that Reed counteracts apathy and indifference with energy. And isn't all creativity about that, the opening up of blocked meridians into energised pathways. Before *New York* it's unlikely that Lou gave much thought to the deprived, although Rachel came from the Philadelphia underbelly, because the divisive was never so extremely pronounced. Reagan and Thatcher, Bush and Blair painted a broad gold central marker line between rich and poor, and Reed's anger set out to explode it with lyric and mashed guitar menace. Not since writing 'Sister Ray', with the messed up persecuted lives of drag queens as his subject, had Lou ever taken up a cause with such vengeance.

In 'Last Great American Whale', Lou uses creation myth as his captivating directive, in fusing the prototype of Melville's *Moby Dick* – the great white uncapturable whale representing America itself in its land mass – with how its physical features become land, as his narrative, a first for rock, about formation and decay as an ontological phenomenon. With the silver-black whale measuring half a mile, and unstoppably voracious in its physical representation of America, Lou self-invents myth to tell us 'They say he would split a mountain in two/that's how we got the Grand Canyon!' You can't argue with this, as its poetry, like Charles Olson's documentation of Melville's quest to harpoon America in *Call Me Ishmael*. In Lou's song lyric, the whale has its brains blown out with a lead harpoon projected by 'some local yokel member of the NRA' as a way of annihilating resistance. And with it, America's a dead land mass.

Does *New York* really deserve its paid-up reputation as a major Reed album, or was its acclaim dependent on rising above a series of uneventful albums, so disappointing as to merit anything smacking of a return to form an intentional masterpiece? It depends on how you hear Lou, and certainly the album's dynamic and outspoken diatribe against a corrupt administration restored rock to one of its significantly forgotten contexts – social protest or revolution.

Consumed by the need to record his own personal problems throughout the eighties, Reed had got locked into a pampered self-indulgent subjectivity – do rock stars really live such interesting lives? – and in the process forgotten social imperatives. New York was literally Reed's redemption, and there's dignity attached to the method in which he takes on novelistic themes like politics, social welfare, Aids when it was a taboo subject, and the hopeless lives of people like Pedro in 'Dirty Boulevard' living in a windowless cardboard-walled hotel, beaten regularly by his father, with nine brothers and sisters all packed into a room that costs $2,000 a month. Lou's sound, a sonic distillation of the streets, was no longer just an instrument of noise, but a weaponised vocabulary of insolent rebuke.

The album also finds Reed in the role of elegist, and nowhere more so than in 'Halloween Parade', his elegy for a New York gay community ravaged by the untreatable at the time retroviral killer Aids; and as such, an observation of the living, and an inventory of the dead. 'Halloween Parade' was the first pop song to address the issue, one given inimitable poetic expression by Thom Gunn in his 1994 collection *The Man With The Night Sweats*, in which he viewed his dying friends as abandoned and incurable as victims of the plague endemic in the 16th and 17th centuries. The song brings Reed's past into alignment with the present, his obsession with drag queens restored by the immediacy of the Aids threat to their decimated numbers, and poses the question as to whether the unnamed figure over whom he worries is Rachel, himself an Aids casualty. Ironically, in gay sexual activities, it is predominantly the passives who get HIV infected by active carriers, and most drag queens are predominantly passive, so Lou's elegy for the vulnerable reduced still further by sickness is additionally moving. It's almost as if Lou is addressing his own status in the song, talking to himself; and the terror of the song is that it will be the same next year, or the same indefinitely, as the infected march towards a prolonged but irreversible death, with only inefficacious AZT as chemical intervention.

It was Reed's intention to chapter *New York* like a novel, with each song leading sequentially into the next, and in narrative terms he was justified in his approach. Always his best eloquent exponent, Reed expounded:

> 'Each song on *New York* sets up the song that is coming afterwards – so when you listen to a song, while you're listening to it, you remember all the songs that came before, which is a lot different to just hearing that song. They're like chapters in a book. There's all

kinds of literary techniques going on in *New York*. For instance, I'm using two characters or more than two, I'm talking from the first person or the third, or I'm having no characters and just talking about concepts and ideas.'

Reed's continual dissatisfaction with rock, and the need to convert the vehicle into something incompatible with its expression, was part of the creative tension driving his new album. 'Maybe I'm not part of rock. Maybe that's what I should consider; that there's Lou Reed music and it's over there, that we can avoid some of the other garbage that goes along with it.' Reed's continual frustration with being constrained by rock's parameters wasn't a new evaluative theme, but there really wasn't another medium into which he could escape and receive corresponding recognition for his work. Public image sticks and so it's intensely difficult to re-identify in another artistic expression.

'Busload Of Faith' is another good upbeat song, held in venomous restraint. Reed's message is that in a disruptive world of homicide, rape and oppression, one can't decide on anyone or anything – except cruelty and effrontery. While the good make 'lampshades and soap', Lou claims that the only constant on which you can depend is 'the worst always happening'. A decade earlier and Reed would have used aggression as his cosh: *New York* is more deadly for its objective focus, and while Reed is removed from the predicament of the poor, he is nonetheless connected to them by social conscience. Any busload of faith is headed direct for the scummed over Hudson brimming with toxic debris. Talking to Tom Hibbert in Q, Reed discussed issues like low esteem and the belief that his gift had deserted him in the seventies, something that increased his dependency on speed in the endeavour to forget. There's no doubt an element of truth in this, although Reed's continual revisions of the past to suit the present make it difficult to separate fact from fiction, and evaluate truth from myth-making. He spoke of being stronger for having survived years of self-abuse and ravaged inner chaos.

'My ability hadn't deserted me. And it won't go away, ever. I didn't understand that so I fucked things around so much that I couldn't do it at all. But the ability's always there if I look for it, and presumably 20 years from now, it will be interesting to hear what I'm doing then, because as someone gets older, it's intriguing to hear what they have to say instead of being inundated with what 14-year-olds have to say. Even from day one with the Velvet Underground we were not aiming at 14-year-olds, because to get my stuff, you have to pay attention to it. And one day when I'm a senile old fart, I'll still be making rock'n'roll records, I hope. Because, after all, how much intelligence does it take to do that? Rock'n'roll is a really stupid medium . . .'

Reed's appeal had never been to youth culture, his intellectualised subject matter, disrespect for the industry financing his genre, and alienation from mainstream pop, meant that he was essentially exo-age and not dependent on youth for his market. Reed's counterculture cult was assumed literary, intelligent and sensible to life as a deepening process of experience that was essentially ageless. Reed, who had always been anxious to dissociate rock from transitioning fashions, discovered in *New York* the exact durable platform from which to consolidate an art expression that reflected age or maturity as its creative basis.

'Well, let's just say that, hopefully, everybody gets better as they get older, as opposed to not learning anything from mistakes, not maturing. That's what growing up is all about and your work reflects it. So often in rock'n'roll, development is kinda reversed and someone who starts out with something to say loses it and winds up as a gibbering idiot. It's disgusting. Back then I thought I'd lost it and I did a bunch of things I was really unhappy with. And I did it all in public and on record and there it is. That's what I did. I just kind of blew it apart because my problem – amongst all the other problems going on that you'd have to be deaf, dumb and blind to miss [i.e. the drugs] – was that I thought my talent was gone. I thought, it's gone and I got real upset about it. I thought it had deserted me and it made me really crazy and suicidal, and I did what a lot of people do about things like that, which was more drugs, and I got fucked up to say the least.'

Once you've accepted there's no other place to go, ageing downstream, as Lou appeared to, rather than trying to oppose the current, then the creative sensibility should really benefit from the process of converting the lived through into artistic reward.

One of the true creative achievements of *New York* is Reed's elegy for Warhol, 'Dime Store Mystery', a song that anticipates the more extensive treatment of this theme in the Reed/Cale collaboration *Songs For Drella* (1990). Dedicated to 'Andy-honey', Reed's attempt to equate Warhol with a suffering Christ integrates Andy's Catholicism into the chaotic conflicting ethos he is describing in New York's big city textures. Words don't substitute for what they describe, anguish over loss, the insoluble question of where the dead go and for what purpose, if they outlive the body. The song is as much a triumph of Reed's guitar as it is of its lyrical puzzling over the philosophic duality of nature, and how we are all split between human limitations and the prompting that we are more than that in our spiritually transcendent aspirations. 'Dime Store Mystery' is possibly the closest to genuine human feeling that Reed ever achieved on record prior to *Songs For Drella*. A personal meditation on death, as well as a lyric that anticipates Warhol's Catholic funeral at St Patrick's, the song carries a profound urgency, a depth across which Reed's guitar howls in solitary pain. Using Christ's bleeding, tortured body as the physical symbol for Warhol's shooting that had left him with permanent abdominal pain, and intestinal damage, so much so that he had to wear a corset, Reed uses the song to question the metaphysical conundrum of death, and what it could ultimately mean, and whatever scrambled thoughts came to Warhol at the end when he knew he was dying. 'There's a funeral tomorrow/at St Patrick's the bells will ring for you/Ah, what must you have been thinking/when you realised the time had come for you.'

Most of us tend to think of death impersonally. That it happens to others and not ourselves is the brain's defensive mechanism of survival; and whatever our last thought we can neither anticipate it nor perhaps ever know it as the brain shuts down and deoxygenates. Reed reproaches his own lost and wasted years in the song, when his emphasis was on hedonistic living without thought of accounting for a deeper psychic meaning to activities, despite his one-time immersion in the mystic writings of Alice Bailey as a companion to speed. Before his guitar bleeds into gesticulated figures of torment, Reed summarises: 'I wish I hadn't thrown away my time/ on so much human and so much divine/the end of the last temptation/the end of a dime store mystery.'

Reed talked at length about the song's inception and its long process of gestation before it found its way on *New York*:

> 'I'd been trying to write that song for ten years. I had the title and I kept starting it, but I could never finish it. Something would happen, and it would just leave . . . So for ten years, all I've got is a title and a vague idea for a song that would take place in a dime store, which is like a cheap store, a bargain department store. And the store would be symbolic of a ten-cent mystery, a cheap mystery. Not a profound one. One that doesn't matter in the end. Anway, I'm writing this album and I'm on the last song, and lo and behold! What do I write down in my book? "Dime Store Mystery".'

Having finally got there and liberated the concept into language, the triggering process having been activated, he said, by watching Martin Scorcese talking about *The Last Temptation Of Christ*, lines from the music stuck with him, and so the idea of integrating Christ's death into Warhol's became a reality. He wrote the song down and then was prompted by an inner voice to rewrite it.

> 'Then I wake up Sunday, six in the morning, with a neon sign in my head blaring out at me this one message: "Your song stinks. This really stinks. You gotta rewrite it. This is not your language at all. This is terrible. Terrible. Terrible. Go over there now and rewrite it." And I really hate rewriting, but I know it's gotta be done. So I have another go at it, and in the rewriting I suddenly end up with the verse about St Patrick's Cathedral which is where they had the wake for Andy. So then this kind of generalised thing about Christ went into this specific thing about Andy, and I had the song.'

The song proved both a departure and a beginning for Reed, for out of it came the extended suite of songs he composed with John Cale, their first real collaboration since the sixties, called *Songs For Drella*: a homage to Andy Warhol and the Factory milieu. *New York* ends on this open wound. 'Dime Store Mystery' pulls the whole thing together, and at the same time suggests a creative bridge tenuously constructed as a gateway into the future. To end on an enigma is to suggest new possibilities, and the album's popularity generated a new global tour and consolidated critical re-evaluation.

Reviewing the album in *Rolling Stone*, Anthony De Curtis compared it, out of context, to Tom Wolfe's novel *Bonfire Of The Vanities*.

> 'But whereas Wolfe maintains an ultimately cynical distance from the urban disintegration he depicts in his novel, Reed is raging . . . At a time when the city's own newspapers routinely evoke Calcutta and Bedlam to describe the Big Apple's rotting condition, Reed's message – powered by a ferocious four-piece band – slams home with the urgency of tomorrow morning's headlines.'

New York isn't great literature, it isn't meant to be, except in Reed's over subjective estimation, but it's a great piece of rock writing, and an album that benefited from the application of craft and rewriting in the interest of the songs. Lou had finally got nearer his declared object of creating novelistic rock, an album that could take on serious subject matter more commonly associated with the novel in terms of character studies, socio-political issues and contemporary events converted by imagination into fiction. If the best of his songs with the Velvet Underground hinted at disparate short stories, then in *New York* for the first time he developed interactive qualities between first and third person subjects sufficient to validate narrative development.

Now dressed like an accountant in recreational leisure clothes, a baggy grey suit, wire-rimmed glasses and with his hair tied back indicative of middle-age, Reed commenced his 1989 world tour by playing six sold out nights at St James Theatre, Broadway, New York, dividing his set into two precise parts: all 14 of the songs on *New York* were performed

throughout the tour as the first act, succeeded in the second by a retrospective of Reed's better received recent songs, together with a selection
of older, recognisable favourites: 'I Love You Suzanne', 'One For My
Baby', 'Doin' The Things That We Want To', 'Rock'n'Roll', 'Video
Violence', 'Original Wrapper', 'Sweet Jane', 'Walk On The Wild Side',
'Vicious', 'Satellite Of Love' and occasionally 'Street Hassle', with no
unpredictables or variants thrown in to disrupt his concisely compacted
professionalism.

Reporting the show favourably, David Fricke, writing for *Melody Maker*
noted:

> 'Reed commenced his two-and-a-half-hour set by performing all 14
> songs in order with a ferocity, acerbic humour and poignant intimacy
> befitting the album's subject and sentiment. The guitars did half the
> talking – raising holy hell in 'There Is No Time' and 'Strawman',
> dropping down into a dry bluesy sorrow for 'Endless Cycle' and
> 'Halloween Parade'. 'Dime Store Mystery', Reed's heartfelt goodbye
> to Andy Warhol, rose in a dramatic arc into a stunning Velvet's
> climax ignited by Rob Wasserman's urgently bowed bass, Bob
> Medici's jungle heartbeat drumming, and, at the end, an ear-splitting
> feedback chorale that must have had Warhol spinning with delight
> up in pop-art heaven.'

The downside was that it was mechanical, a reconstructed Lou delivering
for mega-dollars, the irony being that his songs about urban squalor were
received by New York's cultural elite competing for high-priced tickets
on Broadway, flattening any notions of altruism incorporated into Reed's
richly financed project of doing the album live. And did Lou ever have any
real comprehension that writers, independent of the bestseller blockbuster
market kind, earn almost nothing, poets in particular, and that if he'd
seriously pursued his illusion, he would have been as poor as the victims of
the songs that now earned him substantial financial reward?

Reed, barred from the London Palladium in 1977 because of his drug
reputation, finally succeeded in playing there in June 1989, the stage
decorated with neon and broken glass as a 'New York' tableau; and his

reputation secure as a sanitised survivor of rock's cleaned up professional evacuees from seventies bad boys propagating faggotry. The days of Reed having the crowd wait for an hour while he adjusted his chemistry were a thing of the aberrant past, but he was still capable of sitting down and expressing his disdain for audience chatter by blowing smoke into the microphone and saying, 'While you're talking, I thought I'd do something to match you. Now why don't you shut the fuck up!' Roy Wilkinson commented on Reed's new image as a reformed liberal in *Sounds*: 'Seeing Lou in 1989 is a bit like hearing a new consensus telling you Pol Pot was a nice guy, Caligula a pretty sane bloke.'

But Reed's irreducible ego and professional makeover, while they seemed the constituents of a rock academy designed to mask irreparable age, worked, no matter the man appeared schizoid and dangerously in denial of a past that was still recent history and irreparably attached to his legend. There was something psychopathically frightening about Reed's reform, as though it was an autonomous function he was programmed into pursuing. Not everyone was inspired by a reconstructed, demythologised Reed, and in writing up one of Reed's London Palladium shows in *Melody Maker*, Ted Mico reported on the set as a perfect example of uneventful, professional entertainment, with the contentiously irate Reed and Rathke's guitar menace offset by Wasserman's Clevinger electric upright six-string bass. But sound empty of meaning wasn't the real Lou: it was a survivalist stepping in, a Reed clone.

> 'His versions of Sinatra's 'One More For The Road' and 'Doin' The Things That We Want To Do' both glimmer, but never glisten. The loathsome 'Walk On The Wild Side' is wheeled into the operating theatre, only for everyone to discover the patient is dead and very smelly. 'Satellite Of Love' is cleaned and polished with harmonies and sent into rapturous orbit, while 'Video Violence', the finest track on *Mistrial*, bludgeons and mutilates everything in its path.'

New York was voted Album of the Year at the 1989 New Music Awards show in New York, and news was already circulating that Reed was tentatively collaborating with John Cale on a set of songs by way of tribute to

Warhol, begun with 'Dear Diary' and 'Hello It's Me', a suite commissioned by the Brooklyn Academy of Music. His regeneration as professorial rock Svengali, more revered as formidable for what he knew, rather than what he was currently telling, seemed secure. He was stung by Warhol's growing annoyance at his behaviour, and his deprecatory remarks on Lou's avoidance of him in his *Diaries*, an exhaustingly trivial documentation of Warhol's social engagements and day to day expenditure, largely omitting any reflective insight into his creative process, or the more serious aspects of his life, like the death of his former lover John Gould from Aids in September 1986, or his own declining health problems. Andy's *Diaries* were a monumental assemblage of gossipy trivia, the inanity of which seemed to differ little from his experimental, insistently unedited novel, *a, A Novel*, with Warhol demanding that all typos and spelling errors were left in the published text.

Songs For Drella was Reed and Cale's first full collaborative record since 1968's *White Light/White Heat*, and again a hostile fit of incompatible sensibilities that fed off creative tensions to fire up a moving and versatile song suite as a durable pop tribute to their ingeniously entrepreneurial mentor. According to Lou in his introductory notes to the album, '*Songs For Drella – A Fiction* is a brief musical look at the life of Andy Warhol and is entirely fictitious,' and for Cale:

> '. . . a collaboration, the second Lou and I have completed since 1965. I must say that although I think he did most of the work, he has allowed me to keep a position of dignity in the process. It therefore remains, as intended, a tribute to someone whose inspiration and generosity offered over the years is now remembered with much love and admiration.'

Reed's attempt to construct a fictional life cycle for Warhol from his frugal small town upbringing in Pittsburgh to his commodification of art at the Factory, his misgivings over fame and the questionable entourage it attracted, to being shot by Valerie Solanas and, like Reed, losing inspiration and dying unprepared for the experience at 58, are all lyrically contextualised in rock fiction. The album is complementary to *New York* in that Lou again polarises a specific theme and compresses it into musical narrative.

In 1989, Reed acknowledged Delmore Schwartz and Andy Warhol as the two most brilliant men to influence his life and career. Asked how Warhol's death had affected him, Reed was hardly profound:

'I don't know. How do you measure that? He had no right to die without talking to me first. Put it that way. I mean. How dare he! It was like, "Hey, what? Die? You can't do that." And I was unhappy from a selfish point of view that I couldn't get to talk to him any more. He was perfect. He was perfect all the way up to the end. Just hilarious. He was one of the smartest guys I've ever met in my life.'

Songs for Drella was originally the idea of the artist Julian Schnabel, who approached Cale at the St Patrick's wake and suggested that he write something to commemorate Warhol in music. According to Reed's version of events:

'When Julian suggested the idea of a requiem to John, he dutifully went off and started work on it. He thought it was a great idea. And then when we ran into each other and he was having problems with one part of it, he needed a second opinion. So we got together and decided, you know, to do something together. Just play, you know, for fun. Just us, nobody else around. No Velvet Underground reunion. Just the two of us, playing for ourselves, and we had a great time, a great, great time. Then John called me up and said, "Why don't I put my requiem away for a while and what do you think of the idea of co-writing something, a bunch of songs about Andy?" Then it got commissioned, if that's the word for it – it is the word for it – we were commissioned officially by the Brooklyn Academy of Music and St Ann's in Brooklyn. And we wrote *Songs For Drella*, which was Andy's nickname, and we performed it in St Ann's Church, January 7 and 8. Just the two of us. John had some keyboards and his viola. And I played what I always play. I had my trusty old amp and trusty old guitar and I loved it. I was enormously pleased with it.'

Songs For Drella is arguably the closest thing to sustained musical biography in rock, and due to the inclusion of Cale as instrumental colourist, is more successful melodically, and in variants of mood, than its predecessor, *New York*, modulated by Cale into nuances that were absent from Reed's *New York* as sonic shattering.

Reed's process of estrangement from Warhol over the decades was inevitable, as his solo career adopted its own skewed tangential pursuits, although Reed would never be free of his involvement with the Velvet Underground as the seminal reference by which all his subsequent achievements were judged. Nor perhaps could Lou forget Warhol's *Diary* entry for December 19, 1976, 'I hate Lou more and more' as the expression of mutual antagonism. The two had progressively lost touch after 1976 when a Warhol diary entry reads:

> 'Lou Reed called and that was the drama of the day. He'd come back from a successful tour, he was a big hit in LA, but he said Rachel had gotten kicked in the balls and was bleeding from the mouth and he wanted the name of a doctor . . . I said I'd get Bianca's. But then Lou called back and said he'd got Keith Richards' doctor to come over.'

When someone's dead you can turn the issues in their life into your own version: Reed and Cale's highly subjectivised Warhol is of course a fiction anatomised by selective biographical facts. The indomitable power clash between Reed and Warhol based on control, itself a refusal to concede emotions, was more likely the reason Reed obdurately refused to call Warhol throughout the eighties, when in the interests of systematised celebrity Reed attempted to dissociate from his past. According to Reed:

> 'The main thing was that I wanted to have a normal conversation with Andy and that wasn't possible. He used to tape-record absolutely everything, every conversation he ever had, and I didn't want our talk to end up in some publication which is what would have happened.

He would only talk to me on his own terms. Everything always had to be done on Andy's terms.'

Originally conceived as a live tribute, Reed and Cale performed what was 'a work in progress' at St Ann's Church in Brooklyn, January 1989, then perfected it as a completed project in a series of concerts in late November and early December that year, the commercial product from these performances being the video *Songs For Drella* filmed on location on December 6, 1989 at the Brooklyn Academy of Music. Performing at St Ann's without additional musicians or technology and illustrating the songs with slides of Warhol's paintings and one early, spooky photo-portrait, Reed (in black leather and denim) and Cale (dressed in formal black and looking adeptly geekish) threw shapes that inevitably drew comparison with the Velvet Underground, particularly on 'Images' where Reed's menacingly industrial feedback in contention with Cale's eerily droning viola scored up noise that directly referenced the Velvets' mid-sixties constructive cacophony. 'It was a great opportunity to pick up the threads of the Velvet Underground and draw our original ideas about arrangements and subject matter to a conclusion,' Cale told the *New York Times*, by way of the duo's experimental evocation of Warhol's life.

Asked whether he thought Warhol would have liked the requiem he and Cale had devised for him, Reed coloured up the possibilities:

'I have varying thoughts on that. As long as it wasn't too slick – which we tried really hard for it not to be – he would like that. As far as the stuff about himself, I don't know if he would care. I don't think it would matter to him one way or another. On the other hand, he was a lot more sensitive than people give him credit for. You might have to wait five or ten years to find out what he really thought about that. If he would tell you at all. I would like to think, in his heart of hearts, he would have liked it. Publicly, he would dismiss it. Because that's what Andy Warhol would do . . . Still, I would love him to call me up and say, "Oh I really like it. I think it's great. Congratulations." I don't think for two seconds that's what would really happen. But I would like it to.'

An unfair question to Lou, as it would involve negative self-criticism as a corollary to assuming Warhol wouldn't like the work, and self-congratulatory speculation to assume he would.

The album is as Lou and Cale intended, for serious people, and superb as an instance of intellectualised rock living up to its expectations as audio-biography stripped down to salient narrative basics. Reed of course initialised the album with 'Small Town', Warhol as generic gay misfit, with a formative vision that transcended Pittsburgh, where he studied art at the Carnegie Institute of Technology, remembered there for his chronic shyness and naivety, before leaving for Lower East Side New York within a week of graduating in 1949, as an introverted rebel in the making. Reed gets Andy's intentions right on, his essential ordinariness and low self-esteem masking inordinate ambition. 'When you're growing up in a small town/bad skin, bad eyes – gay and fatty/people look at you funny': and that's the way people always looked at Andy, before and after fame – the platinum hair, albino eyes, the deadpan smart, always a step-change ahead of cool, and the remorseless conversion of work into iconoclastic art and art into commodity.

'Open House' continues the downsized biographical fiction by focussing on Warhol's conditional hospitality, the Czechoslovakian customs picked up from his Catholic mother, his chronic autophobia – no kissing or touching – Marcel Proust was the same, and the apartment above the bar on 81st Street, right across from the subway and the cheap store selling mylar scarves. Continuing on from the meticulously phrased, assiduously crafted songs of *New York*, Lou's writing on *Drella* is sharper, his ear more finely tuned to cadence, his detailed snapshots compressed into portraiture, as though at last he'd got there in his continuously preconceived configuration of elevating rock into a form compatible with literature. And *Drella* remains for me his highest lyrical achievement, pushed by Cale to optimal breaking point as part of it, and got right by Reed in the attempt to validate Warhols's initial belief in him as Factory laureate.

During the fifties, when Lou has Warhol say, 'I drew 550 different shoes today,' Andy gained attention for his loose blotted ink style in drawings of shoe advertisements, examples of which figured in some of his earliest showings at the Bodley Gallery in New York, and the Hugo Gallery. Andy too, in 'Open House', has quickly observed that the stars you look for in New York are not in the sky, but on the ground, as part of his celebrity iconography, his obsessive infatuation with fame and material possessions as the personalised quotient by which he lived. 'Style It Takes' and 'Work' are both songs about Warhol's resolution to succeed as pop avatar by converting brand logos and the glamourised look of contemporary stars into modern art, right on the moment. Warhol's first New York solo pop art exhibition was hosted at Eleanor Ward's Stable Gallery, November 6–24, 1962, the exhibit including works like *Marilyn Diptych*, *100 Soup Cans*, *100 Coke Bottles* and *100 Dollar Bills*. He'd bought a former hat factory on the fifth floor of 231 East 47th Street, and surrounded himself with a patronised and compromised entourage of sycophants, wannabes, those who came to pay homage, stayed to work, or were simply on the transgender scene that fascinated Andy. 'Food does not exist for me,' he informed a *Vogue* reporter. 'I like candies. I also like blood.' 'I'll turn the camera on/and I won't even be there.' Reed has Warhol motion by way of autonomy – that way you get the Empire State Building glowing on your wall for 24 hours. Warhol transposed the concepts of commercial art into pictures, either copying or photographing the subject before starting the self-replicating manufacture of silkscreening the image – his famous Brillo box becomes an art object, even if it's the same one you can purchase in the supermarket, because he says so: meaning is denotational not connotational.

It's in the scorching urgency of 'Work', dominated by Lou's wired guitar savvy, that the real directive of Warhol's work ethic comes through, the inexorable crushing dynamic that drove him to amass a wealth from commodity. Warhol saw work as a moral duty. 'He'd get to the Factory early/if you'd ask him he'd tell you straight out/It's just work, the most important thing is work.' And in the process reproaching Reed for his lack of serious application to writing songs: his failure to work, because time doesn't repeat, and the loss of the moment can never be retrieved, any more than optimally productive years of youth. 'He said, "How many songs did you write?"/I'd written zero, I lied and said, "Ten"/You won't be young forever/You should have written fifteen." Andy's propulsive energies drove the Factory into an unconventional unsystemised empire, the only furniture splash a red Chesterfield, but the workplace torched-up by his instructive dynamic. There's a real argument to be considered that rock music, like good poetry, by its economic phrasing and fractured narrative leaves mainstream fiction obsolete, in that the minimalist crunched ingredients of rock are ideally packaged for the speed of modern life, whereas the novel enjoys long haul travel to arrive at the same place. Popular fiction with its artificial linear narrative is for escapism, redundant by way of saturation, and an album like *Songs For Drella* skilfully compresses the constituents of fiction into accessible flashpoints.

Writing *Drella* saw Reed ruminate on his later vicarious relationship with Warhol, and how most of what filtered through to him came second hand:

> 'I hadn't talked to Andy in a long time but if I got in some trouble I naturally went to him . . . He had always been the big leader. That was his thing and, at a certain point, you want to do things your way. I always felt that if I got to a certain point, I could go back to him and say, "OK, now . . ." But he went and died, and I never did, which was really very stupid of me and which I regret to this very moment. There were all kinds of things he told other people that would come back to me but I wanted him to tell me and he didn't, and I didn't either.'

Drella was in part Lou's compensation for everything left in disconnect, in the way the dead can't talk back to whatever the living may speculate.

Reed was equally forthcoming about the Velvet Underground's indebtedness to Warhol:

> 'He made it possible for us to exist and not change a note. He would sit there and say, 'Oh, that's great.' And because he said it, these other types, who in any other circumstances would have been in there changing things, left us alone? Why? Because Andy Warhol was there, and he said it was great. From that point on, we always knew,

be it with the Velvets or on our own album, that it was great the way we did things and that we didn't ever have any reason to listen to these other people unless we wanted to.'

One can either view this as self-indulgent refusal to be edited, or the debatable conviction that the artist is always right. In 'Trouble With Classicists' Reed champions Warhol's notion that technique limits form, and that the introduction of chance enhanced by input from others created an unpredictable result, with Warhol controlling the parameters during production, and surveying and approving the final result. Reed has Warhol as proponent of street art and graffiti slashes: 'I like the druggy downtown kids who spray paint walls and trains/I like the lack of training/ their primitive technique': Warhol as proponent of using found and available resources in the commodified city is fictionalised by Reed into empathising with kids spraying their own luridly loopy tags over subway trains as art signature. And why not?

There were of course books to contend with that preceded *Songs For Drella*, Ultra Violet's *Famous For Fifteen Minutes* (1988), Victor Bockris' very considerable biography of Warhol, begun in 1983, and Fred Lawrence Guiles' professional biography *The Loner At The Ball: Life Of Andy Warhol* (1989) with Bockris' biography remaining the most authoritative account of Warhol's life and capricious celebrity to date. Looking for the right balance of fact and fiction, biography and invention, Reed spoke to Mark Cooper about the dissolve between the two he'd tried to achieve in writing the album:

'At first the piece wasn't realistic, it was just a genuflect. You have to strike the right balance; you don't want to be non-critically glowing or, on the other hand, a kind of Medusa. We wanted you to meet Warhol in person. He was a difficult man, especially after the shooting when he wasn't doing the art. But I've always believed he would have come back to that because he was so smart. He would have come up with more interesting things because he always saw things differently. I always try to look at things more than once, keeping in mind: Boy – if Andy were here what would he be seeing?'

The concentration of Reed's writing on songs like 'Images', 'Slip Away', 'I Believe' and 'A Dream' are constructed with a meticulous lyrical care Lou had totally lost in the seventies, and for most of the eighties pre-*New York*, when his craft disintegrated into headlining one-liners empty of development. 'Images' is a song Reed and Cale might have stoked into generative storm with the Velvets, and represents a dual creative re-immersion in their volatile co-dependent energies, with the song's vindication of Andy's belief in mass marketing the same image as consumer art, or robotic autonomy. The mechanical process is repeated through the tight cyclical fire of Reed's guitar playing that reproduces some of the restrained anger concealed beneath Warhol's apparently implacable cool.

Hinting at a kind of mature, dignified chamber-rock, inflected by Cale's superb musicianship, *Drella* remains outstanding for its intelligent novelisation of Warhol as self-styled superstar, making it as gay at a time of conditioned social prejudice and homophobia, and indomitably ruling court at the Factory, having relocated in February 1968 to premises at 33 Union Square West, minus Reed and Cale, Gerard Malanga and Billy Name, but retaining in his coterie of Ondine, Brigid Polk, Candy Darling, Ultra Violet, Ingrid Superstar, Nico etc. But the ethos had changed: Joe Dallesandro had tried to commit suicide in Warhol's apartment, Viva had begun to throw scenes in public, the FBI were scrutinising Warhol's movies and the police regularly raided the Factory for drugs, notably speed.

'Slip Away' is Warhol's fictionalised reflection on what would happen if he renounced his open-door policy at the Factory, and his fear that he will stagnate and lose inspiration if the crazy people polarised to his celebrity desert him. 'Slip Away' leads directly into the self-vindication of 'It Wasn't Me', Warhol's denial that he was responsible for the mortality rate of his assistants at the Factory. The reckless drug abuse of a sixties generation, plus the illusion promoted by Andy that his entourage were superstars by association, imploded into the notion that Andy vampirically fed on the ideas of his Factory crazies, ruined them and detached himself from all blame as to the consequences. Reed has Andy exonerate his implied corruption of others by pleading, 'It wasn't me who changed you, you did it to yourself/I'm not an excuse for the hole you dropped in/I'm not simple minded but I'm no father to you all/Death exists but you do things to yourself.' Reed's skill is essentially to allow the two-year period in which he was intimate with Warhol to speak for a lifetime, obviating *Warhol Diary* entries, noting his ignoring him at the 1984 MTV Awards: 'Lou Reed sat in my row, but never even looked over. I don't understand Lou, He doesn't talk to me now.' Commenting on this in an *NME* interview in June 1989, Reed joked, 'I wanted to write a song called "Dear Diary". Then I figured, "Uh? Do I really wanted to get involved in that?"' Cos with the book being out, maybe it's gonna affect the way people look at him. Maybe in some way I should acknowledge that it's out.'

Reed's apparent anger that Valerie Solanas did not go to the electric chair for shooting Warhol is powerfully conveyed through his retributive 'I Believe'. Whether Reed's moral indictment of her is authentic, or a resolution arrived at during writing *Songs For Drella*, is uncertain. Certainly Reed's Jewishness surfaces with his assertion of the punitive Judaic belief of 'an eye for an eye, a tooth for a tooth'. 'And I believe there's got to be some retribution/and I believe an eye for an eye is elemental/I believe that's something's wrong if she's alive right now,' Lou asserts with flaming conviction.

Warhol was shot at the new Factory premises on Monday June 3, 1968. Sitting at his own black glass desktop in the company of associates, Mario Amaya, Paul Morrissey, Fred Hughes and Viva, an unsuspecting Warhol was confronted by Valerie Solanas, who pulled a .32 automatic from a paper bag and fired three times at Warhol, her third shot penetrating Warhol's right side and exiting through the left side of his back. Solanas then shot Mario Amaya through the hip. Warhol was rushed to hospital and pronounced clinically dead at 4.51, having arrived at the hospital at 4.45, 23 minutes after the shooting. At 8 p.m. Valerie Solanas gave herself up to a traffic cop in Times Square. The reason she gave for shooting Warhol was, 'He had assumed too much authority in my life.' Solanis maintained her conviction that Warhol was evil and manipulative. 'Warhol had me tied up, lock, stock and barrel. He was going to do something to me that would have ruined me.' Whether Warhol ever psychologically recovered from the shooting – he was naturally trauma-tised, as well as left with lifelong abdominal damage is debatable: Andy would never trust anyone fully again, and was never to regain his optimal work ethic, although he continued to monetise his work as the platinum-haired enigma of celebrity art.

Warhol's response was understandably one of questioning: why me, why should I be singled out to be shot by a psycho?

'I couldn't figure out why of all the people Valerie must have known, I had to be the one to get shot. I guess it was just being in the wrong place at the right time. That's what assassination is all about. I realized that it was just timing that nothing terrible had ever hap-pened to any of us before now. Crazy people had always fascinated me because they were so creative – they were incapable of doing things normally. Usually they would never hurt anybody, they were just disturbed themselves; but how would I ever know again which was which?'

Solanas, who was committed to Elmhurst General Hospital psychiatric wing, and declared incompetent to stand trial, was finally sentenced to three years for first-degree assault. But Warhol was changed for ever, wore a surgical corset, and told friends that having officially died, he was never really sure after that if he was properly alive. And although he returned to creative activities at the Factory, painting and film-making, Warhol was destabilised and impaired of his characteristic oomph and Andy elan. And some of Reed's indignation, his declaration in 'I Believe' that he would have personally pulled the switch on Solanas, may have arisen from the belief that it could equally have been him who was shot, as the weird attracting weird. Lou's passionate advocacy of the death sentence in 'I Believe' is as controversial a statement as any he ever made in his patchily outrageous career.

One of the truly great songs to emerge from Reed and Cale's repatria-tion on *Drella* is the excerpted cut-ups extracted from Warhol's published *Diaries*, and made into the song 'A Dream', chillingly narrated by Cale in a manner reminiscent of 'The Gift' and 'Lady Godiva's Operation' from the Velvet Underground's *White Light/White Heat* album. Resonant, compelling and intimately disturbing, the tone is used to brilliant effect on a song in which Warhol presciently anticipates his coming death. Warhol wakes in the night to hear Billy Name and Brigid playing underneath his window. Then, deciding to photograph the falling snowflakes, he explores the relationship between his subjective world and the external one. He feels he has lost face with the editors of his own magazine *Interview*. He comments on Billy Name, Ondine, who is now touring and doesn't pay him for the use of films, and on John Cale and Lou Reed. Cale's narration enforces the estrangement between Reed and Warhol, and Warhol's reflections on the contributory role he played in launching the Velvets' first album, and how he had never received financial remuneration for it; the album sleeve he had designed for Cale's 1981 album *Honi Soit*; and all the complex interior motives which emerge over years of separation and occasional meetings, and all the paranoid misapprehensions accumulated in the process.

'A Dream' is arguably the album's high point, with Reed's spookily sourced guitar effects, and Cale's piano stomping for emphasis, having us really believe this is a dream, an oneiric state in which the dreamer reviews his life and sleepwalks through a dark corridor. 'A Dream' leads into its companion piece 'Forever Changed', in which Andy reflects through Lou, not only on the transience of life, but on the irreversible changes brought about by the nature of experience, as the correlative to leaving one's hometown, in Warhol's case Pittsburgh, and moving to the city. 'Train entering the city – I lost myself and never came back/took a trip around the world and never came back/black silhouettes, crisscrossed tracks never came back', and of course you can't, as Lou's lyrics imply, ever repair loss of innocence and security in going out into the world. And the ultimate journey out is of course death, as the physical termination of whatever it is we do in life, have, achieve or aspire to.

Something of Warhol's accretion of fear is quoted by Victor Bockris in his influential biography of Warhol, as a pointer to his confused mental state after the shooting.

'Before I was shot I always suspected I was watching TV instead of living life. Right when I was being shot I knew I was watching television. Since I was shot everything is such a dream to me. I don't know whether or not I'm really alive – whether I died. It's sad. Like I can't say hello or goodbye to people. Life is like a dream. I wasn't afraid before. And having died once, I shouldn't feel fear. But I'm afraid. I don't understand why. I am afraid of God alone, and I wasn't before.'

Warhol's excruciating dilemma – was he experiencing life as someone who was really dead or as, disturbingly, someone who couldn't die and was living in an intermediate state between the two – helped accentuate his already chronically phobic neuroses and misgivings about being a ring master of freaks.

'Forever Changed', made additionally elegiac by Cale's vocals, represent the dramatic culmination of the *Drella* cycle. The postscript that follows it, 'Hello It's Me', is Reed's attempt to reconcile himself to Warhol's memory, a querulous apologia that remains unconvincing as an intended corrective to history notated by Warhol's *Diaries*. 'But I have some resentments that can never be unmade/you hit me where it hurt/I didn't laugh/your *Diaries* are not a worthy epitaph.' Not on Reed's part, stung by Warhol's increasing dislike of him, and defiantly standing his ground over unresolved issues and lingering hostilities that were now irreparable and may have worsened if Warhol had remained alive. 'Hello It's Me' serves as both a valediction to Andy Warhol and an affirmation that Reed had survived, not as a casualty, but as a seriously creative artist, something that in itself was possibly his best tribute to Andy.

The brief rapprochement of the two artists, Reed and Cale, wasn't without hazards and extreme irreconcilable conflict, and Cale's recollection of the sessions in his autobiography, *What's Welsh For Zen*, alludes to simmering tensions. 'Towards the end we were so far apart that we had to negotiate our way out. It was tedious, stressful and makes it hard for me to look back on that album with anything but horror.' Cale too, was apparently coerced into understating his collaborative input into *Drella*. Cale regretted minimising his contributions in the sleeve notes, done apparently to placate Reed. 'I should have changed it,' Cale wrote as an afterthought, 'because my input on *Drella* was at least equal to Lou's.'

Songs For Drella is a neglected masterpiece because of the collaboration, rather than just a rock tribute to Warhol filtered through Lou's sometimes planet-sized ego, with Cale there to modify, diversify and bring a rare musicianship to Reed's rock fiction that doubtless wouldn't have been so colourful solo. *New York, Songs For Drella* and *Magic And Loss* are indisputably Reed's best lyrically crafted and constructed albums, with *Drella* in its fictional characterisation of Warhol coming as close to matching content and form as Lou ever got, in his obsessive quest to match his vision of rock being taken as seriously as the Great American Novel.

9

Now I Have Seen Lots Of People Die

NOW 50, Reed reached mid-life in the midst of a momentous career revival, setting to work on *Magic And Loss*, a harrowingly transcendent album consolidating the verbal craft of *New York* and *Songs For Drella* into an unpitying confrontation with the deaths from cancer of two close friends, the 65-year-old blues singer Doc Pomus (composer of songs like 'Save The Last Dance For Me') and Rotten Rita, a.k.a. Kenneth Rapp, one of Warhol's transvestite entourage at the Factory, name-checked on the *New York* track 'Halloween Parade'. Lyrically, and in the psychological permutation of insighting pain, suffering and the alchemical process or transmutation involved in dying, *Magic And Loss* may stand as Reed's most superbly achieved album of the trilogy begun with *New York* (1989). The economy of phrasing involved in the writing, and his own awareness of its poetic rewards, has a lot to do with the album's sense of being worked on through stages of refinement, with Reed acutely aware of the need to optimise his songwriting resources when writing about one of his admired masters of the genre, Pomus. Poetry, as the minimally expressed carrier of big material, depends a lot for its success on the elimination of all surplus for unit impact. Lou recognised he'd self-consciously achieved that stage in his writing or become aware in the writing of doing it.

> 'But this is, I think, an advance over *Songs for Drella* and over *New York*, along the lines of taking things out. I'm always trying to get the gist of it without an extra word. That's the way the guys played, too. It was all about taking stuff out. Less really is more. I truly believe that. This is an example of another step along that road or that way of thinking. You hear better. So you hear more. And it better be played well. One false step and it falls on its face.'

Terminal illness – and it's hard to find any good in prolonged incurable suffering medically addressed by radically exhaustive and debilitating chemotherapy – is experienced by the patient and observed by the witness, in this case Reed, with the only interface being one of shared compassion, received by one and transmitted by the other. In the attempt to find some form of creative transformation to excruciating pain in his extended hospital visits, Reed looked to alchemy as the key to assigning suffering some sort of positive meaning, with the archetypal alchemical quest of turning lead into gold converted into a symbol of liberation on the individual's part, into self-realisation through transcending pain in the process of dying.

Magic And Loss wasn't the sort of subject rock musicians usually address, and Lou's intense dialogues with twisted physical agony demand serious listening by serious people. In a shamanic, shape-shifting way, equally attributable to alchemy, Reed tried hard to lyricise pain into something cathartic, at least for himself, as the songs couldn't in any way help the dying, or annul the extremes of pain.

> 'I came to understand that the album was about transformation, lead into gold, that was just one example of the process, to be used later to transform yourself. I call the album *Magic And Loss* because that experience can be taken two ways. That's why the song 'Power And Glory' occurs twice, in different forms. A whole different tempo, a whole different way of looking at the exact same thing.'

We come back always to one insoluble problem that art doesn't do anything for the dead, in this case Doc Pomus and Rita, it just helps the artist transform or come to terms with pain he is subjectifying, as his own personal response to intense experience. All elegists are unilateral: they address the artist, far more than the subject, as a form of neural masturbation celebrating aspects of someone or something that usually evokes mutual affinities.

Lou, as always, was obsessed with tech, and with what the listener hears in process, advising:

'Just luxuriate in the sound, it's so thick and defined and dimensional. The writing and performance are one thing, but if the production and the technical side aren't there, and I've got the records to prove it. A lot of my records, till I could get a handle on it, aren't even produced, except in the sense that I wouldn't let the producers do anything, rather than let them do it wrong. And the records are completely dry, 'cause I didn't know how it worked, and I knew they'd fuck it up so I wouldn't let 'em do anything. It takes a long time to learn when you're making a record every couple of years. It's fascinating, but it's like this onion with all these skins, endless.'

Lou's mind, always into what's ahead of studio sound, invariably wanted and heard what wasn't there, his own inner noise.

But for any intelligent appreciation of *Magic And Loss*, Lou was aware he needed listeners who'd been bounced around and off the wall in their own experiential encounters with life. This wasn't an album youth could walk into and proclaim as cool, because it was Lou Reed; access demanded a correspondent quotient of experiential suffering to get there. In 'Power And Glory' Reed extracts from Doc Pomus' chemical cosh: 'The same power that burned Hiroshima/causing three-legged babies and death/shrunk to the size of a nickel/to help him regain his breath.' You won't find that sort of punishing perception in anything else classified as rock, and Lou comes through here as a heroic one-off in his barbed reportorial accuracy, and the sepulchral resonance of his and Mike Rathke's strategic surges of guitar that underline the entire album.

One could presumably argue that *Magic And Loss* is overly academic in terms of rock and pushes limitation to the edge of a new form. Right from the heavy-metal guitar annunciation 'Dorita The Spirit', the album's opening song, an elegiac wail from Reed's interior, Lou contests the day-to-day physical erosion of his two friends through the elegant severity of his art. You can't stop death, so you have to learn to live with it, and music is one way.

Doc Pomus, a.k.a Jerome Solon Felder, was an American blues singer as well as a highly gifted and prolific songwriter, who died from lung cancer at the age of 65 at NYU medical center in Manhattan on March 14, 1991. During the late fifties and early sixties he wrote several songs with Phil Spector, 'Young Boy Blues', 'Ecstasy', 'What Am I To Do', with Mike Stoller and Jerry Leiber 'Young Blood' and 'She's Not You', and also 'Lonely Avenue', a 1956 hit for Ray Charles. Pomus maintained his prolific output throughout the seventies and eighties, writing for, amongst others, Dr Hook, and Reed attended classes Pomus conducted on songwriting in the eighties.

The other friend to inspire Reed's *Magic And Loss* was Rotten Rita, or Kenneth Rapp, an influential denizen of Warhol's Factory, where he was commonly known as 'The Mayor', an opera aficionado and speed-freak, who worked by day in a fabric store, spending nights camping it at the Factory. And it must be remembered that Warhol hated drugs, and while he attracted and remained fascinated by speed-users like Rotten Rita, and Reed himself, Warhol never touched anything that might cause him to lose self-control and his casually disciplinarian hold on the Factory's work assemblage.

The journey undertaken by Reed in attempting to elucidate and chronicle the harrowing body deformations of cancer is one that musically alternates between light and dark in its journeying pathway. And it's the redemptive qualities of tracks like 'Magician' and 'Magic And Loss' that introduce a quality of compassion into his work so noticeably absent from the majority of his output in which objective cool substitutes for emotional response. In 'Magician' Reed's own vulnerability interfaces that of Rita's: 'Somebody . . . please help me/my hand can't hold a cup of coffee/my fingers are weak – things just fall away/inside I'm young and pretty/too many things unfinished/my very breath taken away.'

It took time for Reed to arrive at a place where the heightened awareness of his own mortality, particularly as an inveterately heavy smoker, and Doc Pomus died from lung cancer, met him full on in all its catastrophic terror, and in a way that demanded the mediating response of music integrated into bits of shamanic myth. To his surprise it was greeted with commercial success, *Magic And Loss* charting at number six in the UK, and the single 'What's Good' hitting number one on *Billboard*'s charts. What

Reed was relaying of course was the exacting price of experience in which the banal and the surreal are juxtaposed into an uncomfortable viewpoint of reality: 'Life is like Sanskrit read to a pony/I see you in my mind's eye strangling on your tongue/what good is knowing and devotion/ I've been around-I know what makes things run.' And whereas *Berlin* is irremediably nihilistic and drenched in callous misogyny, *Magic And Loss* beats despair into some sort of malleable, intangible ethereality, in which there might just be hope that there is a purpose in suffering, or some kind of transcendent gain. Reed's dramatised scary theme throughout is it could be me, and why isn't it, a subject he takes up unsparingly in 'No Chance'. 'I'm embarrassed by the strength I lack/if I was in your shoes/so strange that I am not/I'd fold up in a minute and a half.' The paradox, of course, is that what the observer sees and assimilates isn't what the sufferer is experiencing, it's a subjectified interpretation of imagining how it could be: and that's as close as you can get to someone else's pain, and as close as Lou inevitably achieves on *Magic And Loss*, as a stoked distillation of helplessness, pity and revenge through irascible chords. In an *Arena* interview with Steve Beard, Reed stressed an awareness of the importance of individual life, and of his own role as obstinate survivor.

> 'The people I'm talking about would be very disappointed with me if I was off in a corner and not coping. They would certainly expect a lot more of me than that. I would have learned nothing if I came away from this in a negative state of mind, because I've decided how much these people loved the life that others threw away nightly: how they fought for it right down to the last dot.'

Reed had in fact arrived. This album, the summation of a highly crafted trilogy, was never surpassed by succeeding work, particularly the mismanaged pretentiousness of his Poe re-make *The Raven* (2003). The elevated diction of *Magic And Loss* gets nearer to Reed's conception of poetry as he learned it at Syracuse from Delmore Schwartz than anything else he wrote, at last contradicting Lester Bangs' 1975 assessment of Lou's status as a writer:

'The persistent conceit of Lou's recent press releases – that he's the street poet of rock'n'roll – just may be true in an unintended way. The street, after all, is not the most intellectual place in the world. In fact, it's littered with dopey jerkoffs and putzes of every stripe.'

Part bitchy, part true on Bangs' part.

In the album's title track, Reed's disappointment in not having proved himself another Shakespeare, Joyce or Dostoyevsky continues as a stubborn obsession, while he looks to a cleansing, healing fire, rather than one that extinguishes human consciousness at death. 'They say no person can do it all but you want to in your head/But you can't be Shakespeare and you can't be Joyce/So what is left instead/You're stuck with yourself and a rage that can hurt you/You have to start at the beginning again.' Was it lack of reading contemporary literature that had Reed always revert to the past as a measure of greatness, and rarely to the present, or is it that it's easier to praise the dead than acknowledge what's present as a source of literary inspiration? No longer concentrating on the myth of his own disintegration as a source of song material, Reed's success in *Drella* and *Magic And Loss* was to shift his concern to the dissolution of others, a step change towards universalising rather than totally personalising experience; and the change increased his stature as rock humanist, rather than self-preoccupied terrorist.

The concerts to promote the commercially successful *Magic And Loss* were predictable affairs. With the precedent established by *New York*, the whole album was played with little variation from the original. Even an admonitory sign outside London's Hammersmith Odeon stated that he would play no old material and that latecomers would not be admitted into the auditorium after the show had started. All element of surprise removed, Reed settled for surety, a re-creation of the album live with Mike Rathke's accompanying guitar finesse, his Midi-guitar allowing him to create keyboard sounds such as piano and violin, and Robert Wasserman's six-string upright electric bass at times finding the equivalents of classical cello. The format was near perfect, but the academic formality of playing an identical set five nights in a row risked homogenous, samey monotony.

In a review of *Magic And Loss* in *Rolling Stone*, David Fricke thought the album was Lou's 'death letter'. Fricke spoke of it as representing Reed's 'most affecting, emotionally direct solo since *The Blue Mask* (1982), a stunning consummation of that album's naked guitar clamour, and the hushed-chapel intimacy of the third Velvet Underground album', concluding that Reed 'offers no great moral revelations and no happy ever after, just big questions and some basic horse sense.' Jonh Wilde, reviewing the album in *Melody Maker*, was less outright enthusiastic in his sceptical overview of Lou's intentions. 'Crafted from parched guitar fragments, bass trembles, and occasional snatches of percussion, the seriousness of its concerns are signposted by the song titles themselves, which might also invite knee-jerk accusations of ripe pretentiousness from Reed's legions of detractors.'

What about the man behind this comparatively successful trilogy of albums that had redeemed an unbroken run of mediocre eighties work, neither good enough for mainstream authority, nor in any way engaging to Reed's fans who'd largely given up on the idea of his reinvention? Reed was wealthy, married and the dust jacket to his collection of lyrics *Between Thought And Expression* volunteered the information that he had a dog, Champion Mr Sox, and that baseball and bikes comprised his recreational hobbies. Completely normal? Money hadn't given him sartorial elegance or changed his look: the same black zippered leather jackets, dusted up jeans and blackout shades continued to represent an unchanging mode of dress that hadn't really changed since Lou's years with the Velvet Underground. Reed was also working through spiritual disciplines on being calm. 'I practise being calm. Being calm is a good thing. Not excited. Stay out of the way, I really try to do that.' And in a *Vox* interview Reed spoke of his newly acquired habit of distancing himself from criticism. No longer fuelled by a malevolent vengeance to take issue with his critics, he observed a more philosophic art of dissociation from frustration and anger.

'I'm a lot less pigeon-holed than I was before. I try not to read that stuff unless it's nice. So I don't read a whole lot. My wife censors it, says you don't need this impinging on your life. Am I making more human records? Well. I love *Berlin* and *Magic And Loss* is its closest descendent since. It's a coherent whole, instead of 14 disparate songs.'

By publishing *Between Thought And Expression* (Viking, 1992), Reed attempted yet again to reconcile his instanced dichotomy between writer and musician, begun two decades earlier when after splitting with the Velvet Underground, he'd periodically published poems/lyrics in *Fusion* magazine and more tellingly in the *Harvard Advocate*, attempting clearly to convert his depressed state at the time into personally reflective poetry. In the July 23, 1971 issue of *Fusion*, Reed published a despondently mooded poem 'Waste', reviewing his life at 30 as unrealised and partly used-up. 'An education gone to waste/talent left ignored/imagination rent with drugs/someone who's always bored/scared to death of life itself/and even more by death/not fit for company/let alone a wife.' This excerpt from a poem flatly recounting the sterile plateau on which Lou was islanded in 1971 seems pretty much to encapsulate the existential crisis he found it hard inwardly to rise above in the seventies. Disappointment, the conviction of failure, drug damage, sexual confusion, they're all there as pointers to his state of general anxiety and dejection.

In the Fall 1971 issue of the *Harvard Advocate*, at a time when Reed still wasn't sure of his direction in music, he published amongst others the lyrics to 'Candy Says', 'True Love', a surprisingly delicate poem beginning 'If all the beach/ was made of diamonds/sand would be the/stone we value', 'Pain', pronouncing his 'hatred of women', and 'The Coach And Glory Of Love', which is in fact the initial draft of 'Coney Island Baby', only lightly revised and four years in gestation, before Lou recorded it with a special dedication to Rachel in 1975. That this key lyric of Lou's, romanticised through the association with Rachel, remained concealed for four years is still further evidence of how little new material Reed wrote in the seventies, and further confirmation of how he believed his creative gift had deserted him or been partially wiped by drugs. Reed's decision to collect some of his lyrics in *Between Thought And Expression* prompted the writing of anecdotal footnotes to various aspects to his life. Cryptic, humorous, quasi–autobiographical, the reminiscences are couched in Reed's typically deadpan humour. As a note to 'Teach The Gifted People' from *Growing Up In Public* (1980), he tells of his early hatred of authority and his tricky method of avoiding conscription. 'I said I wanted a gun and would shoot anyone or anything in front of me.' These footnotes often read like incidents from Burroughs' *Naked Lunch*, with their hoodlum handgun toting threats, in their dissolve between fiction and fact. As a commentary to 'Afterhours' from *The Velvet Underground* (1969) Reed says that it was in an after-hours bar that he first saw someone beaten to death. He was drinking with Nico when she threw a glass; it smashed in a Mafioso's face. He thought the man behind Reed had thrown it and so he killed him.

In a *Vox* interview given at the time of the book's publication, Reed expressed the view that the book's publication was a significant achievement, a landmark in his career.

> 'That I wanted to do for a long time. It isn't a rock star's compilation. There's no pictures of my home or the band. I didn't bring in some Belgian to paint the cover. It was serious. A lot of the lyrics only existed on record. I don't have drawers full of 'em and I've thrown away my notebooks. I couldn't read the handwriting anyway. The songs are like my diary. If I want to know where I was, the book gives me a good idea.'

In 1992 at the time of the release of *Magic And Loss* and *Between Thought And Expression*, Reed's major achievements had peaked, and the book as a synthesis of his lyrical preoccupations, was also the evaluation of a life committed to a singular genre of intellectually adult musical expression. There's hardly a band, contra Lou's disillusionment, that doesn't owe something to the brief avant-garde supernova which the Velvet Underground represents, a spontaneous happening at full power between 1966 and 1968, part accident, part Warholian manufactured, the reverberations of which have come to be used as reference point for measuring the potential of new talent in indie rock. The sharpness and imaginative risk of his lyrics in this early period are very different in their stripped down form, from his later more richly textured, self-conscious literary diction, employed in the writing of *Magic And Loss*, or *The Raven*, where verbosity can threaten the limited chord structures. 'Chelsea Girls', 'All Tomorrow's Parties', 'Waiting For The Man', 'Heroin' and 'Sweet Jane' are all perfectly assessed lyrics for the social contexts and realities they convey. Maturity and the relentless drive to be taken seriously as a writer had Reed alter his boundaries in the interests of being considered an exclusively challenging proponent of demanding rock be elevated to a legitimate art form.

In one of his more generous interviews, Reed spoke with rare modesty of his lyric intentions. 'There are certain kinds of songs you write that are just fun songs – lyrics that really can't survive without the music. But for most of what I do, the idea behind it was to try and bring a novelist's eye to it, and, within the framework of rock'n'roll, to try to have that lyric there so somebody who enjoys being engaged on that level could have that and have the rock'n'roll too.' Did Lou attach over-importance to his lyric writing, due to too little serious reading of contemporary literature, and is it really that much of a struggle to compress quintessential experience into hooky rock formula? Due to Lou's characteristic, invincible defensiveness, it's difficult to ascertain whether he found writing a difficult process, or whether the module to which he aspired wasn't so easily adapted to rock. And Lou is of course right in that most lyrics don't hold up without music, because the two are inseparably integrated, something made apparent by glaring lack of poetic metre in reading Lou's *Collected Lyrics, Pass Thru Fire* published by Hyperion in February 2000. All the synaptic disconnections needed in a pop lyric, to loosely narrate through omissions, is what makes the form so stimulatingly viable; but it's a different art to poetry where inclusions rather than omissions make it hang.

W.H. Auden famously wrote 'Poetry makes nothing happen', by way of its marginalised expression, whereas rock music does, supported by mediated state-of-the-moment digitised electronics, live circuits and ubiquitous festivals, air-play and a long arm of commercial overreach that diminishes poetry's small outlets. At 50 and compiling a boxed set, anthologising a career retrospective that was exceedingly mean on rarities, Reed was in a position to look back and forwards. In a *Time Out* interview with Neil Gaiman at the time of the anthology's release, Lou made what seems an honest autobiographical statement:

'I thought I'd earned the right; that I knew enough about life at this point, and had gone through enough where I thought stating an opinion about a thing or two would not be soapboxy or preachy, but just hard-won experience trying to communicate to other people. In a lot of the stuff that I wrote about there's no overt moral position, but what's being described speaks for itself and I don't think it needed me to say anything about it – I don't take a superior view or any kind of elitist view toward any of these things; it's life, and that's what we're talking about. But over the last couple of years there's been a change, in the sense that I think that I am capable of taking positions that I'm not going to change my mind about. I think I can justify my opinions. They're hard won and heartfelt.'

Between Thought And Expression, a 3-CD retrospective of Reed's solo career prior to *New York*, consisted almost entirely of previously released material from his RCA period, with Lou taking an active role in selecting tracks and remastering them to put some sort of definitive personal signature on the anthology. An idiosyncratic, eclectic selection, even including a one-and-a-half minute extract from *Metal Machine Music*, confirming Reed's continued belief in its validity as avant-garde signposting, the compilation offered an obligatory number of rarities as a selling point to Reed fans. The outstanding previously unreleased track was the drawlishly brilliant 'Downtown Dirt' from the aborted January 1975 *Coney Island Baby* sessions: a semi-spoken, mean, downturned account of life on the Lower East Side that has Lou sound like he's singing into the bottom of a whiskey glass. 'Leave Me Alone', a lyrically vacuous, stand-offish rocker came from the same disrupted sessions as 'Downtown Dirt': a stunning 20-minute live 'Heroin' recorded on December 1, 1976 at the Roxy in Los Angeles on Lou's *Rock'n'Roll Heart* jazz tour, and originally engineered by Ray Thompson for radio broadcast by station KMET, was the broody diamond in the box for those who'd missed out on bootleg recordings of the show. With Don Cherry flavouring the song with atmospheric trumpet, Lou's melancholy impromptu reading of his epic drug classic reinvents the phrasing to fit with frenetic jazz options.

'Here Comes The Bride', an unreleased outtake from *Take No Prisoners* recorded live at the Bottom Line on May 21, 1978, is uneventful Lou during a high performing but low writing time, and the same goes for 'America' a.k.a. 'Star Spangled Banner', a raucous outtake from *Growing Up In Public* and a dispensable curiosity. 'I don't know why we did it,' Lou commented. 'It would be interesting to know what was going on in the world that would have caused that. It had to be something that set that off. Maybe they were kidnapping Americans, I don't know.' 'Little Sister' from the soundtrack of the movie *Get Crazy* and recorded during the *New Sensations* sessions is another uninspired disposable, and so too is 'Voices Of Freedom', recorded live in London in March 1987 at a benefit concert for Amnesty International, an impoverished rocker that does Reed no credit as a literate songwriter. This wasn't a box for rarities enthusiasts, but given that it's Lou's own personally curated overview of his RCA recording years, it's a valuable document of self-assessment in mid-life at the time of selection.

By the time of the Velvet Underground's complexly motivated reunion in 1993, Reed's marriage to Sylvia Morales was over, and although she continued to manage his affairs, sexual incompatibility was a key issue in the disintegration of marital affairs, despite Lou's implacable denial of his gay past and refusal to address same-sex attraction. We go back again to Lou's prototypical pattern of punishment and reward, shock and non-shock for sexual preference, and for Lou an interzone in which sex didn't exist at all as neutrally safe. If you're neither, you don't have to make a choice, if you're one or the other you're decided.

Environmentally, from June 15 to September 9, 1990, the Cartier Foundation produced an Andy Warhol exhibition – The Andy Warhol System – at Jouy-en-Josas, Ile-de-France. Reed and Cale agreed to play five songs from *Drella* on the opening day, and the contentious Warholian duo were unpredictably joined onstage by Maureen Tucker and Sterling

Morrison to perform 'Heroin' as an unofficial Velvet Underground reunion, the song later released on a bootleg 12" – *The Velvet Underground 'Heroin', Live at the Cartier Foundation, Paris, 15 June 1990* – as an out of the blue one-off curiosity. Intimations of a Velvet Underground reunion were given additional momentum when both Reed and Morrison unexpectedly joined John Cale for an encore at his show at New York University on December 5, 1992. It was an anomalous rumble that hostilities could be repaired in the interests of the big money that Lou was configurating as incentive to reunite for a generation of disaffected indie fans too young ever to have seen the US based Velvet Underground perform live. When the Velvet Underground did finally tour Europe, it was as a rogue Steve Sesnick managed incarnation, minus Reed, a laundered band comprising Doug Yule's assumed leadership, Walter Powers on bass, and original members Sterling Morrison and drummer Maureen Tucker, until Morrison got to be replaced by Boston-based keyboardist Willie Alexander, with the band touring the UK and Holland in support of *Loaded* on the back of their widely propagated infamy. Audience recordings as well as soundboard led to the release of the *Final Velvet Underground 1971–73* – a box set comprising live recordings of their post-Reed inoperative finale.

All over 50, in May 1993, the four original members of the Velvet Underground reconvened for a month of rehearsals, bunkered behind an unmarked wrought iron studio door in New York City's Chelsea district. The brief and contentious reunion that year came with an almost mythic legacy to alienated youth, who ever since punk in the late seventies, and Joy Division's famous reinterpretation of 'Sister Ray,' were generationally fixed on the Velvet Underground's notoriety as misunderstood, intransigent garage fuckers, romantics who'd lost out in the interests of storming the future. With Reed's lyrical panache reconfirmed by *New York*, Cale's consistent cult diversification between pop and classical, and Moe Tucker's continuing to make garage records, three of the Velvets had never really gone away, and if their solo efforts fell short of their integrated sonic attack, then their enigmatically schemed reunion was eagerly anticipated.

Lou was as always unrepentant about age being any impediment to the Velvet Underground or to musicianship in general:

'I sit and play guitar every day, playing that shit because I like it, and I'll do it when I'm 90. Who has the balls to say I'm not allowed to do that? We're not aiming at teenyboppers. People don't come and see us for our looks, that's not what this is about. If you're into costumes and smoke machines, there's all these other things to listen to. I ran through that gamut when I was younger, and it was kinda fun up to a point, but I mean, you lose interest in it after a couple of months, it's just theatrics.'

But what Lou was most anxious to confirm, in his inveterately guarded personal way, was the durability of the songs, and their apparent timeless-ness as subcultural rock classics that hadn't and weren't going to go away.

'Like I said, this stuff holds up. That's a song ['Heroin'] from 1967, but there you go, as contemporary today as it was then. I always tried not to use contemporary slang so the songs could be released tomor-row. That to me is part of good writing. You hear twenties Dixie-land and go, "No way." But you can play our stuff to people today and other than the fact that it's recorded so badly, they'd say "Who's this group?" "Oh, the band we heard in a club a couple of months ago . . ." I hope everyone understands. We're not in it for the money. I really hope we can make a lot of people happy by giving them the chance to see this stuff done live. The fun part's the playing, the gratifying part'll be to turn people onto it.'

Do we interpret this as genuine creative altruism on Lou's part, the assumed lack of interest in money, or simply cynicism given that the three other band members all needed money as an incentive to reunite? For Moe Tucker, who didn't even have a car, let alone a house, 'The money aspect is like winning the lottery to me,' she confessed to journalist Max Bell; while Sterling Morrison confided to *Rolling Stone* editor David Fricke, 'It was pride that kept us apart. But it was also pride that made us do well. Nobody cares more about our legacy than we do.'

No new studio recordings were promised, no apocalyptic flameouts rumoured as part of the band's reconstructed ethic, and Morrison, who was working as a tugboat pilot, was the most philosophic in reviewing the band's stickup history:

> 'It is odd the way the band just sort of dissolved without any seeming reason. There were no big blow ups, no angry fights – people just fell off as it went along. Lou dropped off. It was very strange . . . and since there was never any great apocalyptic moment where we said, "Screw it, enough is enough, no more of this," that's made it possible for us to come back, just as casually.'

It was John Cale who brought anticipations of a renewed band creativity to the reunion, including the hope of new studio recordings, and the avoidance of mechanical re-workings onstage of material by now over-associated with the Velvet Underground's legacy.

> 'When we first came to discuss it, it was important to do some new stuff, so that we could demonstrate that whatever the four of us did before was not inured in 1969. So as soon as we found out that we could do some improvisations, it was roaring away there . . . If you're asking me today do I think we're kicking ass as much as we did in 1968 – not quite, but almost.'

If Cale's interest in mechanical recreation was purely academic, then his disappointment at Reed's lack of impulse to work on new recordings was seminal to the renewed tensions in the band, with only one new song 'Coyote' emerging from their pre-tour rehearsals.

There was also the degrading, insulting and ultimately demeaning behaviour of Sylvia Reed as road manager to the band members, treating them as uniformly subservient to Lou, and as no more than a backing band, with Morrison and Cale reacting furiously to being humiliated, and to the fact that Lou travelled exclusively alone to gigs in a white stretch limo. Cale too was deeply critical of Lou's guitar playing, suggesting in his autobiography it was sub-standard, and let the band down through technical inefficacity. In his autobiographical account of the European reunion tour, Cale recounts how to his mind Lou was incapable of modulating his instrument that was too loud, a volume exacerbated by the fact he would step on the wrong pedal. The regular exchange of guitars onstage by Lou's technician, some for open tuning and others for regular, severely compromised the band's garage banditry and were to Cale's mind superfluous, and to Tucker's inept and gratuitous.

But right from the band's incepted reformation it was Sylvia Reed who was the singular antagonist to any sense of equality, and right on the edge of being jettisoned from Lou's life, her credit cards recalled, her bank accounts cancelled, she attempted to intervene in Reed and Cale's contention about publishing. With Lou angrily stopping the rehearsal, an indignant Sylvia showed up to be faced down by Cale's glowering anger.

> '"This is a band business," I said. "Are you a member of the band? You're not, are you? Right. So why don't you stay out of it?" She said, "I manage Lou Reed." And I said, "Yeah, you do, but you do not manage the Velvet Underground, so there's a slight adjustment of your sights there."'

Whatever the conflicting anxieties and financial rivalries, *Songs For Drella* had proved that Reed and Cale united maximised each other's creative potentialities, with Cale bringing to his largely lyrically based songwriting a musicianship Lou lacked, Cale's facilities as melodist and producer, colouring and, in the case of *Drella*, enhancing Lou's three-chord structures into sophisticated chamber music.

The other problem with a Velvet Underground reunion was that there was nothing the band could do to match the legend that had grown up around it, and that the danger was more in demythologising the past rather than re-mythologising the present by playing old material. Cale's point was that the songs had been done better in their spontaneously raw unproduced originals, and that only by recording and playing new material could the band reinforce its uniquely avant-garde reputation. Cale, unlike Reed, wanted to revitalise the Velvet's resources, rather than recreate material that could never match the originals as deconstructive, untutored garage. Personalised guitar technicians didn't fit into Cale's concept of a still subversively motivated Velvet Underground, regenerated by killer energies and twisted contempt for orthodoxy.

Reviewing the second night of the Velvet's tour at the Playhouse, Edinburgh, on June 2, 1993, John Rockwell, writing for the *New York Times*, singled out Moe Tucker as the band's indispensably forceful drive-unit:

> 'Indeed there was much to cheer. Mr Reed still sings with the same ominous distinctiveness; Mr Cale is still the same multi-faceted musical saboteur; Mr Morrison still contributes a guitar sound of weight and solidity. The revelation on Thursday, though, was the diminutive Ms Tucker's drumming. Standing at her kit and whacking away, she makes a tom-tom-of-doom sound that inspired straight-ahead punk drumming for a generation. The effect is not guilty or amateurish; it is rocklike in the granite sense of that word, the foundation on which the band could build a creative future to match its potently nostalgic past.'

Sadly, the concept of a creative future wasn't to be, as Sterling Morrison's resentment erupted into backstage anger at Lou and Sylvia's disdain for Reed's backing band, treated according to Morrison as abject supernumeraries. Beginning on June 1, 1993, at Edinburgh, the Velvet Underground played two London dates, one at The Forum on June 5, followed by Wembley Arena on June 6, as well as doing the Glastonbury Festival on June 25 as a marginally shambolic uncoordinated affair. Playing Amsterdam, Rotterdam, Hamburg, Czech Republic at the invitation of Vaclav Havel, Berlin, Strasbourg and three nights, June 15, 16 & 17 at L'Olympia, Paris, all of which were filmed for an official live recording, the band underwent the humiliation of supporting U2 for three dates, two in Switzerland, and one at Hippodrome des Vincennes, Paris, before playing the Roskilde Festival, Denmark, on July 2.

Despite the prodigious demand for tickets and the instantly sold out shows, the Velvet Underground predictably lacked explosive frisson, something evident on the live double CD produced by Reed's guitarist Mike Rathke, rather than Cale, and on the commercially released video.

Reed's approach is competently automated rather than improvisational, sullen rather than idiosyncratically flat, and demystification rather than invention is very much the Velvet's ubiquitous branding on tour. By the time the band reached Italy in early July, playing at Udine, Bologna, Milano and terminating at Napoli on July 9, band tensions were detonative and ready to fulminate like the wick in a petrol bomb. Cale takes up the story:

> 'One night in Italy, I think it was Bologna, I was doing 'Waiting For The Man' with a huge orchestral introduction, and I was trying to give them the tempo from the piano but I was too far away. Lou went and told my tech to turn the piano off. At that point I was ready to knock his teeth down his throat. He was getting stranger, and I couldn't deal with that.'

There was the additional problem for audiences too, in that Lou had so consistently exploited the Velvet Underground back catalogue, through the variant permutations of his solo career, from crisp rock to brainfade heavy metal, laconic apathy, diaristic professional, that audiences were inculcated with numbers that had become standards like 'Waiting For The Man', 'Heroin', 'Sweet Jane', 'Pale Blue Eyes', 'Rock'n'Roll' and 'Sister Ray', played for two decades with transitional backing bands, and finally with the reformed Velvet Underground. For some of the audience the indigo was long washed out of the fabric, leaving bleached, no-colour blue jeans. Cale remarks on how flying back from Italy at the end of the tour, he looked across at Lou and had the split-second realisation, 'This guy is empty', meaning of inspiration, something Cale attributed to the intensive shock treatment Reed had undergone in his teens.

Hopes for a proposed Velvet Underground US tour quickly disintegrated in a clash of warring emails between Reed and Cale. Reed's attitude to a projected MTV *Unplugged* show was conditioned by adamant demands that he would only record with the Velvets if he got to produce the resulting album, with Cale proposing the advantages of working with an outsider producer, more attuned to the times. Mashed by Reed's control-freakery, and seething at his patronising attitude, Cale finally terminated relations by sending Reed a nine-page fax telling him exactly what he thought of him from which there was no reparation or return. In 1994 Sire, manifestly displeased with Reed's failure to capitalise on new recordings with the Velvet Underground, failed to renew his contract, and at the same time Sylvia consulted divorce lawyers, cleaning Reed of another slice of his constantly updated life and career. Cale was typically dissatisfied with the live album as redundant product representing a remake of a past it was unnecessary to exhume:

> 'What the live album represents to me is the bare minimum of respect for the capabilities of the four of us. The bare minimum is shown in that. Anybody can play a song the way they did years ago, but to come up with something new? That's another kettle of fish altogether – and I was only interested in that.'

In 1994 Moe Tucker released *Dogs Under Stress*, originally titled *Inexplicably Spanked While Leading A Conga Line*, with Sterling Morrison contributing guitar to five of the tracks, including overs of Bo Diddley's 'Crackin' Up' and Ricky Nelson's 'Poor Little Fool', in the way that Reed had contributed guitar to two of her previous albums, *Life In Exile After Abdication* (1989) and *I Spent A Week There The Other Night* (1991) to which Reed, Cale and Morrison all donated colourful instrumental flavours, while Reed's new proposed solo venture, an album of covers, was turned down by Sire.

The untimely fragmentation of the Velvet Underground, largely attributed to Reed's exploitation of band members, and his irrepressibly autocratic desire to monopolise all financial and band concerns, coincided with Britain's Channel 4 screening an eight-hour tribute to the Velvets and Andy Warhol that registered 400,000 viewers, indicative of the band's continuing high profile cult legacy. Minus the separatist Reed, Cale, Morrison and Tucker reconvened to perform live at the Andy Warhol Museum, Pittsburgh, inspirationally colouring impromptu soundtracks for Warhol's films *Eat* and *Kiss*. Working as a trio, they'd earlier recorded demos for an album, despite Sterling Morrison's still undiagnosed non-Hodgkin's lymphoma, as the virulent cancer strike-force from which he would die on 30 August 1995, the day after his 53rd birthday, still bitter from Sylvia Reeds' brutal slapdown of the reunion to which he'd given consolidated chutzpah and individual firepower.

Morrison, who'd given up an academic life to support his family piloting tugboats in the Houston Ship Channel, was if anything the most subversive rocker in the Velvet Underground, rejecting the notion that lyrics were superior to the driving beat of rock'n'roll, a viewpoint that may have been intended as a denigration of Reed. Referring initially to Elvis Costello's lyric input, Morrison professed the view:

> 'You're rocking to Elvis Costello, but did you ever sit down, Jack, and listen to the lyrics? Well, no, Jack, I never sit down and listen to lyrics because rock'n'roll is not sit-down-and-listen-to-lyrics music. Why is it that the Velvet Underground's celebrated lyricsmith never published a lyrics sheet? Was that to make you strain to hear the lyrics that you never could hear? No. It's because they were saying "Fuck you, if you wanna listen to lyrics, then read the *New York Times*." It has nothing to do with the intellectual apprehension of content.'

Morrison's indignant subjugation of rock lyrics to secondary importance is in direct contradistinction to Reed's repeated endorsement of the lyric content being seminal to and epitomising the band's irreducibly New York cool, as part of the downtown Manhattan art scene, and the sex and drugs danger of the city at night, lyricised into intellectual rock.

Morrison's contempt for Reed's literary pretensions was never more forcibly expressed than after the reunion's irreconcilable disbandment. Morrison regarded rock as primal, beat up noise, the dynamic rhythm the involvement, with the lyrics subservient to the music.

> 'If you're going to rock music to learn something verbally rather than physically or viscerally, then you're in a sad shape, baby. Death to me – and one of the reasons why I wanted to stop playing was when we had to start doing those giant sit down things, where you stood on the edge of the stage and you'd look at people sitting down, gazing up reverently.'

Morrison explodes Reed's belief that the Velvet Underground was an elect academy, somehow intellectualised by his writing into an exclusion zone, in which there was no competition. Reed's self-promoted belief that he was rock's superlative lyricist, while denigrating the medium as semi-moronic, was in itself a confused ethic, inviting the sort of lacerating criticism provided by Sterling Morrison.

While the band resented being intimidated by their own reputation, their reunion did little to enhance or re-mythologise it, their propulsion dependent on the shock that they had chosen to reform at all, and in middle age. With Reed yet again working on a novel that never materialised, and beginning a romantic involvement with the musician and performance artist Laurie Anderson, Morrison's death effectively put an end to the Velvet Underground, with Reed declaring emphatically, 'The Velvet Underground will never play again – not that Velvet Underground, which is the only Velvet Underground.' The band were officially inducted into the Rock and Roll Hall of Fame on January 16, 1996, Lou Reed, John Cale, Moe Tucker and Martha Morrison attending the illustrious inauguration, though one-time member Doug Yule was excluded from the ceremony. As a tribute to Sterling Morrison the band performed a new elegiac song, 'Last Night I Said Goodbye To My Friend', although Cale found it personally unforgiveable that Reed had failed to attend Morrison's memorial service some months earlier, despite his writing a moving article on Morrison called 'Velvet Warrior' for the *New York Times*.

For many critics and fans, the unsung hero of the reunion tour remained the diminutive Moe Tucker, whose indomitably punk drumming came as a revelation to audiences unaware of how she played authoritatively, dominantly, standing up using a simplified drum kit of tom toms, a snare drum and an upturned bass drum, playing with mallets rather than drumsticks. The mother of five who lived in Georgia, and had joined the band in 1965 after dropping out of Ithaca College to work for IBM as a keypunch operator, and who was now working in the computer business, was the real retainer of the band's punkishness, unique in her raw jungle energies, earning from the usually parsimonious Reed the praise 'She's one of the greatest drummers in the world.'

209

'To Lou, everybody's homosexual,' Cale once commented, and as Lou set about recording his new studio album *Set The Twilight Reeling*, his ambivalent sexual life was again thrown into confusion by his unlikely involvement with Laurie Anderson.

10

Sex With Your Parents (Motherfucker)

POST-VELVETS, Reed's next studio affair was a tight urban excursion into churned emotions, the breakup of a badly extenuated marriage, a romantic liaison, and the general kick-about politics and day-by-day concerns of his environmental matrix, New York. *Set The Twilight Reeling* benefits from loud compression, with Reed stoking all guitars and accompanied as a trio by Fernando Saunders on bass and Tony Smith on drums, with occasional resonant horns from Oliver Lake adding to the dark sonic amalgam. The album has a gut rumble, a twitchy thunder-moving–in atmospheric that comes at the listener as disturbing, visceral menace, with Lou's chugging guitar sounding like a car revving in an underground car park, as its firepower chases into you. In many ways the successor to *New York*, the virulent anger expressed benefits from being modified into filtered lowlife menace. The sound squeezes the listener into corners from which there is no escape: *Set The Twilight Reeling* is as rock dystopian as the mashed autopsy of a Francis Bacon portrait anatomised into catastrophic implosion.

As the backstory to some of the album's input, after jettisoning Sylvia Morales from every aspect of his personal and professional life Reed had become involved with the experimental performance artist Laurie Anderson, best known for her 1981 crossover pop hit 'O Superman (For Massenet)', a smash hit in the UK. The two met at the John Zorn Festival, Munich, 1992, when Reed asked Anderson to read something with his band, an experience she described as 'loud, intense, and a lot of fun', with Reed the omnivorous tech geek initially attracted to the Mac she was using at the time for soundscapes. Like Rachel before her, Anderson knew nothing of the Velvet Underground's music and their prototypical influence on most subsequent subcultural genres of rock music. 'I liked him right away,' Anderson recalled, 'but I was surprised he didn't have an English accent. For some reason I thought the Velvet Underground were British, and I had only a vague idea of what they did . . . I was from a different world.'

It seems extraordinary, given Anderson was born in 1947, that as an innovative avant-garde experimentalist she was hardly aware of the impacted musical legacy created by the abrasively edge-pushing Velvet Underground. But things rapidly progressed, and on their first date Lou asked Laurie to meet him in an electronics store where they geeked out at new musical gadgetry, before dinner, catching a movie and walking through the city locked into conversation. It was casual, nothing special, a stroll in New York rain.

Consolidating their relations, Laurie recalled, 'Lou and I played music together, became best friends and then soul mates, travelled, listened to and criticised each other's work, studied things together, butterfly hunting, meditation, kayaking.' It's notable she omits the word lovers, for the more transcendent qualifier, soul mates.

She goes on to tell us of things they developed as a part of intimacy:

> 'We made up ridiculous jokes, stopped smoking 20 times, fought; learnt to hold our breath underwater, went to Africa, sang opera in elevators, made friends with unlikely people; followed each other on tour when we could, got a sweet piano-playing dog, shared a house that was separate from our own places, protected and loved each other.'

If *Set The Twilight Reeling* is about breakup and restart, political tensions and inevitable personal obsessions, its tone is confiding, grave, humorous, big city, and given Reed, assumed superiority over every other possible rock contender. Played loud, the sound tunnels like insistent subway reverb, with Lou's guitar effects spooking the amygdala with rough panic. If the songs are often too long and too wordy to develop hooks, then it's the vitriolic slashing anger of 'Sex With Your Parents (Motherfucker)' that stands out for its shattering of Republicans, including their Presidential candidate Bob Dole. Aiming to slice off their balls, Lou openly brands them with incest as the core of their undemocratic policies. The song's a polemical tour-de-force of seething invective. 'I was getting so sick of this right wing republican shit/ these ugly old men scared of young tit and dick/ so I tried to think of something that made me sick/ and there it was – sex with your parents', Reed unapologetically snarls at his declared enemy. Only Lou would have the audacity to theme a pop song on incest as a central, not implicit theme, and carry it off with such malevolent panache. 'Something fatter or uglier than Rush Rambo/ something more disgusting than Robert Dole/ something pink that climbs out of a hole/ and there it was sex with your parents.'

Designating the whole lot 'motherfuckers', the gynaecological disgust expressed in the lyric is also part of Reed's everlasting sexual fear of women – he understandably never became a father – and partly moved Anderson into his spacious apartment on Christopher Street, the city environment synonymous with being gay.

Produced by Reed and recorded at the Roof, New York City, *Set The Twilight Reeling* is arguably his best vocally recorded album since *Coney Island Baby*, a neglected anomaly displaying not only civic protest, but corrosive riffs that flavour songs that are spiky, romantic and given natural bruise colours by his taut personality. After a trilogy of specifically focussed albums, Reed was anxious to go eclectic and pick up selective material from what was around and happening in his personal life. As he told *Billboard*, 'I just wanted to rock after *Magic And Loss*. I didn't want to post the burden of it having to be thematic on myself, so I told myself, just write whatever. And if it was connected in anyway, that's OK.'

The album's opener, the surreal quirky 'Egg Cream', celebrating a Brooklyn chocolate milkshake that featured in Lou's childhood, and platformed by the low thunder of Lou's guitar, is frothy with free associated imagery and random frivolity. 'Egg Cream', mapping some of Lou's favourite Brooklyn places like Totonno's for Pizza and Becky's for Egg Cream, is also weirdly angled into a drug song. 'For fifty cents you got a shot/ chocolates bubbles up your nose/ that made it easier to deal with knife fights/ and kids pissing in the street.'

Lou's inured sense of urban realism, as though New York is coded into his DNA, is never absent from *Set The Twilight Reeling*, like oxidised grime coating his lyrics and infectiously minatory riffs. It's not surprising the album includes a song called 'NYC Man', given Lou's superglue identification with the city: a number that integrates the insecure ups and downs of his new relationship into its rocky texture. Drug-free, drinking mineral water and Diet Coke, his only concession to alcohol being occasional very good wines, and boosting his depleted system with an addiction to pistachio nuts as health fad, Lou on 'NYC Man' clearly fears Anderson's rejection in lyrics that are lazy, awkwardly forced and don't scan. 'It can only lead to trouble if you break my heart/ if you accidentally crush it on the Ides of March/ I'd prefer you were straightforward/ you don't have to go through all of that/ I'm a New York City man, baby/ say "go" and that is that.' In this instance, Lou doesn't squeeze much lyric juice out of his city with the title promising more than the lyric ever delivers. With Reed over pretentiously dragging a litter of Shakespearean characters into the song, Brutus, Caesar, Macbeth, Lady Macbeth, Hamlet and Lear to qualify his emotional state, his own lyric falls flat by comparison. It's still another example of Lou hijacking literary heritage to no effect other than his own lyrical detriment and adding surface but no depth to his song.

It was a repeat pattern in Lou's life as a homosexual that whenever he met a woman who appeared interested in his potential for bisexuality, he rushed directly into marrying her, Bettye Kronsdat, Sylvia Morales, and now the resistant Laurie Anderson, whose blocking of Lou's romantic path is the inspirational scaffold for much of *Set The Twilight Reeling*. The stormy brew located in its unmitigating guitar weaponry on Lou's part, seems as though he's gunning his depressive aspect into miserable alert to have Laurie concede, though his attempts to reconstruct Velvet Underground and Hendrix feedback are only partial and rarely throw switches on red alert.

'Finish Line', Lou's exit song for Sterling Morrison, lacks the elegiac empathy summoned on *Songs For Drella*, but it is a token gesture towards his old friend and Velvet's noise partner, for whom the reunion was a bitter, creatively redundant experience in which Morrison felt continually sidelined to Reed's imposingly centrifugal domination of band focus. 'Two rented brothers, their faces keep changing/ just like these feelings I have for you/ and nothing's forever not even, five minutes/ when you're headed for the finish line', Reed acknowledges, without ever personally characterising Sterling, or giving us any significant insight into his individuality as someone Lou had known since his Syracuse student days. Lou's allegorical lyric is particularly ungenerous and general, rather than personalised and specific, and his subject deserved better, given Lou's ability to access Warhol's invincibly enigmatic personality and individualised high and low points on *Drella*.

Reviewing the album for *Rolling Stone*, David Fricke was affirmative about his positive listening experience, remarking, 'Twilight is, in its shotgun way, strong, convincing Reed: prickly, confessional, poisonously funny, unabashedly romantic. And it gets under your skin in a cumulative way. The Motown-by-candlelight intonation of Reed's twangy guitar and whispery vocal is a model of minimalist soul.'

If Anderson is the acknowledged inspiration for *Set The Twilight Reeling*, then the colours never come up bright for this addition, but remain in the blue, industrial grey, stormy purple spectrum, with Reed saying of Anderson's emotional support, 'It's a great relief to have that kind of compassion and back-up available, to have someone who understands what's happening and can actually help you get through it.' As a consolidation of their bond Reed duetted on 'In Our Sleep', a track they had co-written for Anderson's album *Bright Red*, while Anderson contributed to 'Hang On To Your Emotions' from *Set The Twilight Reeling*, to my mind Reed's last great urban album, his final ingestion of New York as the menacing physical extension of his guitar facility, the place he'd intrinsically metabolised, and spat out as tough downtown music. Lou wasn't to repeat this visceral eloquence on the album's successor, *Ecstasy*, and wasn't to stoke his three-chord menu to such effect ever again.

Despite being the public recipient of Reed's scorching tongue on numerous occasions, Robert Christgau remained loyal to his inveterately distempered antagonist.

'Ever since *Sally Can't Dance*, if not 'The Ostrich', Reed has been writing stupid-sounding songs that outrage his intellectual fans and probably his stoner fans too. On his best album in over a decade, including three consecutive "serious" ones, this one includes the backward looking 'Egg Cream' (only a self-hater could resist that hook) and the silly-sexy 'Hooky Wooky' ("Reed reveals: 'fucking Is Fun!") and even the defensively macho-cynical "NYC Man" (asshole's confession as asshole's boast). Hooray for Laurie Anderson, either for distracting him from his various higher callings or for urging him to be himself.'

On the title track, Reed looks to reinvention, re-creation, reconstitution, reconstruction of the self, in the light of a new pathway, that while it can help repair psychological damage, can't usually undo its physical counterpart. Lou looks towards a fictional rebirth in the number's turbulent mix: 'Take me for what I am a star newly emerging/ long simmering explodes inside the self is reeling/ in the pocket of the heart in the rushing of the blood/ in the muscle of my sex in the mindful mindless love/ I accept the new found man and set the twilight reeling.'

Something of Reed's orientation towards revitalising his inner energies was of course due to his practice of Tai Chi under Master Ren Guang-Yi, a champion of Chen Tai Chi, who was to instil in Lou an enduring love of Taijiquan martial arts, to which Lou attributed the more transcendent sense of Chi and well-being that came with commitment to his chosen spiritual discipline, even to the point of carrying his classical Chinese weapons with him when on tour. Sensitising his inner resources through ritual practice helped Reed control his normally incandescent anger, itself the residual core of his intolerably repressed upbringing, and also helped divest some of the defensive layers established by Reed to protect his mercurially charged sensitivity. The opening of this pathway too was a necessarily human one if Reed was to establish Anderson as a partner. A note of tranquillity finally colours the title song, 'At 5 a.m. the moon and the sun/ sit set before my window/ light glances off the blue glass we set/ right before the window'; an admission of fragile aesthetic missing from Reed's work for decades.

The anecdotal and the trivial. Colin Summers was a computer consultant whose clients Penn & Teller introduced him to notable New Yorkers, and he regularly encountered Lou enthusiastically browsing the racks at his favourite Bleecker Street Records in New York City's West Village. They would sometimes meet for dinner at Col Legno and, during the time when he was divorcing Morales and the recording of *Set The Twilight Reeling*, Reed recalled a memory of Nico while they were walking together through East Village.

> 'It was when Nico was still with the Velvets and we were invited to some happening. There were some big spaces over here back then. So I am stoned out of my mind, really on every drug I have in my apartment. And I am carrying enough drugs for the rest of the people we bump into at the party. And Nico is high as a kite. We're walking down a street just like this one, with the big flagstones. And Nico is wearing a skirt just like that one', motioning to Jill. 'And suddenly she says, "Lou I have to pee".'

> 'And I tell her we're only a couple of blocks just hold it, but she's so high it's not going to happen. And she's not wearing underwear and hikes up her skirt and squats right there on the sidewalk. I'm stunned, and stoned, and I have to stop walking and I look out into the street, over the row of parked cars, right into the eyes of a cop who has pulled up in his cruiser. I figure it's the end. I have enough drugs on me to keep me in jail for decades. The cop stares at me, then looks past me so I know he can see Nico and says, 'House train her, will ya?' bloops the siren and keeps driving down the street.'

It's a Lou cameo increasing our sense of regret that he never applied his talents to autobiography, a first-hand account of the seminally crazy and creatively innovative years he lived through, which could have been built into inimitably fascinating memoir.

Another important song mapping Reed's personal transitioning at the time is 'Trade In', which integrates the sinister and the redemptive as the familiar lick of *Set The Twilight Reeling*. The song has surreal overtones in common with the Velvet's 'The Gift', 'Lady Godiva's Operation' and

'Murder Mystery'; only it's more punishingly lean and guitar bruised. 'Trade In' is another reintegration song on Lou's past, excising his past in the interests of rebuilding the present, or at least on an imaginative level. Referring undoubtedly to himself, Reed sings, 'He actually was murdered/ I had taken him apart/ And when I put him back together/ I couldn't find his heart/ It was resting underneath a chair/ In a bed of bright tin foil.' With chords that sound like a guitar blowjob, and with Lou reinforcing the song's partly shamanic induction with the line, 'I've met a woman with a thousand faces' and referring to his past derisively as 'a life spent listening to assholes', he struggles through art with the album's unified quest: psychic and physical rehabilitation reinforced by bluesy motivation of a guitar tunneling like storm through the city.

'Hookwooky' like 'Egg Cream' is an infectiously humorous rocker about sex and jealousy, with a scorching guitar solo raised out of the abyss, and was released as a single to zero airplay. *Twilight* is too concertised as a singular suite of songs to excerpt singles, and needs to be listened to in entirety to appreciate its irresolvable variation on a theme: imaginative rebirth, and its physical opposite.

As an incestuous spin-off of their relationship, and with Anderson invited to curate the prestigious Meltdown Festival at London's Royal Festival Hall in 1997, Lou was duly invited to perform and delivered an amplified acoustic affair with moments of hot musical electricity that was recorded for release as *Lou Reed Perfect Night: Live In London*. With Reed as geeky techie, aural obsessive, looking for a unique sound with a newly purchased acoustic guitar, and selecting a career-spanning set performed with appropriate delicacy, the outcome was magical.

As a quasi-unplugged performance, turning up surprises like 'The Kids', 'Kicks', 'I'll Be Your Mirror' and three new songs from the projected *Time Rocker*, a collaborative opera with Robert Wilson, 'Talking Book', 'Into The Divine' and 'Why Do You Talk', as well as retrievals like 'Coney Island Baby', 'Vicious' and 'Perfect Day', the set is quintessential nineties Reed evoking romantic twinkles in the dark.

Lou was exuberant about his new acoustic weapon, given its first live airing at the Meltdown. 'And then I discovered that I can plug straight into one of my amps, and that was the sound I wanted to hear; amplified purity. I had gotten this incredible acoustic guitar, and I still remember in the old apartment plugging it in- what an astonishing sound- and I thought I want everything to sound like this.'

Lou's euphoria over his instrument carried into the performance.

> 'The night of the show, when the band and I hit the stage, I was really pumped. I had an acoustic guitar with the sound of diamonds, a sound that no one had ever really heard before. I had a sound and I knew it, and I was going to be able to share it – me and the guys in the band.'

And putatively the album produces the sound of diamonds in its guitar figures, and while it isn't *Rock'n'Roll Animal* Part 2 in terms of asymmetric metal warfare, the set captures Reed in an accidental moment meant to happen, and delivers Reed as he'd deepened and mellowed into implacable raconteur, but with just the dignity to soften his spikiest acerbic edges.

As a mark of going serious, Lou collaborated with Robert Wilson, the American experimental theatre stage director, best known for his collaboration with Philip Glass, *Einstein On The Beach*, to mixed reception on the *Time Rocker*, taking its inspiration from H.G. Wells' *The Time Machine*, and using the book as the basis of a quasi-modern opera, to which Darryl Pinckney provided dialogue. The fantastic theme, beginning with the disappearance of Dr Procopius from 19th Century London, has their domestics Nick and Pricilla falsely accused of their master's murder, before escaping into time as a giant fish that time-slips from ancient Egypt to a 17th Century opium den to modern day Kansas and beyond as it wormholes through time and space.

The theme didn't really accommodate Lou's lyrical acumen. He is always best as an objective observer rather than subjective empathiser, a commentator rather than creator of imaginative fictions – hadn't he endlessly started novels to no affect? – with the *New York Times* commenting 'profundity eludes Mr Reed's words and the thoughts behind them.'

Wilson, also known for subversively pushing the boundaries of theatre, wasn't into compacted speed or noise (i.e. rock), preferring slow motion theatre through manipulating time. Wilson's *The Life And Times Of Joseph Starling* was a 12-hour performance, while *Kamountain And Guardenia Terrace* was staged on a mountain in Iran and lasted an entire seven days.

The uncompromisingly experientialist Wilson claimed cautiously that working on *Time Rocker* taught him 'to appreciate that the loudness of sound', but Reed wasn't in this instance the best collaborator. Wilson's pioneering was the spatialisation of his shows, and he brought to his performance a deep intellectual conception of what he was staging. 'Spoken theatre seemed to me like a bad lecture,' he commented on his forward-pointing aims. 'I always felt uncomfortable. There was not enough virtual space onstage and not enough mental space in the construction. All that changed when I saw Eastern theatre, when I saw Suzushi Hanayagi, the Kabuki actress.'

It was Lou's irreducible conviction that rock would never be taken seriously as good literature, and the intellectual insecurity it inevitably provoked, that drove him into two collaborations with Robert Wilson, as though to reinforce his lifetime's obsession with creating the rock equivalent of the novel he could never write. Lou simply wouldn't accept the lack of symbiosis between the two forms, which while both may be concerned with narrative as a cross-over lack congruity on the basis of divergent timelines. Rock is of necessity an intensely compressed first or third person narration; limited by length as to its characterisation – Bob Dylan is a rare example of introducing multi-characters into his songs – whereas the novel, by the virtue of length and character development, whether linear or non-linear, occupies a much bigger creative window. Reed's unfounded intellectual insecurity and continuous reinforcement in interviews that he was a Syracuse lit graduate, seemed to imply frustration on a much deeper level, possibly that his university grades should have been higher, and that his dismissal on a post graduate level, largely as the consequence of drugs, had somehow marked him with a sense of self-failure he was forever attempting to redress.

Neatly attempting to reconcile the history of rock and fiction into one comparable genealogy, Reed had argued in 1987 for the compatible unity of the two as one expression.

'All through this, I've always thought that if you thought of all of it as a book then you have the Great American Novel, every record as a chapter. They're all in chronological order. You take the whole thing, stack it and listen to it in order, there's my Great American Novel.'

It's a neat idea, the encyclopaedic cataloguing of the entire chronology of rock interfacing the Great American Novel, but the two don't fit so ideally. The concept or ideal of the Great American Novel, first conceived by the Civil War poet, John DeForest, in an article of the same name in *The Nation*, published on January 9, 1868, evolved into a metaphor for identity, an unachievable quest in both style and theme as being the most accurate representation of the times in which the novel was written or set, exhibiting at the same time a specific language in which to capture the unique American experience, adaptable to the diction of any region.

Never attainable, challengingly and elusively enticing, it was a formidable code for Reed to try and crack through rock. The accepted contenders or practitioners chasing the dream included Herman Melville with *Moby Dick* (1851), Mark Twain with *Adventures Of Huckleberry Finn* (1884), Scott Fitzgerald with *The Great Gatsby* (1928), William Faulkner with *The Sound And The Fury* (1929), Margaret Mitchell with *Gone With The Wind* (1936), John Dos Passos with *USA* (1938), J.D. Salinger with *The Catcher In The Rye* (1951), Ralph Ellison with *Invisible Man* (1952), Jack Kerouac with *On The Road* (1957), Harper Lee with *To Kill A Mockingbird* (1960) and Thomas Pynchon with *Gravity's Rainbow* (1973), to name just a few of the writers who'd left some sort of recognised signature on the trail to nailing this illusory rainbow.

Reed's contentious belief that rock posited equal candidature for the great cultural mirage given palpable form seemed always theoretically to pursue Scott Fitzgerald's design in *The Great Gatsby* to produce in his own words, 'Something new – something extraordinary and beautiful and simple and intricately patterned.'

In terms of indigenous demographic, rock has an equal claim to the title, if it's novelistic, emerging in the US as it did, primarily from a combination of African-American genres, such as blues, rhythm & blues, then called race music, jazz, gospel, Western swing and country music. Early examples of rock were instinctively, presciently contagious, Goree Carter's 'Rock Awhile' (1949), Jimmy Preston's 'Rock The Joint' (1949), Jackie Brenston and the Delta Cats' 'Rocket 88' (1951) and the seminal propagator of the genre, Bill Haley's 'Rock Around The Clock' (1954) that succeeded in inciting youth riots. For Reed with his academic knowledge of rock, and more importantly, there was Chuck Berry's 'Maybellene' (1955) featuring possibly the first electric guitar distortion created accidentally by Berry's small valve amplifier.

The problem for Reed's grandiose aspiration was that his deliberately serious later works failed to match his literary vision, and if in the compressed minimalist space a rock lyric occupies, it's his work with the Velvet Underground that best qualifies for rock being integrated into the context of the Great American Novel, with songs like 'Heroin', 'Sister Ray', 'Waiting For The Man', 'Black Angel's Death Song' and 'Sweet Jane'.

Reed's inability to separate the two mediums, literature and rock, caused him pain and disillusionment, the fundamental dichotomy preventing him from fully enjoying his considerable status as New York's chain-smoking, leather jacketed, Ray-Ban wearing street poet who'd got rich on the back of his incessant pursuit.

The trivial and the anecdotal again, as excerpt. Ed Morales, no relation to Sylvia, tells us:

> 'Back in the early late nineties, when you could still afford to go to a trendy downtown restaurant, I was trying to impress a new girlfriend, so I took her to Indochine across the street from the Public Theatre. Suddenly, a couple of booths down, Lou Reed and Laurie Anderson appeared. It was like the first time I knew they were dating.'

Reed's contributions to the *Time Rocker* fell a long way short of his conceptualised theories, in fact they read and sounded like uninspired cultural commodity, lacking all affinities with Wilson's thematic time slips, and there simply because Reed was again pushing for acceptance by the arty avant-garde, as though the man who had singularly injected decadence into rock was now looking for acceptance as intellectually respectable. Reed's three songs 'Why Do You Talk', a bluesy complaint, 'Into The Divine', a signature rocker, and the best of them, 'Talking Book', a folky, tuneful critique of computers, appear to veer more towards the pedestrian than SF magic, taking us to no special places we've never been before.

Outwardly, despite years of abuse, Reed had changed little, his tightly curled hair cut short, his oddly youthful and angular face carved by wrinkles, like a rehabilitated heroin user, his body still slim, his look unchanged, black T-shirts worn over dark blue jeans, defensive Ray-Bans, rock poet leather jacket, still chain-smoking Spirit cigarettes, and cultivating an implacable base-line arrogance to intimidate audience or interviewers. Lou was to maintain his grizzled ambisexual rock techie signature right up until his death as unmistakably recognisable personal identity, even if the stubborn naivety of his youthful singing voice had coarsened to a punished, leathery, Dylan-like growl. Whatever Lou's dialogue with the mystical through Tai Chi energies, there was no softening of the rude boy attitude he presented to the public.

Reed's successor to *Set The Twilight Reeling* was *Ecstasy* (2000), an album in which the traumatic specifics of relationships, his own and fictionalised, are stripped apart, viciously, compromisingly, disdainfully, unapologetically and worst, sentimentally, in a suite of songs that while lacking the subterranean rumble of *Twilight*, revivify aspects of his affinities with a lowlife demimonde, and the apocalyptic breakdown of his city again into chaotic inequality. Less handgun pointed than *Twilight*, the riffs modified from outward aggro to domestic trouble, *Ecstasy* suffers largely from being too long, and it's extensible parameters don't favour hooks or tight focus in individual songs, particularly 'Tatters' that crosses a prairie instead of a field. Although the semi-confessional themes seem driven by mutual antipathies in Reed's martial relations with Sylvia Morales, and turbulent pockets in his relations with Anderson, the songs reflect the mashed, upended inconsistencies prevalent in most relationships, where good and bad meet a juxtaposed management.

Around the time of *Ecstasy*'s release, Reed gave an interview to *Esquire*, interesting for the light and shapes it threw on what he tried to achieve in his songwriting and what he expected of a pop song. 'I don't mind a repetitive chorus; I mind repetitive verse. I mean, it's the same amount of space. Why should you only have three diamonds, if you can have six? Once you get that idea out of your head, then, if anything, the trouble is not to have 40 of 'em. That's where editing comes in, and rewrites. That's the real secret of everything – rewriting. I always rewrite.'

Lou is of course talking about the process of all good writing being elimination, the extraction of the superfluous phrase for the purposefully compressed, the single exact word replacing a non-specific cluster. Of equal interest in this interview, Reed spoke of neglected songs of his that were amongst his favourites, and both from the mid-seventies, his *Rock'n'Roll Heart* and *Street Hassle* period. 'There's a lot of songs people don't even notice that are my favourites, and they might come under the umbrella of "stupid". Like 'Senselessly Cruel' and 'Shooting Star'. I love that orchestral guitar at the beginning. It's one of the greatest things I ever did, and no one – zero – has ever noticed it.'

And Lou's right, 'Senselessly Cruel' is one of his great, melodic, guitar notated songs of the seventies that could equally have found a place on *Coney Island Baby*, his vocal delivery optimally confident, and 'Shooting Star' quintessentially outpunks punk in its dissipated, relentlessly monotonal delivery, parched, strangulated, dumb.

Reed, who had complained that lyricism deserted him for most of the seventies, either due to a surfeit of drugs and booze as intrepidly hedonistic chutzpah, or due to a preoccupation with cult notoriety that took precedence over work, was at pains in the same insightful interview to hint at bits of his working method that are of course no more than approximate.

'People say, "Do you keep these riffs and ideas and everything? Because then when you make a record, you could just go to the file cabinet?" And I've always thought of doing something like that, but I don't. I just don't do it. I listen to these words flooding by, and once in a while, one just stays' it's very strange.'

Lou in a typically uncompromising pose, Berlin, May, 2003. EAMONN McCABE/REDFERNS

French culture minister Jack Lang awards Lou with the insignia of Knight of the Order of Arts and Letters, Paris, February 18, 1992.
PIERRE GUILLAUD/AFP/GETTY IMAGES

US President Bill Clinton meets Lou following his performance during the State Dinner for Czech President Vaclav Havel in Washington DC, September 16, 1998. RICHARD ELLIS

Lou poses with his Special International Award at the 50th Ivor Novello Awards at Grosvenor House, London, May 26, 2005. GARETH DAVIES/GETTY IMAGES

Lou hugs his partner, performance artist Laurie Anderson, backstage at Arts On The Highwire, a benefit concert for the New York Arts Recovery Fund held at the Hammerstein Ballroom, in 2002. Lou and Anderson would marry in 2008. RICHARD CORKERY/NY DAILY NEWS ARCHIVE VIA GETTY IMAGES

Lou and Patti Smith in 2007. KEVIN MAZUR/WIREIMAGE

Lou and Laurie Anderson perform together at Giorgio Island, Venice, June 15, 2002. CONTRASTO /EYEVINE

Lou practices Tai Chi in New York's Central Park, April 2001. RICHARD B. LEVINE

Lou with his friend and Velvet Underground fan Vaclav Havel, the first democratically elected president of Czechoslovakia, in 2005.
ALAN PAJER/ISIFA/GETTY IMAGES

Lou on stage with James Hetfield and Lars Ulrich of Metallica at the 25th Anniversary Rock & Roll Hall of Fame Concert at New York's Madison Square Garden, October 30, 2009. Lou and Metallica would collaborate on the critically censured album *Lulu*, released in 2011. THEO WARGO/WIREIMAGE

Lou with his friend the New York based British photographer Mick Rock at the launch of their book about the album *Transformer*, for which Rock took the iconic sleeve photo, in New York on October 3, 2013. Two weeks later Reed would die from liver disease. THEO WARGO/GETTY IMAGES FOR JOHN VARVATOS

Lou and Laurie Anderson together at the Azuero On The Harbor fundraising event in East Hampton, September 1, 2012. SONIA MOSKOWITZ/GETTY IMAGES

Writing, I mean considered writing, didn't come easy to Lou, and demanded work and endless revision.

On *Ecstasy*, Lou's cool vocal execution takes on paranoia, masochism, infidelity, sexual humiliation, urban conflict, drugs, broken marriage, all of it meshed in his central nervous system from a lifetime of acting weird. In the diatribe written into 'Mad', Reed's incurable misogyny is unapologetic for being caught in bed with a casual pick-up. Rather than apologise he rounds on [Sylvia], 'Dumb, you're dumb as my thumb/ in the wistful morning you threw a coffee cup at my head/ scum, you said I'm scum/ a very lovely and feminine thing to do.' In the song it's Lou who rights himself on the grounds he was tired of what he had, and comes back self-justifying, like throwing a paint pot over his enraged aggressor. It's Lou who's the incendiary even though he's arguably in the wrong.

If Lou's guitar riffs on *Ecstasy* are less forcibly trebly and flatly staccato than his VU mode that persisted on *Twilight*, it's still sound that scares up disquiet, his chords simulating the nasty electro-shock he recalled as voltage from his teens. 'Tatters' is clearly a fictionalised recreation of Lou's marriage to Morales including all the routinal disharmony in which most couples live, dragged in to emphasise martial discord. What stings Lou in the song is verbal insult, the velocity of a recrimination that can't be unsaid, nor the pain of it ever erased from memory – it's like a bullet he narrates; an incurable hurt. 'But what you said/ still echoes in my head/ and I'm still in the hallway/ downstairs sleeping alone instead.' And what was it so stung Reed – the full on accusation of his homosexuality?

Always his most intelligent New York critic, the esteemed Robert Christgau writing for *Rolling Stone* was spot on in eliciting the album's obsessions and emotional complexity laid down with intermittent explosions of brass.

'Dominated emotionally by dark songs about extreme sex and relationships gone sour, it will once again be linked to Anderson, even though many of its details diverge radically from what everyone knows about the couple's life together – that they have no children for instance. Resist the impulse to turn music into gossip and hear

Ecstasy for what it is – a complex, musically gorgeous synthesis of the obsessions that powered Reed's failed 1973 *Berlin* and his great marriage albums of the early Eighties, especially, *The Blue Mask*.'

Reed never appreciated how fortunate he was in having regular critics like John Rockwell and Robert Christgau who brought an intellectual acumen to his work, and a sympathetic comprehension of his aims, and who are rarely found in literary critics addressing the equivalent constitutes in great challenging writing, the very medium to which Lou aspired. Lou's reputation ran parallel to the consolidation given it by the likes of Christgau, who brought an unusually serious appraisal to the variants of Reed's controversially mercurial career. And neither writer lost patience or belief in an artist who insulted them publicly and often scandalously traduced their appreciation of his inscrutably contradictory motives.

In the title track 'Ecstasy' Lou comes as close to the Velvet's 'Some Kinda Love' – 'put jelly on your shoulder/ and lie down on the carpet' – as he ever got using perverse sexuality as the criterion for lyric. In probably the most melodic of the album's long-haul tracks, 'Ecstasy' documents familiar Reed sexual perversity: 'They call you ecstasy/ nothing ever sticks to you/ not Velcro, not scotch tape/ not my arms dipped in glue.' This could be a Velvet's lyric, overhung with traces of 'Coney Island Baby', and it progresses phrase by deviated phrase into typical Lou: 'Not if I wrap myself in nylon/ a piece of duct tape down my back/ love pierced the arrows with the twelve/ and I can't get you back.'

Ecstasy, although little valued for it, is Reed at his most lyrically perverse, and not since the Velvets had he deviantly mined so decadent a library of obsessive emotional and sexual fetishes, particularly in the twisted, lacerating degradation explored in 'Rock Minuet'.

Reed conducted interviews for *Ecstasy* at Sister Ray Enterprises, a converted loft a few floors above a stretch of Broadway at the northern tip of Soho. Minimally furnished, with polished hardwood floors, the white walls hung with artily framed concert posters and photos of Reed, this was effectively his HQ, with an assistant and office dog called Lola. Lou, if he was to be found there, usually sat at a stripped desk, with a pack of cigarettes and two opaque sky-blue drinking glasses, one containing mineral water, the other Diet Coke. By the time of *Ecstasy*, with the album reflecting the rocky downsides of their relationship, Reed and Anderson were considered old New York cool, both having evolved from seventies downtown art rogues into chilled-out mellower revolutionaries, revered more for their reputations than for what they were currently doing. Both were honorary cool and stood for the sort of Warholian connotations of art experiment each new generation tried to emulate. And what Reed had learnt from Warhol as supremely manipulative pop avatar was to invite fame, while at the same time rejecting it, and to defiantly resist pop definition, while at the same time effortlessly exploiting it, so that his ambivalent relationship with critical attention eluded all attempts at categorisation, liberating him into the enviable position of being admired for a medium he professed to hate. Nobody could get into those cold, expressionless, fuck-you eyes and climb out with easy answers or solutions. What was thrown back was often a smart self-consciousness of faults pre-empting criticism, or an arrogant conceit that overrode all conception of the work. A mixture of vanity and truculence framed by interrogative wire-rim glasses or blackout Ray-Bans, Reed's nastiness also constituted his charm as tough art-boy creation, who exalted transvestites, and used his formidable intellect to trash rock music as a brainless modality for illiterates. Crusty, curmudgeonly, monumentally self-regarding, nobody though should forget the superbly defined architecture of Lou's impossible high cheekbones, the signal of lasting good looks that were his outstanding feature. The aesthetic of Lou's cheekbones deserve a chapter in itself.

Ecstasy has its quotient of star tracks that couldn't have been written by anyone other than Lou, like 'Paranoia Key Of E', that's as playfully surreal as 'I Can't Stand It', and if Arthur Rimbaud attributed a hallucinated colour-coding to vowels in his poem 'Voyelles', Black A, White E, Red I, Green U, Blue O then Lou invents a similarly synesthetic vocabulary of chords in 'Paranoia Key Of E'. 'Now you know mania's in the Key of B/ psychosis in the Key of C/ let's hope that we're not meant to be/ in paranoia Key of E.' The song, a typical Lou-dosed restrained rocker, is expressive of doubt over his apparently cemented relationship with Anderson, who by turning up two hours late and showing signs of disaffection put the jitters in an apprehensive Reed.

But for me, it's 'Rock Minuet', possibly the most outrageously deviant Lou song since 'Sister Ray', that commands focus as the album's twisted winner. The story of a 'piss ugly soul', and clearly a fictionalised account of disturbed incidents in Lou's upbringing, the lyric narrates perversion on an epic scale that only he would dare format into adult rock. Apart from the audio–voyeurism of hearing his parents committing sodomy, Lou is invariably relating his own early gay experiences of anonymous sex, when he writes: 'In the gay bars in the back of the bar/ he consummated hatred on cold sawdust/ while the jukebox played backbeats he sniffed coke off a jar/ while they danced to a rock minuet.'

For anyone who mistakenly assumed Lou had dropped his lyric potential to shock, or had sealed his past into a black box recorder, 'Rock Minuet' is one of the most devastatingly decadent songs he was to ever write about teen trauma, parental discord, and aberrant sex to compensate for incurably demoralising low self-esteem. In 'Rock Minuet' Lou explores the same mental and physical geographies of 'Downtown Dirt', anonymous sex, the needle, outlaws on the cold docks, and the alienation that often comes of drugs and same-sex attracted loneliness. And only Lou could insert into a pop song the graphic details of a guy in the back of a warehouse, who gets his sexual kicks from having his eyes sewn up, an experience that induces orgasm, and with the same fetishised extremes of the psycho protagonist in 'Kicks', whose sexual thrills come from sticking dudes with a knife.

Reed's ability to narrate abnormal sexual pathologies in a bored uninterested tone, as though what's happening is commonplace practice, is of course his incredible individual signature, a white-hot frigidity that unleashes sleaze as normal. And *Ecstasy* is saturated in this attribute of sounding casual about the transgressive, deadened by the amoral. It's the classic Lou, at 23 and 58 the unshockable is the basis of his psychological platform from which to create. It's a take it or leave it dispensation in which everything's permissible if it's your reality, and exposing it isn't

228

shocking, it's really nothing at all. The songs on Ecstasy are filmic; they're about a cast of essentially deranged characters, including Lou, who experience life on the edge as a conditioned state.

In an interview not published at the time, called New York's Prince of Darkness, Simon Houpt turned up at Lou's professional niche Sister Ray Enterprises to get a characteristically resistant and prickly response to the *Ecstasy* programme. What seemed notable to the interviewer was Reed's enthusiasm for a recent Warhol exhibition Shadows, and how he spoke of Andy in the present tense, as though his old mentor in the strategic commodification of art was still around and on the New York moment.

Shadows, put on in 2000, dated back to 1979, when Warhol embarked on a journey to isolate images cast by shadow. With his studio assistant Ronnie Cutrone, Warhol took photos of shadows generated by maquettes devised for the sole purpose of creating abstract forms, using these images to develop a silk screen print series with a degree of diamond dust application.

Prominent in support of Andy as immutable icon, Reed expatiated on the artist's cool.

> 'Listen I was at a show of Andy's over at the Dia Gallery, it was called Shadows. It was, like, so fabulous. So fabulous. It was like 84 paintings. And I think there were a few more they didn't have room for. So one album a year is nothing. Really, it's zero. I should be making five albums a year, but . . . the way the record business is set up you can't do that.'

It's highly significant that the association with Warhol recalls the indictment Reed received at the Factory to work, as Warhol considered him lazy and had an aversion to heroin users as apathetic zombies. The command had stuck, to be repeated as 'work' on *Songs For Drella*, and as an indoctrinated self-reproach Lou would increasingly apply, as he grew older and more consciously aware of biological limitations. If Lou had faced down life with reflective wraparounds, he was only too well aware he couldn't apply the same attitude to death.

The inexcusably long centrepiece to *Ecstasy*, the 18-minute drone 'Like A Possum', with little substantiating lyric to merit its directionless expansion, was also a topic Lou was anxious to accommodate into the interview as integral to the idea of himself as a guitar hero. Lou's declared intention was to spatialise rock beyond its accepted highly compressed timeline into the sort of extended frame he'd given 'Sister Ray', 'Murder Mystery', 'Lady Godiva's Operation' and 'The Gift', all Velvet Underground epics defying every regulation of orthodox rock preconceptions. In order words, Lou as Lou, as Lou, as Lou.

> 'I wanted a long song. I wanted you to have a different view of time. I wanted you to realise that it was going to go on long enough, the rock thing, where you could give yourself up to it. You can't normally do that because it's over in three minutes. I didn't want to complicate it; I wasn't doing jazz. You know what I'm saying? This is straight, basic rock. It's a heavy overdrive guitar, but it's user-friendly.'

And what would Lou's idea of user-unfriendly be, post-Metal Machine Music? Peter Cornish, the British effects wizard had built Lou a customised bank of new guitar pedals to augment his aviation drone, and this contributes to the exaggerated assault of 'Possum'. Aggrandising his studio weaponry, Lou found heavy metaphors to substitute for aural shattering. 'I think of it like a punch in the face from Muhammad Ali. Bang. Like a volcanic eruption. Like the glowing beauty of a hot lava stream.'

Lou's verbal equivalents are quite literally lost in translation, but they give us an idea of how he conceived catastrophic noise in his head and how he wanted it to physically and mentally assault the listener, as feedback directive.

Essaying his private life into chaptered rock, *Ecstasy* is driven by emotional breakage and repair with Lou confiding the intimate menu of Sylvia's domestic violence. 'You slapped my face and cried and screamed/ that's what marriage came to mean/ the bitterest ending of a dream.' For once Lou is prepared to admit to his vulnerability, and to his being the recipient rather than perpetrator of violence, something that would have been unthinkable on *Berlin*, where an insultingly aggressive misogyny defeats the idea of women being anything but passively deserving targets of

Lou's violence, as a confused gay man reminded of his possible inability to sexually perform.

Both *Ecstasy* and its predecessor *Set The Twilight Reeling*, are the closest Reed every got to evaluating his past, and its correlation with the present in semi-fictional terms, - most art is a highly selective combination of fact and fiction- but catapulted out of one marriage into the possibilities of another, Lou was prepared to strip something of his defensive layers in the interest of narrowing in on age, with nicotine congested arteries, to excerpt incidents that were high on his agenda to presumably clarify and in the process open pathways to increased knowledge of the present.

Ecstasy, like *Twilight*, is another environmentally New York album, an urban matrix inspired mix of personal turmoil and dystopian apocalypse, abandoned gutted cars, references to President Clinton's cigar bullet skirt-chasing, and the habitual denial of social inequality that had first surfaced on *New York*, and been so signally absent from his work in the Seventies.

The Incidental and the Guitar techie. On perfect night, Lou used a guitar built by Jim Olsen and a Sunrise pickup; and a Fifties-ish amp called the Tone King; and a feedback suppression devise called the Feedbucker; that was the gadget catalyst for the album's unique tonal sound.

And the sound he was after?

> 'Roy Orbison when he played guitar "Ooby Dooby". That's the kind of playing I go out of my mind over to this day. The solo, James Burton's on Ricky Nelson's "Hello Mary Lou". I never went out and got the James Burton model Tele. I think it's strung with what? 03's? Invisible strings.'

The ostrich guitar. While working as a Pickwick staff songwriter, Lou had seen a guy called Jerry Vance tune a guitar where every string was the same, a technique he came to adopt with his VU tuning.

Lyrics. According to Lou he wrote directly onto a computer, deleting all revisions, as his handwriting was illegible, so there are no notebooks cataloguing draft rewrites.

B minor substitution on 'Sweet Jane', arguably his favourite of his songs.

> 'That's the key to the whole song. That's how it's not 'Twist and Shout' or any of the other three-chord songs that go that way. I remember sitting there playing this lick. To me it's one of the great, great licks to play. And it's because of the B-minor – that little hop to the minor chord. And I said, "Sterling, you gotta hear this. Check this out." It was exciting to do that. I still get a kick out of it. I don't know why.'

Guitar start. Lou originally used a Gretsch that a technician Dan Armstrong customised, and when visiting San Francisco met an electronics geek there who built a repeater (i.e. echo) into it, so that Lou appeared to play faster than he really could. He called it a stereo guitar.

Finger Vibrato. One of Lou's technically improvised practices: finger combos off a chord while doing vibrato – the tone is everything.

Weird Stuff. Take the Velvet Underground's 'What Goes On': the chords D, C and G create a song in the key of G, meaning roughly that resolution to the progression is sustained by G. But being Lou, the band subvert the progression, and by emphasising the D rather than the G, they force the resolution in the wrong place, giving the song its inimitable choppy flavour.

What's good? 'As someone who's always been in love with real old, pre-CBS Fenders, I always kind of judge things from that.'

11

The Sound And The Fury

REED entered the 21st century coming on to 60, undeterred in his driving mission to keep on extending rock frontiers and to perfect his live system by playing still louder in pursuit of the elusive chord programmed somewhere into his neural networks, a power that would rival the nerve-propagation speeds of imagining it. If *Ecstasy* was his millennial statement, and so too the publication of his collected lyrics *Pass Thru Fire*, by Hyperion in 2000, then he was, as always, in the process of moving on to maintain his status as Luciferian hipster of rock's nefarious hoi polloi. Lou's look was now laminated, each of the decades folded into his epidermis like the lived – in layers of his leather jacket. The wear and tear given to both were inseparable.

Living in high-end downtown New York in a loft apartment overlooking the Hudson River that he so loved, its sleazy environs repurposed into ambitiously high-priced real estate, Lou was often to be found in the back room of Pastis, his favourite restaurant, where power-breakfasting or brunching stockbrokers met in a faux-continental interior, the blue frigid light thrown off the Hudson bringing the Atlantic up to the windows. Oddly, and theoretically incompatible with the subtle energies evoked by Tai Chi, he continued to chain-smoke in defiance of his bodily recuperation from drink and drugs: undoing the full potentialities of his chosen inner discipline. Leather and denim remained his constants, including black leather trousers and biker boots to accompany an arsenal of variant leather jackets and coats, as well as a small Mandarina Duck designer handbag often worn over his shoulder. The mixture of macho/camp persisted in his irrepressibly theatrical hand gestures, and spontaneous voice intonations, so too his invincible guard when faced by interviewers: his

233

extensive knowledge of digital technology often being used to deflect questions about his celebrated association with New York's underbelly.

Reed's next project, a courageously misconceived and overblown attempt to re-invent Edgar Allan Poe, without the facility to empathise with Poe's extraordinary inventive and tortuously metaphysical imagination, was the wrong subject given often-brilliant execution. Attracted to Poe's enduring reputation as a mythomaniac, opium habituated, mendacious dissembler, who when he was 27 had married his chronically tubercular 13-year-old cousin Virginia Clemm in Baltimore in 1835, as part of his morbid sexual attraction to illness and early death, Reed looked to pick up on mutually shared bad boy associations with his subject.

Reed's knowledge of Poe's work was manifestly marginal, and the idea for the album was precipitated by theatre, in that Reed had got involved with Hal Willner's Halloween shows at St. Ann's Church, where he'd read Poe's *The Tell-Tale Heart* aloud, and become fixed on the idea of germinating an exhaustive album based around Poe's work and life.

This wasn't so easily facilitated. Poe is often credited as the inventor of the detective fiction genre, as well as emergent SF themes, and is best known for his *Tales Of The Grotesque And Arabesque*, published in two volumes in 1839, which included gothic classics like *The Fall Of The House Of Usher*, *The Pit And The Pendulum*, *The Black Cat*, *The Balloon Hoax* and *The Masque Of The Red Death*. The pathological modality of his sensational themes, the amorphousness of his biography and his defiantly elusive subject matter all appealed enormously to Reed who never gets closer than the idea of Poe as he does in *The Raven*, a compounded understanding of the man's weirdness.

Poe's poem *The Raven*, conceived according to its author as a mathematical exercise in technique, and noted for its hypnotic musicality, stylised language, internal rhyme and overstated alliteration, had shot him to fame on its first publication in the *New York Evening Mirror* on January 29, 1845, its theme being the onset of madness in a distraught lover blown out by his unrequited love for Lenore. Poe, who was broke, was paid only nine dollars for its publication, a fact lost conveniently on Lou in the budget needed to record his conjectured epic with only a tenuous attachment to Poe. But with Lou's tech-head, it would have interested him to know that Poe conceived of *The Raven* with the same intricate knowledge of poetic metre as Lou brought to guitar chords. The poem's 18 six-line stanzas employ trochaic octametre – eight trochaic feet per line, each foot having one stressed syllable followed by one unstressed syllable. According to Poe in his 'The Philosophy Of Composition', referring to *The Raven*, he states, 'It is my design to render it manifest that no one point in its composition is referable either to accident or intuition – that the work proceeded, step by step, to its completion with the precision and rigid consequence of a mathematical problem.'

The poem is of course a triumph of form over content, rather like Lou's album, with the raven acting as occult, nihilistic messenger constantly informing the delusional lover that he will never be reunited with Lenore. Its gothic melodrama won instant appeal on publication, rather like tearjerker ballads would come to do for a pop generation, and for any public reading or lecture undertaken by the itinerant Poe, it became a stage centrepiece.

If it was the life rather than the work that grabbed Lou, then Poe's death at the age of 40, on October 3, 1849, remains itself the subject of specula-tive fiction. Poe's dishevelled body was found in the streets of Baltimore by Joseph M. Walker, Poe being delirious and according to Walker, 'in great distress and in need of immediate assistance'. Never coherently regaining consciousness, and inexplicably found wearing someone else's clothes, Poe was taken to the Washington Medical College where he died at 5 a.m. on Sunday October 7, 1849, having repeatedly called out the name of an unidentifiable person 'Reynolds'.

With no medical records to rely on, the causes of Poe's death have been variously attributed to alcoholic seizures, heart disease, epilepsy, meningeal inflammation, syphilis, cholera, rabies, or being severely beaten up at polling ballots, and the conspiracy theories surrounding his death have accelerated the Poe legend into the sort of continuity that engaged rather than fired-up Lou into the making of *The Raven*, which he saw as the culmination of a lifetime's work to consolidate his individual signature as consummate musician of the American underground.

Originally a commissioned work for a stage production called POEtry, an adaptation of Poe's work by Robert Wilson staged at the Gilman Opera House of the Brooklyn Academy of Music, with Reed's songs performed by the Thalia Theatre in a glacially slow, exhausting production, Daniel Radcliffe reviewing the show for the *New York Times* found the presentation 'painstakingly deliberate and almost clinical in its retelling of stories like *The Tell-Tale Heart* and *The Cask of Amontillado.*'

Like the album, it was too long.

Cameo, Stuttgart, 2003: A black people carrier pulls up outside the Stuttgart concert hall where Lou Reed is performing. A small man in a hooded sweatshirt jumps out, shadow boxes and runs straight inside. He reappears later for a *Guardian* interview, small, worked out pectorals, big belly, tight T-shirt, formidably cantankerous. With a gangster's swaggering B-movie inflation he crumples the interviewer adroitly for asking intrusive personal questions. 'I can't answer questions like that. What is it you really wanna know, because if it's personal stuff you won't get it. So you know, whaddya want?'

Rude, blunt, confrontational, Reed's aggression was always disproportionate to the question asked, sometimes appearing megalomaniacal in his sixties. His diet of green leaf salads, fruit juice, pistachio nuts and the subtle energies induced by Tai Chi did little to curtail the anger he felt at the apparent ubiquitous and continuous misassessment of his work.

The Raven, issued as a single and double CD, 'le grand mal' edition, lost Reed his record label, as it failed to earn back its ambitious recording costs. The unmistakable deadpan Lou vocals, the irate guitar argument between him and Mike Rathke, the stultifying dissonant guitar feedback on 'Fire Music' that Reed likened to *Metal Machine Music* Part 2, and recorded two days after 9/11 in a studio close to Ground Zero are all there. A sonic dirt bomb, Lou said of his seismic reverb on 'Fire Music', 'it's not looped. It's the big brother of *Metal Machine Music*, the next step. What I like is, it doesn't have a key and the rhythm is always shifting – a very free form of music, and a massive real time aural assault'. And 'Fire Music' is Reed's saturated colour moment independent of readings by Steve Buscemi,

Laurie Anderson, Willem Dafoe, Fisher Stevens and Elizabeth Ashley, all of whom lend a certain effect and pretentiousness to the album's escalating scale and inevitable implosion.

Cameo 2003: An Australian journalist is sitting apprehensively in a room on the seventh floor of a Sydney Harbourside Hotel, awaiting a 15-minute interview with Lou. 'A short weathered man walked in and I swear the temperature of the room dropped five degrees.' Scanning the room, Lou despotically demanded, 'I wanna know who everyone is in this room and why they have to be here.' Refusing to sit on the couch where the TV crew has assiduously set up their lighting and camera, and demanding a chair, Lou exploded at a video cameraman who was documenting the interview for the TV show's website, for prematurely starting taping. '"You don't start taping until they start filming," Reed yelled. "Stop! Erase what you have already got. Erase it! Now".'

This unceremonious impetuous anger, an eruptive egomania is probably consistent with how it felt to be the verbal target of Caligula or Nero's reactive capricious paranoia.

Lou's contempt for journalists and critics increased with age to an outright dismissal of their function.

> 'As far as I'm concerned, journalists and audiences want to know one thing, and that's how big your dick is. That's what they want to know. That's the width, breadth, and depth of their interest. I don't know if that's the lowest common denominator. There's still lower, and these are critics.'

Lou's belief in the absolute indomitable imperiousness of the artist over all negative criticism made him hypersensitive and defensively overreactive about his creativity, which in turn set him up as a target for detractors.

Lou was aware that in attempting to rewrite Poe with *The Raven* he was in an unenviable can't-win situation, and that any reinvention would fall short of the original. But it was a first for rock, and as such an audaciously commendable attempt to align his art with a literary renegade who continues to assert a fascinating power over readers.

Reed's rock vernacular, though, often sounds uninspired. *The Raven* doesn't match *Set The Twilight Reeling* or *Ecstasy* for raw, maverick, often shocking lyricism, suggesting Reed was perhaps inhibited by his subject's elevated literary status into writing below his optimal. But the album's strength is rock and not literature, and its virtues are musical and not, in this case, verbal. Ornette Coleman's colourful contributions to the sung version of 'Guilty' allowed Reed direct contact with one of the major instrumental experimentalists informing his youth, and indirectly on his free form guitar playing. In a Hollywood interview, Lou spoke of Coleman as a catalytically formative influence on his discordant music and a hero, and how at the time of recording *The Raven*, Coleman was fortuitously living only a few blocks away from the studio. According to Lou, 'When I was a kid, I used to follow him around from gig to gig when he played the Village, because I couldn't afford to see his shows.'

Anticipating his *Berlin* remake, Lou included a version of 'The Bed' on the expanded version of the record, presumably equating the suicidal impulses of Caroline with the speculatively troubled marriage of Poe and the unworldly adolescent, Virginia. Antony Hegarty covered Lou's 'Perfect Day' with idiosyncratic finesse, the two remakes acting as familiar signposts to fans otherwise lost in the exhaustive mapping of a fictional Poe who failed to come convincingly alive, except in the sonic terror scared up by 'Fire Music' that could arguably be the rogue hurricane that demolished the House of Usher, crashing it into its surrounding lake as exploded debris.

Of *The Raven*, Lou said, typically dictatorially, 'This might be a nice way to say goodbye' although in theory he'd already done that with *Ecstasy*, the last of his seriously written conceptually urban albums, in which the personal reflects the general or universal state.

An album of subversively gorgeous instrumental passages – Lou like most bluesmen, and in this case a post-modern one, got better with age – *The Raven* surely isn't in his estimation 'the culmination of everything I've done', but rather an experiment that went asymmetric rather than symmetric in the process of assemblage and lacks memorable hooky tunes. I suspect that rather like Scott Walker's later albums, *The Drift* and *Bish*

Bosch, the self-indulgent lack of critical self-perception integral to their construction, makes *The Raven* similarly, a one-off listening experience, rarely repeated for lack of commanding differentials in the song writing.

While *The Raven* remains an innovatively guesting slab of experimental adult rock, Reed would have benefitted from researching other Poe reinventions, particularly those anthologised in *The Man Who Called Himself Poe* (Doubleday, 1969), in which remakes of Poe's stories, like *The Man Who Collected Poe* by Robert Bloch, *The Lighthouse* by Edgar Allan Poe and Robert Bloch, *Manuscript Found In A Drawer* by Charles Norman, *The Valley Of Unrest* by Douglas Sherley and *The Dark Brotherhood* by H.P. Lovecraft and August Derleth all imaginatively reconstruct, rewrite or radically modernise Poe's lugubrious mapping of pathological obsessions in ways that may have proved inspirational to Reed, whose writing on the album often sides with tired clichés.

A quintessential New Yorker, who despite his stonewall hostility to journalists, fans, critics, other musicians etc, and his assumed anti-socially intimidating aura, Lou used his city optimally to socially network, attending gallery openings and Broadway shows, formed serious friendships with Julian Schnabel and Richard Belzer, Robert Wilson and Sam Sheppard, and was regularly to be seen out walking his dog by the moody blue Hudson River. And central to his life was the spiritual discipline of Tai Chi, qigong and kung fu, methods he'd begun in the eighties with Eagle Claw master Leung Shum, who taught him for 15 years before retiring, initially as an effective method for breaking the destructive patterns of addiction. Reed had begun with practising the Wu Hao style, before being introduced to Chen style Tai Chi Chuan, and to his second master Ren Guang-Yi. Reed's power incentive associated Chen with the intensity of motorcycles and dynamic rock'n'roll, as well as benefitting from its health rewards, self-defence techniques, and the philosophical/metaphysical input the discipline enhanced. Reed's master Ren Guang-Yi had immigrated from a poor province in Mainland China to New York City, surviving various menial jobs before gradually asserting himself as a virtuoso tai chi teacher, sharing with Reed an easy friendship, a real camaraderie, a mutual respect and a drive to perfect their respective art forms.

Reed's incisive musculature as a result of martial arts gave him the sustained physique of a 30-year-old, in outward physical contrast to the lasting internal damage he'd incurred from decades of drug-induced hepatitis, and chronic abuse of alcohol, drugs and nicotine. Reed had so severely compromised his health by his forties, when he first adopted Tai Chi, that his surviving another three decades must in part be attributed to his devotion to Tai Chi as a form of regenerative energy, a highly disciplined basis from which to continue.

Reed's mind constituted a neural library of referential rock – he was an academician of rock'n'roll – which tended to mean that he invested the subject with unconditional authority and a seriousness that sometimes undermined his aims. But Lou's fundamental doubt over the durability of rock in general led him in the last decade of his life to devaluate his strengths by trying to integrate them into theatre concepts that simply didn't display him at his best, or advance his work culturally in the manner he clearly wished. That he was so constantly insecure about his legacy led him to intellectually agonise and theorise about the limitations of rock and the public conception of its dubious significance. 'Anyhow, how much can you pack into a rock'n'roll record? Or, for that matter, how seriously will people take a rock'n'roll record? Apparently not very seriously at all.' That's Lou framing and answering his own question speculatively. And maybe it was his formative experience of writing bubble-gum pop on demand as a staff writer at Pickwick Records had him doubt the cultural authenticity of two and three minute rock songs, and to his mind the banality of most lyrics characterising mainstream pop, where a hooky chorus line often masks an absence of engaging lyric input. It's interesting that no other rock star has so openly debated the meaning and infrastructural nuances of popular music in the way it obsessed Reed.

> 'It's just you take the lyric and you push it a little forward so that it speaks to you on a personal level and still keeps the beat, because I'm not talking to you about having discussions on nuclear disarmament. You can even just make it a dialogue between men and women. That could keep you occupied for the rest of your life.'

Lou's incessant analysis of his craft, rather like a creative writing instructor sterilising a poem by deconstructing its components to a reductive zero, at times killed off spontaneity in the interests of an overcritical self-scrutiny of what he was doing, rather than letting it happen.

> 'I think works of art can change the world. Certainly they can change your life, a thing of beauty is a joy forever and all that. I think a rock'n'roll song can be just that, so that in a sense it can do anything. Maybe we should treasure records of people who do things like that.'

Lou needn't have worried so acutely, the legacy to date of most outstanding blues, pop and rock artists has outlived and continued to influence successive generations of musicians and fans – as presumably Lou will continue to do, as prototypical garage progenitor of unrivalled constructive VU noise. In the end everything goes, you can't continue to outlive what's culturally disposable like a red gas giant burning out in deep space.

Two of Lou's inerasable career grievances, the critical scar tissue left behind by the negative reception given to both *Berlin* and *Metal Machine Music* were to be re-addressed in his last decade, in the attempt not so much to revisit these controversial musical sites, but to rehabilitate them to new acclaim. Almost ubiquitously in interviews Reed had used *Berlin* as the criterion by which to prove his critics wrong, as though its initial dismissal to his mind, as a slab of depressive overload, was a lasting point of contention he was determined to redress.

Berlin was never the commercial flop assumed in Reed mythology. Its original release in 1973 coincided with an acute literary preoccupation with suicide, instigated in part by Sylvia Plath's taking her life 1963, and the publication of Al Alvarez's seminal book on suicide *The Savage God* (1971), in which the alienated creative sensibility, living at variance to the capitalist socio-economic state, is arguably liberated into the autonomous right to exit, because living in a systemised world is ultimately untenable to the compromised individual. On a miniature scale, *Berlin*, the narratives of mangled abuse and violence shared by Jim and Caroline, who commits suicide, was suitably themed for the times, when prescription drugs and enhanced psychological focus on the disaffected outsider made suicide for the first time a morally debatable option.

Lou's decision to revisit *Berlin* and recreate the album in full was incepted by Julian Schnabel directing and filming Reed and his band over five nights at St Ann's Warehouse, Brooklyn, in December 2006. Dressed in a red T-shirt, blue jeans and his trademark professional wire-rimmed specs, and bookended by 12 choristers and a 30-strong band, including Steve Hunter returned to weaponise blazing guitar riffs, Reed's understated vocally shot delivery found new angles into this material contemporaneous with aging. As a 1973 rehabbed classic, a small-plot melodrama pursuing its original arrangements, with more space for Hunter to propel virtuoso figures, *Berlin* sounded re-energised and apposite to the times, rather than maudlin and time-bound by Jim and Caroline's mutually inflicted abuse. The characters who do drugs, domestic violence and custody battles, before Caroline kills herself, are timeless in their messy déclassé lifestyles, so the plot holds up as a rock short story, and Reed's commitment to staging and touring it on a grand scale helped prevent the predictability that so often comes from playing an old album in full to an audience grown accustomed to the original. But there's the question as to whether an essentially claustrophobic and hermetic album made to listen to alone really benefits from being put into the arena of public performance as detached, disillusioned raconteur of marital discord.

For Reed the *Berlin* remake was a vindication of an album he'd always assumed disparaged and unappreciated, and which he'd revived in part in his 1979 and 1980 tours, but still felt lacked its due critical acclaim. With Bob Ezrin, the album's producer onstage in a white lab coat reading BERLIN on the back and maniacally conducting the band, Lou managed to stoke new energies from what he saw as his neglected masterpiece.

About his creative prerogative to recreate *Berlin*, Lou remained defiant that the work's durability was comparable to Burroughs' *Naked Lunch* in counterculture signposting, and if you looked for justification to question the rewrite of either, you were in for big trouble. A prickly defensive Lou simply wasn't having it in his *Spin* interview. Asked if people's feelings had changed with time about *Berlin*, a foursquare Lou replied:

'It's making me think, like, if you were talking to Bill Burroughs, would you have said, "Now Bill, they put together the new version of *Naked Lunch*. What do you think? Do you still feel the same way Bill?" Can you imagine being put in a position where you're trying to justify *Naked Lunch*? . . . It's such a simple idea [*Berlin*] that it barely qualifies as an idea. Instead of all the songs having different characters, why not have the characters come back and deal with each other?'

In this case the intended analogy doesn't work. *Naked Lunch* is a visionary drug-fuelled myth-making excursion across inner and outer geographies, coloured by an opiate habit converted into extraordinary non-linear fiction, chaptered by streaming visual imagination. *Berlin* by contrast is a set of rock lyrics, unexceptional in terms of writing, but overtly themed by a nihilistic mood with which Burroughs would arguably have sympathised, but there's no cross-over in the writing, just a brutally shared lived-out misogyny held in common, as hard defensive.

As a departure from his regular rock output, and intended as an adjunct to meditation, Lou's next excursion into unpredictability was the contemplative compass *Hudson Wind Meditations*, a lyric free slice of deviated ambient, both subtle and tonally challenging, which in his own words was 'music to play in the background of life – to replace the everyday cacophony with new and ordered sounds of an unpredictable nature.'

Recorded at Animal Lab, New York, largely using a Moog Analog Voyager to create real rather than sampled sound, the album comprises four pieces, 'Move Your Heart', 'Find Your Note', 'Hudson River Wind (Blend The Ambience)' and 'Wind Coda', as aids to exploring the sort of inner places Reed set out to locate in his practice of Tai Chi Chuan, and at a time when he'd actually quit smoking to enhance the deep breathing modulations seminal to any form of reward from meditative disciplines. If hypnotic electronic wavelengths of music assist in cutting out everyday brain chatter and accumulative white noise, in the same way for instance as Brian Eno's ethereal *Music For Airports*, then Reed's experimentation with the form does precisely that, islanding the individual from busy noise invasion by helping the mind create internalised silence, and a cut off point from continuous thought associations.

You can't ever assess anyone else's quality of meditation, you can only evaluate your own and imagine theirs, but never really know. What layers of meditative experience Reed entered, we'll never know, but the music he made to massage his angle on mindful meditation is a valuable pointer to inner spaces he inhabited or found meaningful.

Avoiding all association with benign, floaty, gently arpeggiated New Age music, with its usually bland synth notations, Lou was still aware of the need to record an original and sometimes unsettling record in response to his inner directives. And because celebrities invariably seek attention for meditative practices most people keep private, there's the additional criterion that this, after all, is a Lou Reed record carrying his brand name, and not necessarily an honest interpretation of Tai Chi Chuan brush-strokes of white-on white music.

In an interview with Valerie Reiss, Reed made the interesting observation that, as New York is an island it's a good place to meditate, as well as being an energy centre. Contrary to expectation big cities make good meditation locales, maybe because the vibrant collective energies can be fed off and filtered to necessary exclusion levels by the individual partici-pant. It's like downsizing the cosmos to the universe, the mass population to one.

As always in his interviews, Lou was into tech specifics.

> 'The activity is way up there, but it's also . . . the better your speak-ers, the better you can experience it. There's some really wonderful things happening in the bass area, the bottom, that you should physi-cally feel if you have speakers that can carry it. The high end thing, that was enormous fun to play.'

The easiest of the four movements to go with is 'Move Your Heart' with its tranquil harmonics, minimalist variations and ambient waves of electronic sound that I associate with sea fog rolling in imperceptibly, only its vaporised texture distinguishing it from air. The thing about abstract music with only subtle undulations is that it doesn't think for you like rock, but rather you think into it and with it, creating your own thought patterns in response to the music, like painting on empty space.

The spookier, more oscillatingly active 'Find Your Note' is closer to a chilled out *Metal Machine Music*, complete with modulating feedback, the sinusoid rhythms fractured by overtone, but the whole thing is studiously controlled into focusable shifts in tone, although the prowling bass is at times menacing, and not conducive to Tai Chi bodywork or spatialised meditation. But there wouldn't be a Lou Reed album without departure from form, and elements of Reed's frustration with cool enter into his rotating drone piece, with the listener half-anticipating an abrupt squall of feedback aggro to shatter the music's stability.

The sequence closes proceedings with wind noises off the Hudson River, two ambient miniatures that introduce elemental energies into pre-occupation with inner space, a sound Lou must have regularly heard in his Hudson River penthouse apartment as a raw transitioning force.

Reed's guitar-free soundtrack to his own subjective response to Tai Chi isn't so much a great album, but another instance of his mutable explora-tion of sound that fits the pattern if you're acquainted with the notorious *Metal Machine Music*, and ironically the Velvet Underground's drone quotient. As a break in the routine guitar dissonance of his rock albums, and Reed was already ill with the liver cancer that would aggressively spread five years later, the experiment, not even an attempt to upgrade New York underground flagship pioneers of minimalism like La Monte Young and Tony Conrad, and its very simplicity following on from the overblown production of *The Raven* as failed epic, *Hudson Wind Meditations* was a strategic drop in temperature, a hiatus in rock combat to accommodate something else – the potential for music without noise.

For Lou, surrounded now by New York's art luminaries, including Paul Auster, the author of *New York Trilogy*, taking yourself too seriously became a problem of over aggrandising rock's meaning, which is essen-tially simple communication of everyday life and emotions. Reed's in-security – he was incapable of doing an interview now without mentioning he had a degree in literature – became apparent in his cultivation of an arty ethos, that didn't so much feed his work as knock it out of proportion.

Some of Reed's interviews when touring the *Berlin* remake are self-regarding to the point of fatuousness, as though the album was the indubitable resolution to every art algorithm ever devised. This was a long way from the bad boy attitude and deliberately cultivated mystique that had been a large part of Reed's appeal in the seventies to punkish audiences even if he resisted the term. It was also a long remove from the 'highly strung, intelligent, fragile kid in a polo-neck sweater, rumpled jeans and loafers . . . bruised, trembling, quiet and insecure' – John Cale's description of Reed at the time of their first meetings, when Lou was only allowed into Manhattan at weekends. The inwardly disturbed youth who first found some sort of acceptance at the Factory, which as he admitted, fed him fruit at night, as he lacked money for food, had graduated, despite the stability afforded by his relationship with Anderson, into a morose, humourless rock avatar, rich, celebrated, but seemingly locked into a permanent grey-mooded despondent ennui, the equivalent of Charles Baudelaire's equally abject spleen.

With his well-muscled body, the product of martial arts, Reed was also studying a form of meditation taught to him by a Tibetan Buddhist lama, Mingyur Rinpoche, although outwardly he appeared resistant to the brightening, usually uplifting sense of well-being that is just one of the affirmative rewards of sustained meditational practice: a blue sky ceiling.

Reed saw the ethereal designs of *Hudson Wind Meditations*, with its sound absorbent textures masking New York noise pollution, as an oblique descendant of his much aligned *Metal Machine Music*, an album he was now in the process of rehabilitating in much the same way as the equally misconstrued *Berlin* to prove his critics wrong with the passage of time. Reed's geek obsession integral to *Metal Machine Music* had famously extended to arranging his first date with Laurie Anderson at the Audio Engineering Society Convention, a conglomeration of amps, cables and shop-talking electronics, in the microphones concession, as the focus of his continuous preoccupation with gadgets and the analysis of electronic sounds.

In 2002, Ulrich Krieger, much to Reed's astonishment, had transcribed *Metal Machine Music* and arranged it to be performed by a German nutbar orchestral collective Zeitkratzer, with Reed contributing a cameo drone guitar over the third act of the performance at Maerz Musik Haus Der Berliner Festpiele on March 17, 2002, for a CD release by San Francisco's Asphodel Records in 2007.

Reed was again into the wordless, the notion of feedback as a complete style of playing, almost as the elusive aural vanishing point he'd been pursing since his first distorted guitar work with the Velvet Underground, as stratospheric drone.

> 'There couldn't be a better time to be a musician than right now with all these astonishing instruments available. I mean, someone's going to put this stuff together in a different way, somebody really smart, and just bust it open.'

This, of course, is what the Velvet Underground had accomplished in the mid-sixties, combining elements of garage, rock, doo-wop, classical and avant-garde minimalism into an anarchic amalgam of lawless tuneful noise, but Lou didn't have the expansive horizon to reach that platform again.

Reed had once given *Vanity Fair* his definition of abject misery as 'being interviewed by an English journalist'. *The Daily Telegraph*'s Mick Brown, in an interview at the time, described Reed as perpetually morose, his misanthropic voice drained of anything resembling enthusiasm. They met in a Greenwich Village Café, with Reed wearing a white safari jacket and jeans, and too impolite and uninterested to even bother to answer questions that didn't appeal to him, picking up momentum only to talk convincingly of three favourites, Doc Pomus, Andy Warhol and Hubert Selby. What had so flattened Reed? Was it the knowledge he was seriously ill, or the general dejection that comes with ageing, or exhaustion with a musical genre he'd pushed to personal limits without a sense of self-fulfilment? But in the interview Reed said something acutely perceptive about Hubert Selby, author of *Last Exit To Brooklyn*, by now a notorious underbelly classic, that was equally applicable to the lyric contents of a rock song. In talking of the directness of Selby's writing, which is also its speed, Lou was quick to make the association with rock music. Referring to the fact that he had personally interviewed Selby, Reed volunteered:

'What I wanted to know was how long had he practised doing dialogue without quotes, so you know who said it by the tone of voice. Because that's one of the things that I thought about with *Last Exit* . . . you just know who's talking.'

One could argue the same about the Velvet Underground's narrative songs like 'Sister Ray', 'Murder Mystery', 'Lady Godiva's Operation', or for that matter 'Walk On The Wild Side', or any of Lou's more complexly characterised songs, in which his singular tone has to carry the song's action.

'I say, no Selby, no anybody – that's the way I see it. Because he was a straight line between two points; no fucking around over there; no polysyllabic anything – it's just, God . . . if that's not rock'n'roll, what is?'

Reed is far closer to Selby in the lyric content of his songs than he is to Burroughs, whose essentially non-linear prose succeeds by the association of poetic imagery, rather than direct unmediated thrust, like we find in Selby's brutally realistic fiction.

From June to July 2007, Reed toured *Berlin* across Europe, anxious to consolidate his conviction that the album was a conceptual rock classic, a neglected masterpiece that wasn't so much depressing as hard-core real, flavoured with melodrama; an exercise he was dutifully to repeat in the summer of 2008. His 2007 tour took in six select US dates, and included on its European leg, the Palais de Congress, Paris, Tempodrom, Berlin, as well as two nights at London's Hammersmith Apollo on June 30 and July 1. But an album that had begun life as an intimate listening experience, a claustrophobic bedroom luxury for moody teens, was now transformed into a theatrical show, often saturated to disadvantage by Hal Willner's production, with the films being so literal they're barely inseparable from the action, the characters depicted too beautiful for the sordid milieu of the songs, and with Lou ending songs with a jut of his hand and trading guitar riffs with Hunter's mercenary figures. In London, the onstage presence of seven of the London Metropolitan Orchestra, and

12 New London Children's choir singers, again tended to cushion the open nerve wrist-cutting of the original album's oblique existential misery soaked in whiskey and Valium.

Reed was 31 when he recorded *Berlin* as his third solo album in London, and 65 when he took it on the road as a composite suite of songs, and while the voice remained the same dispassionately removed instrument, there was inevitable emotional distance from the raging breakup of Lou's violent, short-term marriage to Bettye as parasuicidal victim of the mess. Up to a point in interviews Reed was willing to confess to the dark core of jealousy and rage that fuelled the album, and to trace its origins back to his student days, when an ambiguous sexuality had clearly torn up attempts at relationships, and instilled in him what John Cale had observed as an ability to seek advantage for himself by congenitally bringing out the worst in people, by antagonising them. This time round Lou confessed both to jealousy and problems with women constituting the building blocks of an album also fired up by capricious alcoholic temper.

> 'What *Berlin* is about is jealousy, rage, humiliation . . . There are some real problems with women that we all go through; that's the way it is. Unfortunately for me there were a couple starting in college. Terrible. If nothing else in life, I hope that never happens to me again – that kind of relationship, that terrible rage.'

Meanwhile, Reed, still the sunglasses-wearing hipster, had taken over a warehouse in the West Village as a workspace, and remained a regular at John of Bleecker Street, 278 Bleecker St, between Jones and Cornelia Street, managed by Mike Frank who remembered Lou from his days of being a waiter there. Lou would come in for pizza and Diet Coke (nutritionally antipathetic to Tai Chi), and for years Frank was 'afraid even to talk to him, because he seemed so serious', finally breaking the frigidity by mentioning *The Blue Mask* at which Lou's face lit up. 'I think he was surprised I even knew it,' Frank adds.

Reed was also a regular at Joey Campanaro's restaurant The Little Owl, where he liked the music, at Ceci Cela Patisserie, 55 Spring Street, famous for its quiche, sandwiches, croissants, and pain au chocolat, and at Café

Figaro in Greenwich Village Sidewalk, where he hung out with his regular cappuccino or Diet Coke. Clearly none of Reed's meditation teachers had advised him on a diet conducive to optimising subtle energies in Tai Chi practice.

Interestingly too, Reed had provided VH1 archives with a list of his favourite records. Asked to submit a list of 100, Reed settled for eight, an immensely valuable insight into the inspirational mapping of what he personally favoured in music, his choices excluding all Reed wannabes, collaborators or pretenders. In order of priority Reed listed:

1. 'Stay With Me Baby'   Lorraine Ellison
2. 'Outcast'   Eddie and Ernie
3. 'Loving You Too Long'   Otis Redding
4. 'River Deep Mountain High'   Ike and Tina Turner
5. 'Georgia Boy'   Al Green
6. 'Belle'   Al Green
7. 'That's Alright Mama'   Elvis Presley
8. 'I Can't Stand The Rain   Ann Peebles

Lou had also become passionate about photography, bringing the same tech-head obsession to digital cameras as he had guitars, using a camera adapted to "see" in the infrared zone, and a customised German lens for special affects. Asked by *Vogue* as to what New York personally meant to him through the transitioning decades, his direct attention leapt to photography.

> 'My favourite moments in the Village are always with the beautiful sun drifting over the Hudson River. And, as I look out, I am taking photos in my mind or with one of my cameras. It's always great for me to start the day with a beautiful photo and then three hours of Tai Chi, all these golden moments in the Village.'

With a Jersey country retreat comprising two big bedrooms, two palatial bathrooms, a spacious living room with an open fireplace, sparkling professional kitchen, formal dining room and a screen porch, Lou's environmentally realistic photos oscillated between urban and rural landscapes in pursuit of an aesthetic that rarely entered his lyrics – beauty.

Photography was also a way into silence that complemented meditation, a noiseless gadgetry unlike muscled feedback, but a fixed retrieval of the visual moment, rather like a song is immutably time-framed by studio recording. Both modalities exist in the continuous present when accessed – whenever you hear a song it's in your space now – and viewing a photograph is the same in that you're seeing the past as present, and neither can deviate unless one is remixed and the other digitally repurposed.

Quickly becoming a camera geek, Reed in the last decade of his life published three books of photography, *Emotion In Action* (2003), *Lou Reed's New York* (2008), and *Romanticism* (2009), discovering in his unpeopled landscapes a preoccupation with light and movement and a gravitation to empty spaces largely absent from his busy music. In *New York*, with most of the photos selectively taken from his apartment window, brilliant sunsets and hot neon surges predominate, whereas the black and white three-dimensional landscapes of *Romanticism* attempt to recreate atmospherics inspired by the 19th century Romantic painter, Caspar David Friedrich and, with no use of Photoshop, explore uncultivated nature, the shots taken variously in Scotland, Denmark, Spain, Rome and China, as well as New Jersey.

In interviews, Reed spoke of cameras like he did guitars, confessing to owning a Leica medium format with just the body costing $24,000, and to having a 119 on order, as well as using an Alpa with a Schneider lens and a medium format Hasselblad with Fuji lenses. Lou's gallery of cameras was like silent guitars, and his practice of having two different cameras looking at the same thing to achieve two different results, wasn't so far removed from the aural methods applied to *Metal Machine Music*. And what's more Reed was starting to discover elemental colour blocks and nuances in skyscapes that had him compulsively shoot sunsets over the Hudson River in their explosive Jaffa orange reds. Referring to a particular lens on a Contax Camera, he likened it to a piece of jewellery beautiful enough to make into a ring, and looking through the viewfinder to being in a movie theatre. If Reed was a skilled amateur photographer, a recreational though serious snapshotter largely of landscapes without figures, then the expression cultivated an aesthetic that had in large been repressed by his music, where deviant humans are the norm, and the underworld their environs.

If one views *Ecstasy* (2000), as Reed's last consolidated album triumph, then photography as a minor pursuit in the last decade of his life ran parallel with his music schemas that weren't so much progressive as a return to old sites with their intended restoration.

So back to noise, and Reed's inextinguishable obsession with *Metal Machine Music* as constructive drone predator in need to re-evaluation to endorse its rogue sonic menu. Incapable of ever letting go his intellectual validation of the project, Reed was up for its reinvention as classically infected academic thesis, having admitted in 1975 that not even he could listen to in its entirety.

Cameo, noise insertion: When John Cale revisited his old Ludlow Street apartment in 2013, he recalled: 'When we rehearsed we weren't too loud. We only had acoustic instruments and the most basic amps. We stole electricity from other apartments, so wires snaked all over the place. Besides, the people downstairs were always blasting music on the radio, so no one in the building heard us or complained.'

'Fire Music' on *The Raven*, three-minutes of scorchingly deranged feedback, a drone metaphor for the torched Twin Towers, was Reed's way back into *Metal Machine Music*; a deregulated cacophony that issued from Reed's guitar like an electronic river.

Re-affiliated to *MMM* as his noise umbilical, Reed spoke of the thrill of hearing 'Fire Music' on huge speakers. 'I was up at Bob Ludwig's where he was listening on these huge speakers . . . and that thing just rises up like this huge sonic wave, it's amazing. If there wasn't a wall to catch you, you'd be still heading south.' It was in fact Reed's feedback response to the two Al-Qaeda hijacked Boeings, American Airlines Flight II and United Airlines Flight 175, that were rammed nose first through the North and South towers respectively, of the World Trade Center complex in New York City, with both towers collapsing in eruptive plumes of orange and black smoke, and almost 3,000 people dying in the attacks.

Cameo: New York burning – Warhol's original Factory, 231 East 47th

Street, demolished in the sixties – is now a parking lot in the well-groomed Midtown district of Manhattan; a vehicular site for the rich. And the corner of 125th Street and Lexington Avenue, the most famous of Reed's specific lyric locations, with 26 dollars in his hand to score heroin: the place is a corner of pilgrimage for Reed fanatics, who often hang out by Duane Reed pharmacy.

With the formation of Lou's band Metal Machine Trio, his return to feedback formula was re-pitched into guitar technics, and the advantage of multiples, like cameras to create integral pluralities of tone feeding off each other. Lou was anxious to assert in a Pitchfork interview the physicality of the sound of the original *Metal Machine Music*, evolving from the fact that most of his guitar solos with the Velvet Underground were saturated feedback, without a key or tempo, and essentially constructive white noise interpreting dystopian urban ethics. Lou explained his method of knock-on collisional sound carried to extremes in *Metal Machine Music*.

> 'I had two huge amps, and I would take two guitars and tune them in a certain way and lean them against the amps so they would start feeding back. And once they started feeding back both of them, their sounds would collide and that would produce a third sound, and then that would start feeding and cause another one and another one, and I would play along with all of them.'

Encouraged by the revival of his allegedly ridiculed drone masterpiece, and its reissue in 2008 on 180gms vinyl, Reed in the same year founded Metal Machine Trio for improvised performances of noisy abstractly textured music, incorporating a workable cocktail of free-jazz, minimal music, noise, electronica, ambient, with Ulrich Kreiger on electric saxophone and Garth Calhoun on various electronics that also processed his fellow performers in real time.

With this in mind, Lou issued a statement of purpose to accommodate his newly founded trio: 'We have formed a recording unit called Best Seat In The House. We intend to put out different types of music – from industrial to meditative to songs to subway stops in between.'

Anxious to initialise their essentially live strain of impromptu talents the band premiered at Redcat, part of the Disney Concert Hall Complex in downtown Los Angeles on October 2 and 3, 2008, under the title 'Unclassified: Lou Reed and Ulrich Krieger', with a live double CD of those shows, *The Creation Of The Universe*, released on December 22, 2008, on Reed's own label.

The band returned to live performance on April 23 and 24, 2009, at the New York Blender Theatre at Gramercy, with the official flyer stating 'No songs, no vocals'. With Calhoun sitting centre-stage as the electronic controller facilitating a Continuum Fingerboard and a Kyma workstation, and tickets selling at $50, the band issued a continuous low-frequency distortion, with Reed's VU influenced atonal guitar solos slicing across Krieger's panicked sax in the general distressed frequencies of the music. Metal Machine Trio touch few comfort zones in their eclectic ranging, and like the original album Creation Of The Universe isn't a work you'd regularly revisit unless you're a drone exponent like Lou.

In 2010, the trio undertook a short European and UK tour, playing London's Royal Festival Hall for a night of deep noise, with the *Guardian* reviewer claiming of the show, 'It reaches a climax when Reed whacks a gong at the back of the stage: incredibly it's the loudest and most startling sound all night.'

If nothing else, the experiment was a partial vindication of a sound that was originally prototypically industrial, and arguably the first album to take metal as its thesis, and soak the listener in squealing feedback. Lou had lost none of the resource as the originator of guitar drone, his affiliation to the Velvet Underground's garage squall, still the unstoppable sound on which he fed as pioneering noise progenitor.

Unstoppably controversial and noise regenerative in his unrepentant late sixties, Lou teamed up with the thrash metal heavies Metallica at the Rock and Roll Hall of Fame's 25th Anniversary Concert, to pulverise at aviation levels 'Sweet Jane' and 'White Light/White Heat'. Next Lou conceived the idea of having Metallica join him in re-recording a bunch of previously unreleased tracks he'd written over the years, including a collection of demos composed for a play called *Lulu* that taken to the next level was to lead to the apparently incongruous collaboration between the two, as the pyrotechnic concept album *Lulu*, released as a double CD on October 31, 2011.

The idea for *Lulu* germinated from two avant-garde transgressive psychosexual plays, *Earth Spirit* (1895) and *Pandora's Box* (1904), by the Munich born playwright Franz Wedekind, whose degenerate work explored lesbianism, homoeroticism, incest, group masturbation and, in *Pandora's Box*, an encounter with Jack the Ripper, a role Wedekind played himself in the original production, having at the age of 34 served a nine-month prison sentence for the libellous and defamatory content of a collection of satirical poems entitled *Simplicissimus*. The *Lulu* plays formed the basis for G.W. Pabst's acclaimed silent film *Pandora's Box* (1929), starring Louise Brooks as Lulu, and Alban Berg's inspired incomplete opera *Lulu* (1937).

The story of *Lulu* as archetypal femme fatale, a stripper who uses sex to socially network, only to end up as a degraded prostitute sold as a sex slave, also find correlatives with the uninhibited sexuality implied by Marlene Deitrich's portrayal of Lola in *The Blue Angel*, as libidinous, licentious hottie with indomitable style: the déclassé hooker who is punished for her unequal relations with men though selling sex.

The theme of the ruined, voraciously self-destructive woman, so appositely explored by Reed on *Berlin*, provided ideal subject matter as lyric narrative, with Reed's evident rage on record shared by Metallica's hyperactive riff aggression. But right from the start, even before the album's release, Metallica fans took online objection to the rogue collaboration, with Reed reporting on his website:

> 'Metallica's fans are threatening to shoot me, and that's only because I showed up. They haven't even heard the record yet, and they're recommending various forms of torture and death.'

The album, recorded spontaneously live at Metallica's own studio in San Raphael, North California between April and June 2011, was promoted online with no advance review copies sent out. Music journalists were obliged to visit the Manhattan offices of Metallica's management QPrime, and ushered into an office where *Lulu* was driven at volume through band-approved Genelec speakers, given the derogatory classification of Radio Shack CD speakers by Reed.

The resulting 89-minute intransigent mismatch of rock intellectual and metal warriors needed no apology, despite a uniform negative reception on the part of the critics, who largely saw its misconceived, tortuous contents as inflicting irreparably lasting damage on Metallica, while having little adverse effect on Reed's legacy as a deliberately deconstructive advocate of in your face rock permutations like *Metal Machine Music*. With his usual audacious cool Lou shrugged off the album's crushing put-downs by claiming, 'I don't have any fans left. After *Metal Machine Music* (1975) they all fled. Who cares? I'm essentially in this for the fun of it.'

Only Reed could launch into the album's opener, 'Brandenburg Gate', with the line, 'I would cut my legs and tits off' as nonchalant throwaway, or in the Ripper Song, 'Pumping Blood', have Lulu declare, 'I swallow your sharpest cutter/ like a coloured man's dick/ blood spurting from me/ blood spurting from me', as a means of inviting being slashed and eviscerated by the Whitechapel alley prowler. In fact the album invited some of Reed's most brutally perverse writing, even though the material is mostly sung first person through empathising with Lulu, while adopting the same contempt for her as he had done for Caroline on his noir classic *Berlin*.

Too many of the songs risk being tediously overlong by default, with Lou's limited vocal strength straining to climb above Metallica's punishing riffs that sustain remorseless thrash. Reed told the *Guardian*:

> 'This has so much rage it's thrilling. I've waited for a long time to have a shot at doing something like this with the right people. I'm energised and jacked up. Sometimes I find it so emotional I have to get up and turn it off.'

It was a stylistic detour for both parties, although Reed had pretty much initialised aspects of metal with the Velvet Underground. The album shot to number 36 on *Billboard*'s Top 200, selling 100,000 copies in the first two weeks of release, despite the animosity with which it was reviewed as an aberrant catastrophic failure, an exhaustive, asymmetric churn lacking in listener appeal and direction. Lou:

'Whatever the thing is, it exists in the playing. Feeling is everything to me in rock – to make it really happen and not degenerate into pop music. That's not to put pop down.'

It's an honest statement on Lou's part, although his vocals on the album often sound like rant in conflict with shattering. When precisely the demos were written, Lou didn't divulge, and some of them differently arranged, wouldn't sound out of place on *Berlin*. Certainly Reed matched moral depredation with equally uninhibited lyrics. In 'Mistress Dread' Reed writes, 'I beg you to degrade me/ is there waste that I could eat/ please spit into my mouth,' that takes us right back to his mid-seventies fascination with coprophiliac drag queens who picked up in neon drenched Times Square. Reed's unimpeachable sleaze-gene remained a constant right to this, his last studio recorded album. The band photo on the studio album is literally era-less, with five guys sharing different generational decades seated at a wooden plank table, all wearing blackout shades as defensive eyewear, and all dressed in black. Lou wearing a chunky gold chain heads the convention, his ravaged features carved like land scars into his epidermal tissue. He looks a thousand years old, but the high cheekbones have kept him unmistakably Lou Reed, so too the short wavy black hair maintained like that since his days with the Velvet Underground. Two of the band with their sunglassed look and shoulder-length hair look like sixties outtakes from the Manson era Californian desert, anomalously slipped into the present, while Metallica's lead vocalist James Hetfield poses as uncrossably hard, short groomed beard and gated contactless eyes giving him an indomitably thuggish air, reciprocated by the drummer's bearded scowl, as a don't mess image. The collective impression is one of forcible determination, like you don't question their resolve to kick up a storm on *Lulu*.

It's an extraordinary photo of mean integrated into resources, with Lou looking like the appointed elder statesman of rock, the light on his reflective Raybans substituting for eyes. The utility table's bare; no drinks, no cigarette packs as stereotypical accessories. The impacted attitude is a vocabulary of intention to explode any preconceptions of what the work may or may not entail. It's a rock tribal gathering frozen into silence as the antithesis of the album's discordant thrash. And it's suitably in black and white for grey mood affects, grey being the colour of brain matter and Californian sea fog. Lou told *GQ*:

> 'The stuff is mainly cut live, so I went wherever it went, leakage and all. The genius of these guys, my metal brothers, they built this beautiful studio that's based around the idea of leakage, so everybody's sitting in a big circle, singing and playing.'

But I keep returning to that photo and Lou's last on a studio album. Did he know in the back of his mind his diagnosis? That microscopic cancer cells were migrating from his liver as metastatic rogues? Because it's a group photo something of his undermined state is diffused into numbers. If you confront someone wearing reflective sunglasses you invariably think they're looking at you even if they're not. They induce a compulsion on the part of the observed to keep looking at the suspected observer, because the radius of their eyes appears to have expanded to the size of the lenses: it's what we call fascination. And as a point of fascination, Lou focus. Would Rachel have recognised Lou in that photo, if he was still alive?

The answer's probably yes, and whatever Rachel had experienced as the transitional pathway into death, Lou was narrowing in on as an inescapable shut-down phenomenon: the irreversible corridor where nobody is privileged by fame, but simply the psychic carrier of what they've done in terms of self-realisation. You can't take nothing and you leave everything behind, that's death as the ultimate disappearing act. 'I heard it through the grapevine,' sang Marvin Gaye, and that's all we know of death, intimations, contradictory ideas of outliving ourselves, but no concrete evidence of post-human survival, Lou or anyone, all we know is we are so uniquely individual we can never be twice the same physically, or presumably mentally.

You can't do 'Sister Ray' in death, but I'm hearing it now, 'Duck and Sally inside . . .' and so on and so on to 'She's too busy sucking on my dingdong'. You know the story, the dealer's just got back from Carolina, said he didn't like the weather. Do you?

12

Slow Dazzle

IN the early months of 2013 Lou Reed suffered chronic liver failure, due to decades of alcohol and substances abuse, accentuated by recurrent Hepatitis C induced by intravenous drug use in the sixties and seventies with shared or contaminated needles.

Reed was operated on in April 2013 at the Cleveland Clinic in Ohio, where Dr Charles Miller, Programme Director for Liver Transplantation, who'd overseen more than 175 living donor transplants since taking up his appointment at Cleveland in 2004, performed the transplant on Reed in the hope of extending his life. 'This is the end, beautiful friend,' Nico repeated so often live, and so memorably on record, covering Jim Morrison's ophidian lyric, with a blue snake materialising on the road, and it was almost that for Lou. According to the National Institute of Health, 79 per cent of liver transplants survive the first year, 67 per cent make it to five years with five to zero per cent having a 15 years survival rate. Lou's was to be six months.

According to Laurie Anderson, Lou underwent 'big surgery which went very well. You send out two planes – one for the donor, one for the recipient, at the same time. You bring the donor in live; you take him off life support. It's a technological feat. I find certain things about technology truly, deeply inspiring.'

The seriousness of Lou's condition, that he had liver cancer at the time of the transplant placed him in a small minority survival rate. Discharged from the clinic after three weeks, Reed posted a message via Facebook optimistically affirming a full recovery and continuity.

'I am a triumph of modern medicine, physics and chemistry. I am bigger and stronger than ever. My Chen Taiji and health regime has served me well all these years, thanks to Master Ren Guang-yi. I look forward to being onstage performing, and writing more songs to connect with your hearts and spirits and the universe well into the future.'

To prove his regenerative status Reed, a week after discharge participated in a Q&A session at the Cannes Lions International Festival of Creativity, in France, before suffering an immediate relapse. Returning home, Reed was rushed to a Long Island hospital following an emergency call for an adult male suffering from chronic dehydration and kept in for three days. This was the first clear indication that the donor organ was starting to be rejected by Lou's compromised organism.

While Reed was forced into cancelling his two April 2013 gigs at Coachella in California, and the three sideshows he had booked between the annual festival's two weekends, he'd turned up unannounced at a March 4 listening party for his *Transformer* album in a New York City bar, and actually been conversant with fans. On March 19, a few weeks before his liver transplant, he'd read a poem in an almost inaudible voice at the City Winery, 155 Varick Street, New York, indulgently drinking red wine, emaciated, and climbing the three steps to the stage with a painful arthritic shuffle.

Lou hadn't played a full concert since his appearance at London's Meltdown Festival on August 10, 2012, when a cantankerous, musically misanthropic Reed, as inspirational antihero and art rock irritant, had delivered a two-hour set, mixing uncompromising slabs of *Lulu* with Velvet Underground classics like 'Sweet Jane', 'Waiting For The Man' and 'White Light/White Heat' submitted to loud permutations of the originals. Reed's authority appeared undiminished, when facing down a heckler one number in, he retorted to a rebuke, 'Not loud enough for you asshole' – having opened with a squalling 'Brandenburg Gate' as unsettling crowd attractor.

Lou was clearly ill and suffering adverse side effects from Interferon injections given three times a week to help combat Hepatitis C and liver tumours. Synthetic interferons are proteins made and released by host cells in response to the presence of pathogens such as viruses, bacteria, parasites or tumour cells. While not directly killing viral or cancerous cells, interferons boost the immune system response and reduce the growth of cancer cells by regulating the action of several genes that control the secretion of numerous cellular proteins that affect growth.

Lou with his analytic tech-head would have taken this in and worked it out for himself. His side effects or contraindications were the usual: fever, chills, headache, muscle aches and pains, nausea and general malaise. Reed was back at the Cleveland Clinic in September, due to liver malfunction that appeared to Dr Miller to be approaching an untreatable end stage, or rather the options were thought to be too distressing to administer, and unlikely to substantially enhance the patient's life expectancy.

At 3 p.m. on September 21, 2013 at an office in Washington Street, New York, Reed gave his last filmed interview in a conversation shared with director Farida Khelfa, after Reed had hired his sonic expertise to Parrot, adjusting the balance of the Parrot 2ik headphones so they'd be better suited for rock, an exercise he conducted with acutely fine-tuned professional acumen. Remarking on the necessity to improve the bass, his voice a strained whisper, Reed commented:

> 'I wouldn't want to hear Beethoven without beautiful bass, the cellos, the tuba. It's very important. Hip-hop has thunderous bass, and so does Beethoven. If you don't have the bass, it's like being amputated. It's like you have no legs.'

Still totally focused on sound as the universal heartbeat, Lou spoke of what he considered to be the appalling sound quality of most CDs, claiming he'd re-mastered every album he'd made to take advantage of the new technology. 'I am very emotionally affected by sound. Sounds are the inexplicable. There is a sound you hear in your head, it's your nerves, or your blood running. It's kind of amazing to hear that.'

Lou claimed in the interview to have bought his first guitar when he was nine, totally disparaging his father for not contributing to its cost, or giving him anything, and having taken up with sound then, and how progressively to manipulate it for his own highly idiosyncratic purposes.

Visibly weak and failing, but intellectually unimpaired, Lou concluded the interview by saying something significantly memorable about sound as universal signifier in the context of human continuity, and also something deeply moving, given that he was dying.

> 'The first memory of sound would have to be your mother's heart-beat, for all of us. You grow up from when you were a peanut, listening to rhythm.'

Crumpled into a deeply lived-in leather jacket, this was Lou's last ever interview, before flying back to the Cleveland Clinic to be told his condition was untreatably terminal. Reed chose to spend his last weeks at home at Springs, Long Island, New York, observant as always of the big blood orange – red Hudson River sunsets, and the busy river traffic he so loved, and aware too of Manhattan's consolidated ambient white noise. It was important for him to die centred in the city out of which he'd made a lifetime's music as the energised expression of his creativity.

In a valedictory essay to her partner published in *Rolling Stone*, Laurie Anderson spoke of how as mediators, they had both prepared for Lou's end, and its actual finality. Lou had weakly managed to make it outside to the terrace, presumably knowing he was dying. 'I had never seen an expression as full of wonder as Lou's as he died. His hands were doing the water flowing 21-form of Tai Chi. His eyes were wide open. I was holding in my arms the person I loved most in the world and talking to him as he died. His heart stopped. He wasn't afraid . . . I believe that the purpose of death is the release of love.'

Lou Reed died on October 27, 2013.

The serene manner of Lou's death, as reported, would have appeared inconceivable to his seventies fans infatuated by his wired speed-freak, anti-social butch image as king of weird and advocate of every gay litany; but the creative side of Lou never disowned his past, and his work right up to *Lulu* remains a defiant counterculture outlaw's vision of reality's B-side or underbelly. Inwardly too, Reed nurtured his subtle energies into pathways that provided him with a necessary discipline to restrain self-abuse. If he hadn't undergone detoxification in the early eighties, it's doubtful he would have survived that decade, with his injected use of speed and his chronic alcoholism often involving a bottle of spirits a day. But no matter how extreme his toxic programme, his intellect never lost focus in its treatment of rock as academic pursuit, and his interviews, no matter how renegade, remain the singularly most intelligent and thought provoking ever provided by a rock star, even if they risk being a triumph of theory over sublimated achievement.

Reed will always remain integral to rock legacy, as one of its seminal innovators, and expressive of an attitude that defined cool to a generation screened out by his dark glasses. Nobody was going to work one on Lou; his sharply analytical intelligence didn't allow management the chance, or permit band members ever to violate his rules of conduct. Even at the time of his worst excesses, Reed stayed on top of things, taking action against any traces of management fraud. And then there was the ambiguous sexuality that confused both men and women, in that Lou could flip from one to the other impulsively. Rather like his shades, you risked encountering contactless response. Like Burroughs, Reed was too cerebral to be easily physicalised, and music for him was a far closer identity than sex.

Creatively, Lou Reed is optimal circa 1965–1978, a marginalised artist feeding on cult status, and what follows, despite a trilogy of great albums, *New York*, *Songs For Drella*, and *Magic And Loss*, is an impressive but diminished curve, cross-infected at times by the need for mainstream acceptance to vindicate his influence on contemporaries who had overtaken him commercially on the way. 'I do Lou Reed better than anyone,' became his declared credo. And of course, he did, but it takes time to get recognition, and Reed had to reorganise his energies and tone down his bad boy image to find media tolerance. It was a transition that disappointed his real fans, but allowed him to go forward, and keep on making records, although to the general public he remains forever identified with 'Walk On The Wild Side', his sole commercially popular hit.

I suspect nobody ever really got into Lou's head, because he was inured to suspect a trick, or an ulterior motive like duplicity or insidious subterfuge. His homosexuality left him innately defensive with his parents, and strains of paranoid suspicion continued to condition his human relations all of his life, so that he admitted to the assumption that he lied in response to what he assumed were misconceptions of his character that were in themselves lies. The real Lou, where do we find him, partly in this book, partly in his music, but there's no definitive Lou, there's facts and how we subjectively interpret them?

LOU REED THE GREATEST. Read this sentence in 30 years, it will still be the same, the same, the same. LOU REED THE GREATEST.

Acknowledgments

The author wishes to thank the editors of *NME*, *Melody Maker*, *Sounds*, *Creem*, *Rolling Stone*, *Penthouse*, *The New York Times*, *The Guardian*, *The Observer*, *The Independent*, *The Daily Telegraph*, *National Screw*, *Pitchfork*, *Album Tracking*, *The Village Voice* and *Circus* magazine. Thanks also to Mick Rock, and to Michael Bracewell for his interview with Lou Reed that included the quote about this book, and innumerable blogs for online anecdotes.

The following books offered helpful signposting: *The Diaries Of Andy Warhol* (Simon & Schuster, 1989); *Psychotic Reactions And Carburetor Dung* by Lester Bangs (Heinemann, 1989); *Lou Reed & The Velvet Underground* by Diana Clapton (Proteus Books, 1982); *Growing Up In Public* by Peter Doggett (Omnibus Press, 1991); *The Rough Guide To The Velvet Underground* by Peter Hogan (Rough Guides, 2007); *Love Goes To Buildings On Fire* by Will Hermes (Viking, 2011); and *What's Welsh For Zen* by John Cale (Bloomsbury, 1999).

Index

Singles releases are in roman type and albums are in italics.

Index